SERIOUS
BASS
FISHING

D1605469

Winning Secrets of Advanced Bass Anglers

by Mike Folkestad and Ron Kovach

MARKETSCOPE
BOOKS

119 Richard Ct.
Aptos, CA 95003
(408) 688-7535

ISBN 0-934061-20-3

Illustrations: Meredith A. Kovach

Dedication

To become a serious bass fisherman,
you need serious support from the people you love.
Thank you, Sheila and Linda, for encouraging us
in our pursuit of these little green fish.
You made our dream possible!

We also want to thank the following
manufacturers for their continued support:

Advanced Angler Technology
Angler's Choice
Berkley
Costa Del Mar
Delco Voyager
Eagle Claw
Luhr Jensen
Minnkota
Normark-Rapala
Penn
Ranger Boats
Yamaha

About the Authors

Mike Folkestad is a professional bass fisherman and businessman. He is a former U.S. Open victor and has qualified for the prestigious Bassmaster Classic. He is also one of the premier technicians in this sport.

Ron Kovach is one of the foremost angler-educators in the country. He is the founder and director of the Eagle Claw Fishing Schools and Penn Fishing University. He is also a renown outdoor writer and consultant to the sporting goods industry.

Contents

Contents (cont.)

Introduction: Serious Bassin'—
A Dual Perspective

Introduction: Serious Bassin'— A Dual Perspective

Bass fishing remains one of the most popular types of angling in the United States. These little green fish are found in almost every state. No matter where you go, they remain a challenge to catch. Although the various bass species can be caught all year long in most locales, limit days for many anglers remain far and few between. Without a doubt, bassin' persists as a highly "cerebral" endeavor.

Professional guides and tournament anglers take their bass fishing seriously. Both, in different ways, have reputations and money on the line when they launch their bass boats. The professional guide is being paid by clients not only to teach them the tricks of the trade on a specific body of water but, more importantly, to *find* the fish for the customers to catch that day. The guide perhaps has it toughest since there is no place to run, no place to hide following a day on the water. He must be prepared to face his customers at the end of both good days and bad. This can be serious "pressure time."

The tournament angler, on the other hand, fishes against other professional bassers and most often bankrolls himself for the contest. Occasionally, in the upper echelon of the sport, the top level pros may receive some sponsorships that help offset tournament costs. Still, there are usually considerable time, reputation, and travel costs involved for those who try their luck on the tournament trail. Unlike professional guides, however, the tournament basser can quietly "disappear" from the weigh-in area following a disappointing day on the water, only to return for another challenge on another tournament day.

Touring pros learn regional patterns and inside tips from local guides. Veteran guides, in return, learn from the pros some of the new hot secret strategies that are initially previewed on the professional bassin' circuits. This can be a great symbiotic relationship where considerable information may be exchanged.

Ron Kovach and Mike Folkestad represent these two different kinds of serious bass fishermen. Ron Kovach is the veteran guide who paid his dues finding fish for his clients on the tough, small Southern California weekend lakes. He is one of the most well-known angler-educators in the West, founding both the Eagle Claw Fishing Schools and the Penn Fishing University.

Mike Folkestad, in contrast, rose from the ranks of club level fisherman to become the most prominent name in professional bass circles on the West Coast. Having won the U.S. Open, Bassmaster Florida Invitational, and qualified for the prestigious Bassmaster Classic, Folkestad has "done it all" and is recognized from coast to coast as one of the foremost technicians and strategists in the sport. He is considered to be one of the founding fathers of the so-called "finesse" style of serious bassin'.

Ron Kovach and Mike Folkestad have also spent literally hundreds of hours on the water together, analyzing different lakes, conceptualizing diverse techniques, jointly working to "demystify" this complex fishing endeavor. By joining forces, Mike and Ron feel that as touring pro and guide, we bring a unique combined perspective to our readers on how to catch not only more, but larger bass.

This book is not a beginner's text. Instead, we assume that the reader has some understanding of the basics of bass fishing. What we want to do is take your bassin' up a "notch" and share with you the "serious" dimensions of the sport. We want to give you some of our insights into the "inner game" of serious bass fishing, examining the finer points of the sport that serve to separate the occasional, recreational angler from the angler who routinely posts the best catches and is perhaps interested in guiding or fishing tournaments. We hope you will find this book both informative and useful in your pursuit of these little green fish.

Serious Strategies

Serious Strategies

So much of becoming a successful serious bass fisherman depends upon developing certain strategies that will allow you to attack a particular body of water in the most efficient manner. "Strategizing" in this sport involves using your head more than using any fancy equipment or hi-tech bass boat. Characteristics like memory, intuition, patience, and perseverance are much more important to serious bassin' than the accumulation of quality tackle and gear.

Examining Pre-Pattern Variables[1]

Recreational bass fishermen are often amazed at the way accomplished pros and guides are able to tame a lake and nail a limit of fish. Bassers in this class are able to do well by deciphering what kind of "pattern" the bass are on. For example, do the fish want a 4 inch earth tone-colored curl-tail worm pitched off points, or a compact chugger in shad finish worked along the green tules? These are both examples of specific "patterns." Most serious anglers feel that the ability to pattern their quarry in this manner is the foundation of the sport.

Learning to pattern the fish, however, is not as simple as it sounds. If the angler takes into account some basic factors beforehand, the primary feeding pattern may be easier to isolate. There are certain pre-pattern conditions we review, sometimes for days prior to when we launch. We will examine the lake's general history, emergent weather patterns, water conditions, and differences in species behavior *before* we even make that first cast.

Assessing these pre-pattern variables gives serious bass fishermen an idea of how to select and prepare their tackle prior to an important outing. This knowledge also allows the anglers to draw up more precisely an articulate game plan for the day. They can begin to formulate in advance the probable baits and techniques to use as well as the best potential spots to try. Much valuable time can be saved and unproductive water eliminated when the serious bass fisherman reviews these variables *before* working the lake.

Lake History

Most impoundments demonstrate certain seasonal characteristics year after year. Some are recognized, for instance, as stellar worm lakes in the spring while others are early season spinnerbait havens. Some reservoirs are known for summer moss beds, while others are famous for a deep structure wintertime bite. These are examples of generalized seasonal patterns that seem to hold true for long periods of time on a given lake.

Taking such history into account can often provide the angler with some reliable starting points in attacking the water. Such common knowledge among veteran bass anglers helps them to get an initial "handle" on the water as they look for more specific patterns.

Ron and Mike also keep detailed logs. All of the principle elements that affected a particular outing are entered into a journal. Over a period of time, some enduring features of a specific lake may become evident. With such historical and seasonal information, serious bassers can begin to narrow down their tackle repertoire for an upcoming day on the water. Specific lures, retrieve options, and traditional fish-holding spots are considered as the pros and guides design their strategies. They then lay out the appropriate rods, reels, and lines, assembling the diverse outfits they feel they will need to start attacking the water.

Emergent Weather Patterns

Some serious bassers frequently listen to weather reports days before setting out to the lake. Bass are an extremely

[1] Portions of this section previously appeared in *B.A.S.S. Times*

temperamental species. There is considerable evidence to indicate that these fish are affected by climatic changes.

Sometimes we will actually utilize weather broadcasts to monitor both prevailing and emergent conditions on the lake we are planning to fish. We always watch for low pressure storms coming into the region. We prefer to fish before it starts to rain. This can really generate major bass movement.

Checking the weather reports for an upcoming tournament or guide trip can also influence *how* you decide to present your baits. For instance if we hear reports of bad weather, we know we will have to focus on areas of the lake that we have the most confidence in from past experience. We will look for bass holding tight to structure and concentrate on making precise casts, wasting little time and focusing on normally high-yielding spots.

Thus by parlaying such information about the weather into our overall line of attack, we waste little time exploring "dead" stretches of water or trying out useless methods.

Water Conditions

If possible, try to also acquire some knowledge about the water conditions of the lake you are traveling to. Ask questions about water levels, clarity, movement of current, pH, and surface temperatures. There is a wealth of information to be gleaned from reviewing these variables prior to your trip.

Sometimes we even call the lake marina operator or dam manager to check beforehand if there is a lot of water being put in or drained out of the lake. This can be an integral component in establishing a fishing pattern.

For example, on desert lakes in the West we sometimes call ahead to ascertain information on water flow. If we find that a lot of water is being run through the lake we will expect the bass to move out of the main river channel where the current is ripping. We then concentrate on the coves where there is less turbulence. This eliminates considerable unproductive water as we attempt to establish a complete pattern.

There are also situations where we will key in on water levels. We set out a different line-up of baits for the situation, depending upon whether the lake's water level is high or low. For example, if the lake is real high and flooded, we prefer a bigger lure that covers a lot of territory like a spinnerbait or crankbait. A subtle finesse bait such as a darter head or tubebait works best at times when a lake is low. It helps to study topographic maps before arriving at a lake to determine different depths of structure such as channels, drop-offs and humps.

Invariably, we find that we rely upon information about the specific impoundment's water conditions to decide what tackle to bring and what sort of initial strategy to devise once we arrive on the lake. By assessing this pre-pattern variable, the angler is once again able to limit his approach and focus on the potentially best areas using the potentially best baits.

Species Differentiation

Ron and Mike review the different aspects of bass feeding habits in lakes with multiple species present. Some reservoirs can have Florida largemouths and spotted bass, for example. Others may have smallmouths and spots living together. A bass is not just a "bass." Each separate species has distinct behavioral traits.

Accounting for these differences in feeding habits before you reach the lake can also help to isolate a certain pattern. Sometimes you might be fishing a lake with multiple species. Review your logs and compare the previous methods you have successfully employed for largemouths and smallmouths. Then rig up the right baits for both species the night before. Thus, if one species is not active, you will always have rigs ready for the other. The larger baits will usually nail the largemouths. Then switch to little baits for smallmouths if the largemouths are tough to catch.

In this situation, serious bassers learn to "cover all bases," by carefully analyzing the bass species s they are stalking. By carrying an arsenal of lures and rigs to accommodate each species, the veteran tournament pro or guide is then able to respond to a full range of possible patterns.

Successfully patterning bass on a given impoundment takes a lot of forethought with a measure of skill, experience, and luck thrown in. Considerable guesswork can be eliminated if these pre-pattern variables are assessed prior to leaving for the lake.

When to Throw Out the Book

We think that most of you will agree that compared to other types of fresh and saltwater angling, serious bass fishing is a tough sport to master. Weekend traffic, including pleasure boaters, water-skiers, sailors, and local bass club members impact this fishery tremendously. Few recreational anglers ever tally that elusive daily limit on most lakes.

These fishermen are not alone. Even the hard-core tournament-level angler or professional guide with his $25,000 rig, hi-tech electronics, and an arsenal of rods, reels, and lures, feels the effect of all the pressure. We, too, often show up at the dock with an empty live well after being shut out for the day.

We both have had the opportunity to guide and fish tournaments under routinely tough conditions. Like other serious bassers, we have frequently been able to pull a "rabbit out of our hats" and come up with a way to catch fish. This, we might add, often occurs when most recreational fishermen are stymied.

There are some common denominators that serious bassers share that allow them to nail bass under the most trying conditions. They are meticulous with their equipment. They spend considerable hours on the water each month. They have great perseverance, stamina, and a winning attitude. Above all, bass fishermen of this caliber know when to "throw out the book," so to speak, and take a chance with an innovative game plan.

Bass fishing is far from an exact science. Many dedicated bass anglers like to talk about how they have a particular lake "wired." This is based on repeated successes over many years fishing a specific pattern at a specific lake. Frequently, this kind of historical confidence can back the angler into a corner. We have witnessed too many situations where the patented techniques associated with a certain lake or set of conditions simply failed to produce. Lake regulars stubbornly persisted, however, in staying with the time-proven methods because they had worked in the past.

In contrast, the serious basser knows when it is time to bail out—to "throw out the book" and try to shake up the program with some radical innovation. By breaking out of these routines and doing something dramatically different, bass that are heavily pressured are given a new lure, retrieve, action, or silhouette to look at. It is often this radical presentation that can suddenly excite bass into striking after they have been bombarded all day by a routine menu of baits.

Forget Seasonal Strategies!

Take Lake Castaic for instance. This body of water located an hour's drive from downtown Los Angeles is one of the most heavily fished impoundments in the country. It has reached notoriety nationwide in the past year by kicking out two world-class Florida largemouths topping the 20 pound mark. Most locals who fish Castaic feel that if they are to have a chance at scoring under this kind of pressure, using light line and the ever popular split-shot technique is the best option day in and day out.

When fishing in the summer at this lake, most fishermen will be working tiny split-shot worms and reapers out over 30 to 40 foot ledges. Instead of getting locked into the "split-shot syndrome," you might try, for example, summertime spoonin' in 8 to 12 foot depths. Spoons will work at lakes like Castaic in the summer if the bass are feeding on shad. Show them a lure that has some erratic swimming action combined with flash to generate a reaction strike.

Now we all know that spoons are a wintertime lure. They are made for slow vertical yo-yoing in deep water. Few anglers will use a spoon as they would a jig, hopping it in shallow water and covering a lot of territory—and in the middle of the summer doldrums no less. Serious bass fishermen sometimes choose to ignore the obvious. Highly pressured fish need to see something different. The spoon becomes a dramatic yet rarely used alternative to the split-shot strategy among "traditional" bass fishermen at Lake Castaic.

Bass fishermen often have a tendency to get locked into seasonal patterns more so when the weather turns extreme. For example, veterans who fish popular Lake Perris near Riverside, California, feel it is common knowledge that the worse the weather factor is in the winter, the better the chances are for scoring on a trophy Alabama spotted bass. There is also the widely held belief that the spots primarily root on crawdads in 25 to 40 foot water during the height of winter. This is the basic "book" for Perris and its world record spotted bass fishery.

While fishing Perris, we discovered from lake locals that other approaches sometime work even better. We were fishing worms and jigs over deep structure in typical winter fashion. Sometimes a small school of shad would puddle on the surface right at the bank in the dead of winter. Since we weren't getting bit, we decided to switch to surface plugs—a strategy that definitely is not recommended by the book for bassin' in the dead of winter.

In fact, this tactic worked in sub-50 degree water with big spotted bass crashing on a wintertime top-water bait! Here again, you must be willing to take a chance and "throw out the book."

Forget the Local "Scoop"

Other pros recurrently "throw out the book" for a local lake and persist in doing it their way using more obscure strategies. Expert worm fishermen are often seen casting 10 to 16 inch "snakes" racking up not only big fish but limits as well when other anglers are split-shottin' every piece of shoreline with 4 inch finesse baits.

Trophy hunters similarly throw larger 7 to 9 inch long saltwater minnow-shaped plugs like #18-F Rapalas, Bomber Long-A's or Smithwick Rogues to wake up the 10 pounders into hitting. Big fish like these may be getting tired of seeing the tiny little poppers that so many recreational bassers seem to throw these days.

Proficient structure fishermen who typically work deep underwater breaks and ledges might confuse a lot of lake locals when they position their boats next to the bank and present their lures *uphill* instead of downhill like 90 percent of the weekend crowd. A lure worked in this manner can often trigger strikes from sluggish bass moving up from deep water. Again, this is throwing out the traditional "book" on structure bassin'.

Top-water specialists who persist in throwing buzzbaits in the middle of a summer day when most anglers are content crawling worms or jigs hoping the bite will pick up invariably limit out by creating a major disturbance and forcing the fish to attack the lone buzzer. Here is another illustration of how it pays to throw out the book and pave new ground when conditions turn difficult.

Fish the Extreme!

There are other situations where traditional-size bass lures fail to get bit. Here is where the shrewd angler might want to delve into his troutin' box and try some ultralight plugs, spinners, or spoons with fine diameter 4 to 6 pound mono. Although these minuscule lures were designed primarily for trout or panfish, we have seen them produce phenomenal results many times on highly pressured bass lakes. When teamed with the gossamer mono, the tiny baits frequently draw strikes from hook-shy largemouth, bronzebacks and Alabama spots because of their subtle profiles. This is yet another example of discarding conventional wisdom and giving the bass a radical new array of lures to look at.

These are all classic examples of the ways in which serious bassers are willing to deviate from the popular patterns associated with a particular lake, a season, or a set of conditions. By "throwing out the book" and taking a chance, these are the guys who routinely post those stellar limits on otherwise tough impoundments.

It is important to emphasize that taking chances, being experimental and innovative, is not relegated only to special lakes, regions or conditions. There are only so many fish-holding spots on a given lake or river where the bass will most likely be found. As you would expect, these prime spots, whether located in the West, South, North, or East will inevitably get hammered by angling pressure.

When you encounter this type of situation, take a chance, "throw out the book," and give the bass something new to look at. Both limits and lunkers may result!

Challenge Unfamiliar Water[2]

For many bass anglers, one of the toughest challenges they may face is encountering totally unfamiliar water. It doesn't matter whether it is a small 1000 acre impoundment, a massive lake, or a complex river system—there can always be a fear of the unknown upon launching your rig on new water.

There are a number of options worth investigating simply by using your eyes, looking for potential visual targets to throw at. Let's examine some of the more obvious ones, focusing in on how to select the most viable targets.

Points

A stretch of shoreline that extends out into the water is always one of the prime areas to find bass. The fish utilize points as a major staging area for migrations from deep to shallow and back again.

In late winter and early spring, bass typically position themselves on these outside points in deeper water. Then, with warmer weather, the fish move up from the deeper zones, traversing these points on their way to the shallow banks. During the hotter months, the bass move from the shore by midday along the points situating themselves in the cooler deeper water found at the end of these ridges.

Schools of baitfish may also intermittently be pushed up against one side of the point or the other either by the wind and wave action or while seeking sanctuary on the shady side of the ridge. Points can be quickly surveyed using crankbaits to probe the sides and the end of the ridge. This is a good strategy to use if you are on a new lake with numerous points that jut out from the bank.

On other lakes, however, you may see only a few such structures. Here it might be better to try a more concentrated approach, canvassing all facets of the point with slower methods such as crawling plastic worms, hoppin' a jig, or finessin' with a tube bait or tiny darter head jig.

We should add that a pair of polarized sunglasses can be extremely helpful in positioning yourself along a point when you can't rely on sophisticated electronics. Frequently, what might appear to be a small rocky outcropping from the bank may actually be a more elongated point with as much as 80 percent of the structure underwater.

Polarized lenses help reduce glare and let you see to some degree underwater, as well as helping you to see differences in water color. Usually darker water is a sign of a drop-off of some sort.

[2] Portions of this section previously appeared in *Bassmaster Magazine*

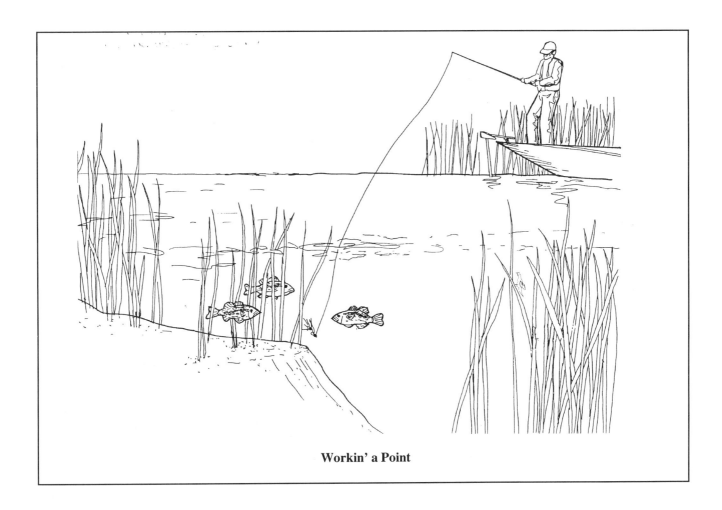

Workin' a Point

Current

Whenever you find some type of dramatic water movement — fish it! One obvious source of current is where a creek or river empties into a lake. Similarly, eddies, tailouts, and converging tributaries in a river also generate dramatic fluctuations in water movement.

While fishing extensive river or canal vegetation, always try to focus in on areas evidencing current. Sometimes you may have to look for more subtle signs of current. On some smaller reservoirs, for example, there are underwater conduits placed in these man-made lakes used to pump fresh water and, hence, aerate the impoundment. All year long, baitfish gravitate to the churning, oxygen-rich water near the aerator unit. Bass will follow.

Often, the water being aerated by the submerged pumps only appears as an eerie-looking mass of swirling current on the surface. This is prime vertical spoonin' country, as the bass may stack up in clusters in the moving current. You can also fish current quickly and efficiently throwing crankplugs, spinnerbaits, and various tail-swimming jig combinations.

Riprap

The rocky face of a dam or a stretch of bank that has a concentration of rock is another place to start when bassin' on a strange lake. In the winter, the fish find warmth from the rocks that retain radiant heat. Crawdads also like this kind of terrain. Later in the year, schools of baitfish frequently suspend over the riprap with bass coming out from the rocks to ambush prey.

The problem with a long stretch of riprap is that it all pretty much looks the same. Here again, a crankbait in the hands of a skilled serious basser allows him to methodically run down the bank quickly firing off cast after cast through the stretch of riprap.

Roadbeds

Ron and Mike are always on the lookout for submerged roadbeds as key areas to explore. These are most easily discovered using topographical maps of the lake. However, even without the help of electronics or the benefit of the topographic map, you may still be able to home in on this prime terrain using your eyes.

On many reservoirs, for example, there are visible signs of old roads that have stopped at the lake. Most of these impoundments are man-made, flooded basins contained by a concrete or rocky dam. Before they were flooded, various country roads criss-crossed this terrain. It is a good bet that when you see a road abruptly end at the water's edge, that it actually extends out under the water.

On lakes characterized by bland, muddy bottoms, these roadbeds offer the bass broken asphalt or gravel as a form of subtle structure that stands out from the softer bottom. Shallow shoreline roadbeds such as these are excellent spots to slow down and crawl a plastic worm, grub, or jig across. This type of topography is especially suitable for the popular split-shot technique. Small reapers, grubs, and worms can be S-L-O-W-L-Y dragged over the broken asphalt or gravel, slightly suspended above this bottom structure.

Sun and Shade

Climatic variations can also be a key component in setting up a game plan to fish an unfamiliar lake or river. In the winter months it usually helps to concentrate on the shallow zones that receive the first sun. This may be the sector of the lake or river that warms quickest where the bass will naturally move towards.

In the hotter months, areas that hold shade may be key in both the early morning and late afternoon period. Light penetration can be intense during this time of the year and the bass are going to situate themselves into shadier comfort zones.

A shallow cove that receives first sun in the summer, for instance, may be a poor choice for throwing a topwater lure. Your better option might be the coves on the other side of the lake that receive sunlight a few hours later. The bass will be more prone to attack a shallow surface plug in the darker, shadier water where they find sanctuary from the early light.

By midday, you may have to look toward the end of those long extended points or the sheer steep canyon walls where considerable shade can be found along with cooler deeper water.

Keep in mind that we should not always think of the sun as a nemesis. Sometimes it can be an ally when it comes to bass fishing. During the colder months, certain types of shoreline benefit from direct exposure to sunlight.

Many bassers are convinced that red clay banks, for instance, retain radiant heat overnight longer than other types of terrain. Hence, this is a potentially good fish-holding spot on a cold morning.

The riprap that lines the face of a dam, or a concrete or asphalt launch ramp, may also evidence similar heat-retaining qualities on a winter's day attracting bass to the immediate area.

Rubble

On many lakes, the shoreline terrain is stark and barren. Therefore almost any slight deviation in that topography can be a virtual "oasis" in the desert. What Mike and Ron sometimes look for in challenging unknown waters is small clusters of "rubble."

Rubble is nothing more than larger boulders or broken rocks that are intermittently scattered along small concise stretches of the bank. Like visible roadbeds that end at the water, it is a good bet that the rubble you see on the bank most likely extends further into the water.

In a low water year, for example, if you carefully look at the bank, you may see the tiered levels of the various water lines that remain as the water has dropped further and further. You will probably also see some structures that were once underwater but are now high and dry on the bank. Usually where there is one cluster of scattered rubble there are others nearby in slightly deeper water. This is an excellent place to work a plastic worm, jig, or finesse bait trying to make precise contact with this isolated piece of structure.

Look for even the smallest amount of rock or brush that might break up a barren shoreline. Realize that it doesn't take a lot to hold bass on these muddy bottom lakes.

Transition Banks

This is one of the more difficult, yet important pieces of real estate to focus on when attacking new water. Look for subtle changes in the bank as you motor along. Too often, there is a tendency to focus only on the obvious stick-ups, broken rock, or riprap that line the shore.

Again, all of this structure is likely to be overfished. Instead look for sections of the bank where gravel becomes sand. Keep your eye out for the place where scattered rocks meet an expansive tule line. These are transitional banks. They are subtle yet distinct variations from the dominant complexion of the shoreline.

Crawdads, shad, and other indigenous baits are often found where the underwater terrain begins to change. Bass will consequently use these small, isolated areas as a "feeding oasis" where competition from the rest of the gamefish population is minimized.

Gentle Inclines

Always be on the alert for stretches of shoreline that gradually lead into deeper water. These can also be excellent places to fish in the winter when many anglers are working well off the bank over deep structure.

Gentle sloping banks such as this can serve as a major highway for both crawdads and bass moving from deep to shallow during colder periods. The fish may not move all the way up into the most shallow water, preferring to remain at 5 to 15 foot depths.

The best way to canvass an incline like this is to position your boat near the bank in the shallows and cast out towards deeper water. Using a slow-moving lure like a worm, grub, or jig, retrieve the bait uphill. Positioning in this manner allows you to make excellent bottom contact while bringing the lure up the sloping bank. Look for this type of terrain to hold bass, especially when it lies adjacent to steeper rocky shoreline.

Mud Lines

One often overlooked area is the muddy stretch of shallow water where the wave action has stirred up the water diminishing clarity to a considerable degree. Recreational bassers often pass up this kind of water, figuring that it is too muddy to sustain life.

Actually, some of the best midday action can occur in the mud line. If you look carefully toward the bank, you can actually see where the muddy water stops and the clearer water begins. Light intensity is minimized here and the water ironically may be fairly oxygenated from all the prop chop. Baitfish and bass often move into these mud lines.

This is the kind of area to throw a lure that generates significant flash, rattle, or vibration. It takes a modest amount of commotion to "call" the fish into the lure due to reduced visibility in the mud line. This distinctive break in water clarity also occurs on many impoundments that experience heavy water-skiing pressure.

Serious bassers who own electronic fish-finding devices can increase their chances significantly over those anglers who depend solely upon a visual approach when fishing new water. Electronics allow you to pinpoint the most subtle types of structure sometimes found well off the bank where bass may congregate. Here then are some of the basics to look for when using electronics in unfamiliar territory.

Ledges and Breaks

Deeper underwater ledges are similar in importance to points that extend out from the bank. A ledge or "break" may be a prime place for the deep-structure fisherman to concentrate.

These drop-offs may be dramatic as an underwater ledge "breaks" from 20 to 35 feet or they may be more subtle as the bottom terrain is structured in a stair-step effect "breaking" in shorter 5 foot intervals. Sometimes the major concentrations of bass to be found in a given body of water will hang on these ledges.

As you motor around the lake and discover one of these breaks, look for signs of baitfish nearby. It is common for the bait—and the bass—to situate themselves on the edge of the drop-off. This is a perfect place to try a vertical approach ranging from doodlin' a tiny worm, bouncin' a jig, or yo-yoing a spoon.

Humps

One of the most subtle types of underwater structure you may encounter is a gently "hump" or mound that rises above the muddy bottom. Frequently these humps are found on many shallow lakes that evidence few, more dramatic ledges or shoreline structure. These gentle unassuming mounds may thus become the major structure-holding spots on a reservoir.

Ditches

Similarly, many lakes feature a series of small, narrow crevices or "ditches" often located in shallow water a short distance from the bank. Unlike breaks, these small underwater cuts may drop off only from 3 to 5 feet. This may be all you need in the way of viable structure, particularly on a lake with a monotonous muddy bottom.

The Key: Patience and Confidence

The two key ingredients in attacking a new body of water are patience and confidence. It is important for the serious basser to take some time to get a preliminary lay of the land.

Motor around for a while before you start casting. Use your keen sense of vision to look for riprap, old roadbeds, rubble, points, shade and sun. Leave you electronics on and monitor for those distinct ledges and more obscure humps and ditches.

Retain confidence in your ability both to find fish and catch them as you do on your home lakes. More than likely, many of those same techniques you have already mastered will work in this new environment. Try to avoid the most obvious places to begin with. Aggressively seek out and explore the more subtle spots where bass may be found. Challenge unfamiliar water!

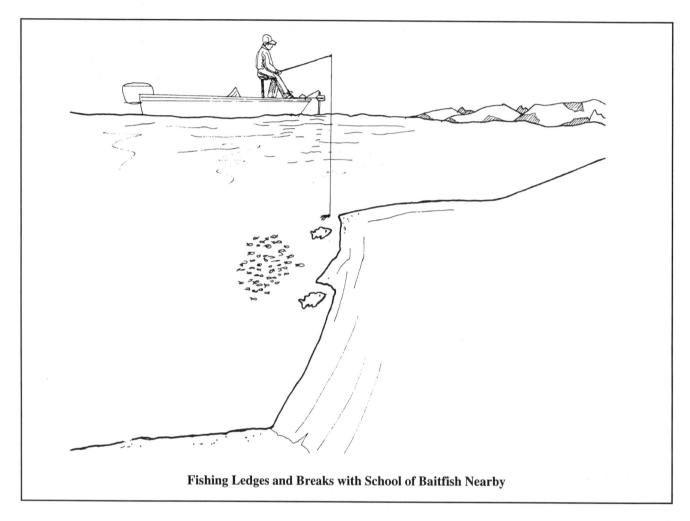

Fishing Ledges and Breaks with School of Baitfish Nearby

Strategies for Small Lakes

If bassin' is often a difficult proposition, things can get even tougher when you fish small impoundments that serve as multi-use reservoirs.

In some parts of the country, local promoters routinely stage major two-man team tournaments on tiny trophy lakes. Weekend anglers are lured to these smaller 1,000 to 2,000 acre impoundments because they are close to home. Many of these lakes also kick out some extraordinary trophy-class bass on a regular basis. Hence many area bassers reckon it may take only one big fish to win the contest.

Still the pressure on such small waters is immense. There can be over 100 teams in the tournament. An additional fleet of 60 or so rental skiffs will be taken by recreational fishermen. There are typically another 100 shore anglers, a few dozen float tubers, and at least 50 pleasure boats all sharing the water the day of the tourna-

ment. Put simply, this scene has all the earmarks of a virtual "zoo" as far as serious bassin' is concerned.

Serious bassers learn to accept this crowding as a feature of their environment. The successful competitors carefully evince strategies to work around this congestion.

Learn the Spots

Most of these small lakes are characterized by stark shoreline cover. There are a few minor targets to throw at such as boat docks, scattered boulders, or the riprap along a dam. Count on seeing boats blanket these visual targets immediately at the start of the tournament.

The other primary spots are found mostly on outside structure, often some distance from the bank. Your electronics will help you find ledges, drop-offs, submerged islands, and gentle "humps" as previously mentioned. Most likely, you will not need topographical maps to locate the spots you failed to find with your electronics. There will already be boats on them. There are few secrets left to be discovered on such small lakes.

The Strategies

To begin with, if you think you can attack a 1,000 acre lake by quickly running down a shoreline, you will probably not do well. There are too many other boats you will have to maneuver around. In addition, the bass will be extremely wary after the first hour following boat launching. The boat traffic will definitely inhibit these fish from readily striking a reaction bait used in a rapid-fire presentation.

In these conditions, fish the more subtle baits such as a reaper, a small grub, or worm, with 4 or 10 pound test line, a 1/16 to 1/8 ounce slide sinker, split-shottin', and all those similar techniques. It takes these kinds of baits, because the fish have so much pressure with the boats running around.

If you persist in using the larger reaction lures associated with a run-and-gun approach, you may not even get a single strike on these highly pressured waters. However, it might pay to fire off a few casts in the morning or late evening with a spinnerbait or crankplug as you approach a spot during that time. There is always a remote possibility at this time of day of finding one bass that is aggressive enough to attack a larger lure.

One alternative to the run-and-gun strategy is to locate a good spot and practically "camp" on it. The theory is that the bass in the lake will invariably use that particular location as a major feeding area *sometime during the day*. Anglers who camp on such a spot believe that it will only be a matter of time before a movement of bass occurs in that area.

Sometimes this strategy really pays off. Both large bass and a volume of fish can often be taken from a single spot. Trophy-class Florida bass generally demonstrate two movements. One occurs in the morning and the other in the evening. The Floridas will typically move up in the late afternoon. There are spots that we have found through trial and error that this species will use as a feeding shelf or ambush point. Wait long enough, "camp" on the spot, and they will come.

The trick is to place your boat in position to take advantage of the best presentation possible. For instance, it might be better to work a spot uphill instead of the more commonly used downhill retrieve. In this situation, it would be wise to keep the boat close to the shore and work uphill.

Similarly, it might be important to anchor on an outside flat and fan cast the adjacent area. The anchor keeps the boat fairly stationary. The anglers won't have to fight the elements while they concentrate on every inch of the immediate terrain in casting distance from the boat. This is another method that sometimes accounts for limit catches on these little reservoirs.

Another option is to plan out a "rotation sequence," which will allow you to cover a greater amount of productive water. Design a game plan before you visit the lake. Pick out a half dozen prime spots that you figure should hold fish. Try to get to those locations during the time of day that they have historically held fish.

The object is to rotate from spot to spot hoping to intercept the bass at the time they move on that particular area. This tactic is risky since quite often most of the productive areas have boats on them when you want to fish that spot.

Forget the Obvious

Most anglers will thus relegate themselves to fishing the most recognizable "hot" spots by either "camping" on the area or rotating between a small number of normally productive locations.

Instead, consider taking a dramatically different approach. Look for some of the least obvious water you can find. Head for a prime spot if you can launch early. These are spots all the good bass fishermen know. You can run to that spot and sit on it all day. If you get out late, you probably aren't going to get on any of the good spots. What you do then is look for little subtle structure between the good spots where the boats don't fish because it looks real poor. If you scrutinize these areas carefully, you will find a little rock pile, maybe a little rough spot, something that holds one or two fish.

So, intentionally focus on otherwise bland nondescript stretches of bank that might be overlooked by locals working the primary spots. Above all, employ a slow meticulous presentation. The bass will more often than not be highly selective with regard to the baits they strike. They will have seen virtually hundreds of offerings all day. Pick the lure you have confidence in and fish it slowly.

Take some time to work these less obvious stretches. Continue to move from one to another, picking off a bass here and there. Five separate stretches can hold five solitary fish. This can translate into a respectable catch for the day!

Take It to the Bank

Many recreational bass fishermen assume that they will be at a major disadvantage if they do not have a boat. This is simply not true. Across the country each year many lunkers are caught by anglers fishing from the shore. Serious bassers who own hi-tech bass rigs may often learn valuable insights from observing serious bassers who walk the bank.

On any given lake, you will actually find that many of the fishermen with sophisticated bass rigs invariably end up working their baits and lures right next to the shore anyway. Many bass pros and veteran guides are firm believers in the adage that—regardless of the time of year—there will always be some fish feeding in the shallows. Bank fishermen can thus readily take advantage of this situation.

Another reason bassin' from the bank can be so productive has to do with the presentation of the lure or bait. Shore fishermen throw out into deeper water then retrieve their offerings uphill. Lures or baits presented in this manner make excellent contact with the bottom. Typically this is where feeding bass live. Quite often boaters casting from deep water up to the bank find that it is difficult to keep their offerings close to the bottom as they retrieve their line in a downhill direction. The difficulty in keeping the bait on the bottom increases as it returns closer to the boat.

Catching bass from the bank still requires a certain level of expertise. There are certain areas that will be routinely more productive than others. Similarly there are different techniques that lend themselves to shoreline bassin', each with its own specific presentation.

Viable Areas and Tactics

It is estimated that 90 percent of the bass are located in 10 percent of the water. Hence it is important to key in on those areas of the lake, pond, or reservoir where the fish should be. This entails learning to "read" the water and to thus eliminate unproductive "dead" stretches of shoreline.

Again—Look to Points. While walking the bank, submerged points are probably the best place to start looking for bass day in and day out. The fish migrate up from deeper water along these points all through the year. Casting from points as they extend out from the bank, gives the shore angler considerable access to deep water.

Points are also excellent places to try in the wind. However, interestingly most fishermen make the mistake of moving off the windward bank of the point to seek shelter on the lee side. The wind and ensuing wave action pushes the bait up against the point. Water clarity is also broken up with the chop on this windward side. Both of these factors make the bass more prone to feed along the side of the point facing the wind.

A multitude of artificial lures or live baits can be effective fished off these points. Plastic worms, grubs, tube baits, and feather-shaped reapers are effective crawled on a Texas rig, split-shotted or teamed with small 1/8 ounce jig heads. The full gamut of reaction lures such as crankplugs and spinnerbaits are also all worth trying off the points. Switch to jigs for casting out into deeper water, hopping this lure up along the edge of the point back to the bank. Both the traditional pig 'n jig combination and plastic tail-swimming jigs are effective for this uphill tactic.

Coves. Regardless of the size of the body of water you are fishing, coves like points, may also be potential hot spots. Winds will frequently force bait into the backs of coves. Here again, the bass will follow the bait.

During the spring, the warmest water on the lake or pond is often found in the shallow backs of coves. This is a prime area to look for more aggressive spawning fish.

This shallow water also warms first in the dead of winter. Bass will frequently make a short midday foray this time of year seeking warmth in the shallows. Feeding activity during the cold months is limited but can sporadically increase in the shallow water.

Plastic worms, reapers, and grubs are excellent for fishing shallow coves from the shore. Lures will remain fairly weedless, especially in coves with moss beds when rigged with either Texas or Carolina setups. Surface plugs and buzz baits are effective in warmer waters.

Stair-Step Slopes. Many larger impoundments have certain stretches with steep banks that are layered like a series of stair steps. Often the effect you see above the water also extends out into the lake.

Look for these stair-step inclines and work your bait or lures uphill. These steps typically lead to deeper water. Bass will traverse these different layers, particularly in summer and winter, moving from deep water up to the bank. Worms and slow-moving jigs are excellent for this type of terrain.

Riprap. This is another type of structure that can be potentially good from the bank. The rocks that form the face of a dam or a jetty leading into a marina, for example, can be excellent fish-holding structures. During the winter in particular, these rocks can to some extent retain radiant heat over night. This will then be one of the potentially warmer spots on the lake to try in the early morning hours.

The problem often facing the bank fisherman in working riprap is that sometimes the rocks comprise long stretches of shoreline that basically look all the same. So, where do you start and how do you fish this terrain effectively?

A good place to begin in walking along the riprap is in the corner where the rocks lie near another type of terrain. An example would be where broken rock converges with a sandy bank. This is a distinct transition in the shoreline and can serve as a staging area where bass may begin a migration from one type of bottom to another, triggering a new feeding mode.

A crankplug is a valuable lure for the shore fisherman to use to explore the expansive riprap. Walk the bank firing off casts with your favorite crankbait until fish are located on a particular stretch of shoreline. Try to cast parallel to the bank in your presentation. Once you catch a bass with the plug, consider slowing down. Concentrate on the precise area where you found the fish. If you no longer get any strikes from the crankbait, consider changing to a slower moving offering such as a plastic worm or a jig. You may have caught the most aggressive bass in the area with the plug, while other more sluggish fish remain. The worm or jig may generate additional strikes.

Docks and Piers. These man-made structures function somewhat similarly to a natural point. They give the bank fisherman greater access to deeper water.

Here again, a deep-diving crankbait can be highly effective when casted from a dock or pier. The best strategy is to first make a few casts alongside the wood or concrete pilings. The bass sometimes use the pilings for ambush points, usually resting on the shady side of the structure.

After covering the immediate vicinity of the dock, move towards the end and throw out into deeper open water. Fish may be suspended in the outside water normally not within casting distance from the bank. Make a series of "fan-casts," moving from left to right to thoroughly blanket the area. If the crankbait proves unproductive, try a bottom-bouncing jig or plastic worm for a slower survey of this deeper water.

Vegetation. Anywhere on a lake, pond, or reservoir that you can find vegetation there is the likelihood that bass will be nearby. Plant life can provide increased oxygen, shade, and sanctuary. Many smaller community lakes and ponds have bulrushes, reeds, and lily pads or tules growing along the bank.

Bass can be found nestled in aquatic vegetation all season long, especially if the water is fairly shallow. Weedless spoons, spinnerbaits, plastic worms, and grubs are recommended for fishing the "weeds" while casting from the bank. Surface plugs can routinely draw strikes in the warmer months for the stealthy shoreline basser carefully stalking the weeds.

Another intriguing option is to actually try the flippin' technique from the bank in chest-waders, or even in a float tube, for probing vegetation like this. Remain out of the direct sunlight, and quietly approach the tules. The bank fisherman using a 7 1/2 to 8 foot flippin' rod can be in for some terrific action! Quite often the bass may be rooted too far into the interior of the weeds for the boat fisherman to reach. By coming in from the bank side of the tules, the shore angler can gently drop a jig or worm directly into the major strike zone. This usually requires using a baitcasting reel with 20 to 25 pound test line teamed with a stiff flippin' rod to quickly yank bass out of this shallow cover.

Inlets. Another prime area the bank fisherman should look for is anywhere the water flows into the lake. A stream, canal, culvert, or irrigation ditch that empties into a larger impoundment can bring considerable forage bait plus oxygenated water within casting distance of the bank. (More on this in later chapters.)

These are excellent spots for a full spectrum of offerings: crankplugs, spinnerbaits, top-water lures, plastic worms and grubs, jigs, and of course live bait. Be on the lookout for moving current in the form of eddies or gentle white water ripples. The bass will move into these "feeding funnels" aggressively attacking bait caught in the flow.

Roadbeds. As you walk the shoreline, look to the hillside terrain for evidence of old dirt or asphalt roads that may have been covered up with the formation of the lake or larger pond. Many of these submerged roadbeds are composed of broken rock, chunks of asphalt, or gravel. Both threadfin shad and crawdads are frequently found on these surfaces, usually within casting distance of the bank.

A plastic worm with either a Texas-rig or a split-shot setup is perfect for crawling over these submerged roadbeds. If the path seems to lead into deeper water, crankbaits or jigs can also be used. Look for bass to move up into the shallow portion of the roadbed during the spring and winter, following forage bait into the shallows.

More Tips

To reiterate, once you develop a sense of what to look for in terms of viable stretches of shoreline, *remain mobile*.

Don't get locked into only fishing shallow coves or fan-casting off docks and piers into deeper water. Bass are highly temperamental creatures. They will migrate with the bait—both shallow and deep.

We mentioned how both professional guides and tournament anglers talk about looking for a particular "pattern" that the fish are on so they can narrow their options down in a given day on the water. Shore-based fishermen should try to discern feeding patterns as they focus their attention on the environment of the bank. Again, be prepared for patterns to fluctuate during the day with emergent changes in weather.

Also, it is imperative to put your lures and bait where the fish live when pounding the shoreline. It is obviously difficult to retrieve an offering once it is snagged while casting from the bank. A majority of bass will be on or near the bottom, so be prepared to occasionally lose some of your baits.

Routinely check for nicks and abrasions on your line. Use an uphill approach when casting from the bank to be sure your line makes optimum contact with the bottom. This means greater wear on the monofilament in contrast to casting from a boat.

Finally, learn to fish the shoreline with confidence. Use a limited selection of lures or baits. Focus less on repeatedly changing offerings and more on looking for prime water to fish with baits you have confidence in. Be precise and meticulous in your presentations. You may not be able to cover as much territory as the fellow in the hi-tech boat. You may be able to concentrate on key spots with intensity that the boater can't reach. There are many limit days possible while bassin' from the shore. Take it to the bank!

Match the Hatch

To become accomplished fly fishermen, anglers must develop some skill at selecting their flies to replicate small aquatic or terrestrial insects. Members of this sophisticated angling community refer to this selection process as "matching the hatch." In many ways, serious bass fishermen do the same thing when they use artificial lures.

Crankplugs, spinnerbaits, surface lures, jigs, plastic worms, and spoons are all made to resemble indigenous creatures found in or alongside warm water lakes, ponds, or rivers. Expert bassers, like their fly fishing cousins, employ a similar selection technique to pick the best lure for existing conditions. Bass anglers basically use three lines of attack when trying to "match the hatch" for their particular quarry: natural coloration, proper silhouette, and simulated action.

Let's focus on each of these three dimensions to get a better idea of how this selection process works.

Natural Coloration

Choosing the proper color scheme is perhaps the most critical variable in lure selection. Before bassers can decide which color to use, they must have some fundamental knowledge of the natural forage baits in their regions.

Keep in mind that there are two baits that bass feed on across the country: shad minnows and crayfish. All of the major species of bass, to one degree or another, forage on shad and crawdads. The dietary patterns of the fish depend upon the overall availability of the bait as well as the time of year.

For example, bass at times will key in on slow-moving crayfish and shad in the colder months. Fish evidence a decrease in metabolism as temperatures plummet. In the wintertime, the bass become more lethargic. They feed less and move shorter distances to attack their prey in order to minimize energy expenditure. A crawdad is the perfect meal for sluggish fish this time of the year.

As water temperatures increase, so does the bass' metabolism and appetite. The fish are prone to move further to chase down faster moving baitfish.

Thus, the time of the year plays an important role in proper bait selection. Don't underestimate the fish's propensity to unexpectedly switch preferences regardless of assumed seasonal patterns.

A simple way to select colors that most closely imitate these two types of natural bait is to think in terms of light versus dark. Lures in shades of white, yellow, pearl, clear, smoke, and silver appear shad-like underwater. Chartreuse is also included in this category, since baitfish often assume a greenish tint in the colder months. Darker, more opaque patterns including brown, black, purple, blue, red, or orange are more akin to the crayfish that crawl along the bottom.

The light versus dark distinction applies to all kinds of artificial lures. For instance, smoke-colored plastic worms are designed to mimic shad minnows whereas purple worms are colored to look like crayfish.

However, don't limit your selection of lure colors only to duplicating natural shad or crawdad finishes. There are other panfish, amphibians, and insects that can comprise a major portion of the bass' diet, depending upon the different waters you fish.

Panfish such as bluegill and warmouth, for example, are often the primary forage in small farm ponds. Lures in blends of blue, green, and yellow come close to matching the coloration of these panfish species.

Similarly, amphibians like frogs, salamanders, and newts can be the major food sources in certain rivers and streams. Lures in frog patterns are typically in yellow and green combinations. Keep in mind that frogs often assume other colorations including mottled brown, black, or green. Obviously, the shrewd basser who observes these amphibians in their natural habitat should try to replicate the color of the frog as closely as possible rather than simply opting for the traditional green and yellow mix. Browns, blacks, purples, and orange combinations in soft plastic lures are the common colors used to duplicate salamanders and newts.

Other larger fish sometimes offer a hefty meal for big Florida bass. It is not uncommon to see smart anglers throw lures in rainbow trout, baby bass, or golden shiner tones if they are stalking the big Floridas. The crankplug, spinnerbait, spoon, and surface plug manufacturers now market an array of lures in these three finishes. Soft plastic worms and grubs are also being produced to appear similar to trout, bass fry, or shiner minnows.

Climatic Conditions

Accomplished bassers also take into consideration the weather in selecting the most effective lure color. If the sky is dark and cloudy, then it is necessary to choose a bait that once again presents a prominent silhouette as the bass looks at it from below. Lures in black, brown, and purple would be an excellent choice for this situation regardless of whether you are using a plastic worm, crankplug, or top-water bait.

Conversely, for bright sunny days, switch to lighter, more translucent lures that present a more subtle silhouette to the fish. Baits in shades of white, gray, yellow, silver, smoke, or clear are recommended for this type of weather.

Proper Silhouette

Many weekend anglers become adept at matching lure color to the natural baits found in the area. It is equally important to scale the lure so that it approximates the basic size and shape of the forage bait.

In various areas of the country, biologists have conducted extensive research on the feeding habits of the different bass species. One study in particular generated a highly important piece of information relevant to lure selection for freshwater bass. After dissecting numerous fish, the average prey was found to be roughly 3 inches in length.

Now this is an intriguing finding. We know from experience that larger baits tend to catch bigger bass. There are times when smaller artificials will equally take larger fish and in greater numbers. This is due to the fact that diminutive lures in the 3 to 4 inch class more closely replicate the size of the shad or crawdads found in the water.

A classic example of this relationship comes to mind. In California and Texas, the transplanted Florida bass are extremely finicky feeders. They are difficult to fool with artificial baits. In recent years, local bassers have scaled down further and further when presenting slow-moving soft plastic lures.

Three or 4 inch hand-poured worms, stubby curly-tail grubs, and the tiny three inch feather-like reapers have put a significant dent in the Florida bass population out West. Lures in this genre present a silhouette to the fish that compares favorably to the size of the shad and crayfish found in these impoundments. In addition, more compact crankplugs, floating minnows, spoons, buzzers, and jigs are now being used to replicate the size of the crayfish and threadfin shad.

Once again, we want to caution the reader not to take anything for granted. Bass fishing is far from being an exact science. There are times when a larger lure nails the lunker fish. For example, in the spring when terrestrial critters such as snakes and lizards tumble off the bank, a longer 6 to 10 inch plastic worm would be a wise choice. Similarly, it takes larger plugs, spinnerbaits, spoons, or jigs to properly duplicate the silhouettes of bass fry, shiner minnows, small trout, panfish, or frogs.

The basic rule of thumb is to try to match, as closely as possible, the *current* size of the bait found in the water you are fishing. We emphasize current size because some natural baits such as shad change in length as they grow through the year. Hence, we may start out in the spring throwing a floating minnow in a 3 to 5 inch length. By fall, fishing the same lake, we may switch to an identical plug in a 7 inch model to imitate jumbo, mature shad. Crawdads also increase in size through the year. If it appears that the lake is being overrun by magnum 4 to 5 inch 'dads, then certainly consider scaling up to a lure with a slightly larger profile.

Simulated Action

Even after the angler has decided which lure to use in terms of color and size, the final ingredient is often omitted from the selection process. It is critical to choose artificials so that their actions are similar to the movement of the natural baits.

Most crankplugs have a diving action that is made to simulate a swimming baitfish or a crawdad. Top-water plugs are designed to look like a struggling minnow, frog, small panfish, trout, or large insect. Spinnerbaits in light shades are thrown to mimic shad. Dark-colored spinners are worked near the bottom to replicate crawdads. Spoons will sink and flutter, imitating a dying baitfish. Jigs are plowed along the bottom to parody either shad or crawdads. Finally, soft plastic worms, grubs, reapers, or similar lures, are made to act like slow-moving minnows or crayfish.

Understand that quite frequently anglers must impart some of their own actions to insure the lure is moving on parity with the natural bait. A dark plastic jig, for example, can be hopped down a ledge to act like a crawdad. The same lure in a light shade can be casted and retrieved without pausing to give it the illusion of a swimming baitfish.

Similarly, a surface plug can be twitched, creating the effect of a wounded minnow or it can be popped to sound like a frog. The point is that the serious bass fisherman has to be selective in not only picking the right color and silhouette for the lure, but also the proper action.

In summary, it is important to envision precisely what it is that you want your lure to replicate in the water — a minnow, crawdad, frog, snake, or whatever. Try to pick an appropriate color scheme and profile to match this "hatch." Then make sure that the lure is designed properly so that you can make it move in the water in imitation of the natural prey.

Be Color Innovative!

Frequently, even the most ardent bassers will find themselves in the field without the proper color in a particular lure. With a small collection of felt-tip marking pens and a pocket knife, there are a few simple tricks you can use to custom-color your baits while on the water in an effort to either match the hatch or to simply create something out of the ordinary.

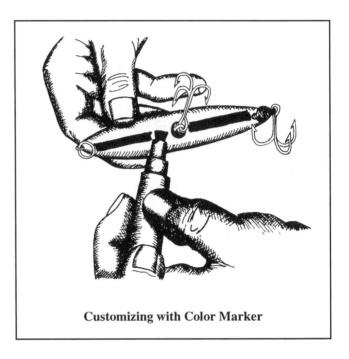

Customizing with Color Marker

Keep permanent markers in black, brown, green, and chartreuse in your tackle box at all times. These can be purchased at most stationery or art supply stores.

The black pen probably has the greatest utility. To begin with, in a pinch you can change practically any light-colored plug, spinnerbait, or soft plastic lure into a darker shade if you are caught short fishing in off-colored water or under dark skies. You can also add a dark dorsal or ventral vein to both soft and hard plastic lures to create a contrast the manufacturer may have overlooked.

Use the markers in brown and green to create the mottled tones on both hard baits and soft plastics. This particular coloration has been widely popularized in the West as the "green weenie" look. This is one of the best combinations of color and shade to duplicate crawdads anywhere in the country.

A small pocket knife can create similar miracles in the field for hard baits that are not getting bit. Sometimes "subtle" is the answer. As we mentioned, frequently bass in pressured waters become accustomed to seeing the same parade of lure colors day after day. Take your pocket knife and scrape away some of the paint on your favorite stickbait, chugger, popper, or crankplug. Most likely, you will now be throwing a bait with much more subdued color and shade, offering the bass something new and interesting to see and possibly more akin to natural coloration of potential prey.

The Color-C-Lector

In recent years, Mike and Ron, as well as many other anglers, have begun to rely upon the Color-C-Lector to help them choose the proper color lure.

This simple device functions as a photosynthetic light meter. As the angler lowers a light-sensitive probe under water, the meter reads the primary color that will be most effective at that location, time, and depth to which the probe is submerged.

There are 26 primary colors that the Color-C-Lector can discern appearing along a circular band that gives readings for clear, stained, or muddy water. In addition, the meter also provides the angler with both secondary colors appearing on each side of the band and an optional fluorescent color appearing above the main band. This permits the bass fisherman to choose an artificial lure with a combination of colors and shades that will be most visible and appealing to the fish under precise conditions.

For example, if the probe was lowered to the bottom in 20 feet of stained water, and the needle reads the color " N ", a light violet worm fished at that depth would be an excellent choice.

But, on each side of "N," are the colors "M" (purple) and "R" (dark green), respectively. Our choice can be made even more effective by adding a purple colored worm sinker and coloring the tail slightly with a green marking pen. Now, both the primary and secondary colors are included in our bait selection.

Always remember that meter readings vary from one location on the lake to another based on water clarity, atmospheric conditions, and depth surveyed.

Serious Mechanics

Serious Mechanics

Now that you're armed with some core strategies for challenging your favorite bass lake or river, let's look at some of the more subtle aspects of utilizing all the hi-tech gear you've accumulated. To begin with, Mike and Ron both agree that bass fishing is not an exact science. Nevertheless, the adage that "10 percent of the fishermen catch 90 percent of the fish" seems to hold true for this sport. Why is this the case?

You will find that the best, most serious anglers have developed a precise repertoire of tackle and artificial lures. They study and diligently practice the latest sophisticated techniques devised to fool bass. In addition to these ingredients, the accomplished bass fisherman also learns to take care of the "finer points" of his game, both in terms of tackle selection and procedures he incorporates.

These are the subtleties frequently neglected by the recreational angler. Paying attention to these minute details is what separates the serious basser from the weekend novice. Starting with the basic components of line, hooks, and lures, let's examine some of the less obvious things the pros do to "fine tune" their game and their mental attitude.

Why Trigger-Grip Rods?[1]

Most bass fishermen learn to use a baitcasting reel, teamed with a relatively short 5 1/2 to 6 foot long pistol grip rod. This kind of bass fishing rod has been the staple for the sport for decades. In recent years, however, more serious bassers are adding the newer trigger-grip models to their rod lockers.

When trigger-grip rods were initially introduced, they were earmarked for the more specialized flippin' techniques. The typical flippin' rod measures 7 to 8 feet in length and is primarily designed for the shallow water attack.

Now, rod manufacturers have added a full array of lighter trigger-grip models to their line-ups. They are suitable for practically any type of bassin'. These rods are marketed in 6 to 7 foot lengths with a wide spectrum of actions. There are clearly some definite advantages worth considering to switching to one of these rods from the older pistol-grip models.

Besides the flippin' approach, a trigger-style bass rod is particularly comfortable for pitchin' baits. In 6 to 7 foot lengths, this blank design allows the angler to make quick underhand or sidearm pitches to shoreline cover while maintaining some distance from the target. The reel itself is usually held with two hands—one on the grip and one on the reel. This helps to give the basser a strong powerful two-handed hook set with strikes near the bank.

Plastic worm aficionados may also find a long trigger-grip rod to their liking. A graphite blank in the 6 to 7 foot range will pick up slack line more quickly than a shorter 5 to 5 1/2 foot baitcasting rod. This can be a critical feature for successful worm fishing. Too much slack line on the set can lead to a swing-and-a-miss.

A trigger-grip wormin' rod in the longer 6 to 7 foot lengths can also double for flippin' or pitchin'. Quite frequently, bass get spooked in clear shallow water. Flippin' with 20 to 30 pound mono and a jig may fail to produce. Use a lighter 6 to 7 foot trigger-grip rod matched with a baitcaster filled with 12 to 14 pound test line. Gently flip or pitch worms in place of the pork frog to tempt skittish fish to strike.

Many pros and guides also point out that the longer trigger-grip rods—including the 7 to 8 foot flippin' models — are effective when greater casting distance is

[1] Portions of this section previously appeared in *B.A.S.S. Times*

needed. These rods are perfect for overhead, two-handed casting. This tactic is similar to two-handed saltwater surfcasting. The extra length of the graphite blank, combined with the thrust and power generated from a two-handed presentation, can translate to added distance. This is particularly the case when it comes to throwing large bulky lures such as magnum willowleaf spinnerbaits, big cigar-shaped surface plugs, and buzzers.

This style rod is also suitable for casting the new generation of ultradeep diving crankbaits. These lures can be cumbersome to throw with shorter, pistol-grip baitcasting models. It takes less effort to retrieve these jumbo-size plugs with the longer blank and the more comfortable trigger-grip working for you. As an added bonus, you can drive these big baits down even deeper by extending a 6 to 8 foot long trigger-grip rod into the water with the patented "kneel-and-reel" strategy.

Tournament anglers relegated to the backseat position may greatly benefit from switching to the longer trigger-grip models. As noted, the two-handed casting style will help increase distance. This may serve to somewhat "neutralize" the advantage of the front-seater, especially when chuckin' or windin' down a bank with some sort of reaction bait.

Finally, if there was any major drawback with using a trigger-grip rod in the past, it was that the additional length of the grip was awkward to hold against the body for long periods. Most new models have remedied this with shorter grips that do not extend very far out from the body. If an even shorter length is desired, a section of the rear portion of the grip can be cut to obtain a custom fit.

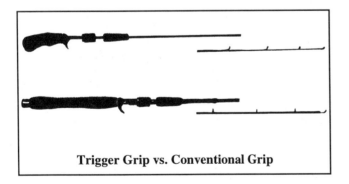

Trigger Grip vs. Conventional Grip

Why Spinning Reels?

In 1935, the first fixed spool spinning reels were introduced into the United States from Europe. These strange-looking contraptions vaguely resembled an old-fashioned coffee grinder. They were a radical departure from the then popular knuckle-bustin' baitcasting reels with the basic revolving spool.

It wasn't really until the end of World War II that the open-face spinning reels we use today were widely distributed. Die-hard knuckle-busters initially viewed these foreign imports with great suspicion. They soon learned, however, that the spinners opened up an entirely new world of fishing opportunities.

To begin with, the fixed spool concept was a major breakthrough in reel design. In contrast to the revolving spool found in the casting reels, the angler no longer had to use his thumb to apply braking pressure at the end of the cast. Thus, the spinning reel's main advantage was that it would eliminate the potential for annoying backlash.

The post-war spinners brought angling to the masses. They made casting a simple and enjoyable experience. These innovative reels also accommodated the newly introduced monofilament that replaced linen lines. The fine diameter mono could be spooled more easily onto a spinner than on a baitcasting reel. Novice fishermen could now go out and compete—at least in terms of casting—with the most seasoned anglers.

Nevertheless, we know that today some hard-core bassers still resist using the spinning reel. Many serious anglers feel that these models are simply too flimsy and not strong enough to withstand the rigors of serious hawg huntin'. They note that the typical open-faced spinner can't accommodate the heavier test lines needed to drag bass out of dense underwater cover. Furthermore, serious bass fishermen do not trust the drag mechanisms of the lightweight spinning models. They prefer the traditional star drags found in the heavy duty baitcasters when big fish or tournament moneys are on the line.

Well, as they say, the times are a changin'. There is a growing legion of dedicated bassers who are finding tremendous applications for these "coffee grinders," including these two writers.

Let's examine some of the sophisticated techniques practiced by Mike and Ron and how they lend themselves to using a spinning reel.

Light-Lining

On deep clear lakes, fine diameter monofilament is a necessity for fooling hook-shy bass. For many Southern pros, "light line" means 10 to 12 pound test. For their Western counterparts, many tournaments will be won with 6 to 8 pound mono. Mike and Ron prefer Berkley Trilene XL, Ultrathin and the new Select monofilament for their light-line approach.

Spinning reels team well with light line. In clear water there is a lot of pressure on the bass. Frequently, you will get bit more with 6 to 8 pound test mono. The spinning reels of today have precise, sophisticated drag systems that are good enough to tame lunker bass.

Heavier, revolving spool, baitcasting reels will not as easily accommodate this gossamer line. The latest trend has been for line manufacturers to extrude even finer diameter mono with considerable limpness. This new generation of fishing lines lies best on the spinning reel. It also takes a lot of this ultrathin mono to fill the average baitcaster.

Minuscule Lures

Combined with the light line approach is a wealth of scaled-down artificial lures used to seduce bass under the toughest conditions. These baits are difficult to throw with the casting reel simply because they are so light. Perhaps, more importantly, lures in this genre also "swim" better and evidence more action when they are teamed with light, 4 to 10 pound test lines.

The latest evolution of tubular baits such as the Berkley Power Tube or Gitzit are examples of lures that perform best with light line and spinning gear. Tube baits are commonly rigged on tiny 1/16 to 1/8 ounce lead heads. It takes more effort and greater casting expertise to toss these with baitcasting tackle.

A similar rage in past years has been the 3 to 5 inch curl-tail grubs. These are also threaded onto a small lead head jig. Grubs can be cast great distances in super clear water with a spinning outfit. These stubby lures have terrific swimming action, but it is enhanced only with the small diameter monofilament.

Other Spinning Lures

In addition to little grubs and tube baits, there are some other key lures that seem to perform better with spinning tackle. For example, the ever-popular plastic worm has a definite niche in the spin fisherman's arsenal. When the bass are especially twitchy, it often helps to select a worm in reduced length. Numerous West Coast lure manufacturers now market tiny, spaghetti-thin plastic worms in 2 to 4 inch models. These compact baits are superb fished on a small lead head or worked Texas-style with a 1/16 to 1/8 ounce sliding sinker. Here again, these worm variations can be casted and presented with optimal action on light lines and spinning combos.

Spinning Tactics

There are some specific situations that call for using a spinning rod and reel to maximize your chances of nailing a limit of bass. Many accomplished bassers now prefer to use spinning outfits when they fish bulky floating minnows on or below the surface. Rapala, Bomber, and Smithwick make a variety of 3 to 5 inch minnows that are made to be danced or twitched near the water line. These modest-sized baits can be thrown with considerable accuracy on 6 to 12 pound test line and a medium action spinning setup. Popular models include the Rapala #7, #9, and #11, Bomber Long-A, and Smithwick Rogue.

Once again, in windy weather, it is much easier to run'n gun a shoreline with these minnows using spinning gear rather than baitcasting tackle. Floating minnows like these will also generate more wiggle and enticing action with the lighter mono.

6 Pounder on a Spinnerbait

Spinning reels are also excellent for skipping lures into hard-to-get-to spaces. It is now common to see top-level bass pros using spinning combos to gently skip tube baits, darter worms, and tiny grubs under boat docks, piers, or overhanging brush.

Moving out into deeper water, the smart guide finds that spinning tackle for his customers is highly suitable for the popular split-shot method. This is nothing more than a simplified version of the Carolina rig, simplified with spinning gear for those being introduced to this methodology.

A 1/16 to 1/4 ounce lead shot is crimped anywhere from 12 to 48 inches above a diminutive plastic bait. Small 3 inch feather-like Reapers, 3 to 4 inch hand-poured plastic worms and short 3 inch curl-tail grubs have been putting a major dent in the bass population across the country with this method.

Here again, spinning gear excels at properly presenting this distinctive setup. Many anglers feel that it is considerably easier to cast the cumbersome, long-dangling leaders intrinsic to the split-shot rig with a spinning outfit rather than baitcasting tackle.

Also, there are times on deep clear impoundments where the fisherman needs to use not only a scaled-down lure, but to make an extraordinarily long cast as well. Here, too, the spinning reel is a valuable asset.

For example, it is not uncommon on lakes to see bass crashing on shad near the surface some distance from the boat. If you motor too close to the schooling frenzy, the fish will sound. Similarly, if you toss a bait that is too large or bulky, the bass will also spook.

Shrewd bass anglers will often rely upon small spoons or spinners normally associated with trout fishing to fool these school bass. Keeping away from the surface commotion, they will cast tiny 1/8 to 1/4 ounce spoons or spinners into the boils. As is often the case, some of the best catches of the year are tallied in this manner, thanks to light lines, little baits, and spinning outfits.

Live Bait Fishing

Spinning tackle is also a real boon for live bait fishing. Many bass anglers like to fish with live crawdads, night crawlers, or minnows. With smaller natural baits, you can carefully lob your offerings using minimal sinkers, if any. Extra weight might otherwise impede the movement of the creature. Crawdads, minnows, and 'crawlers also move more naturally and freely when they are fished with light monofilament. The bass obviously have a greater tendency to strike an unencumbered live offering.

Buy Quality Reels

Spinning reels definitely have a place in the serious bass fisherman's tackle repertoire. Be careful not to cut corners and scrimp when purchasing this style reel. It's important to stay with top quality models to insure maximum performance from your equipment. Reels like Daiwa's 1300 or Penn's 430SS exemplify this type of needed technical product of the serious basser.

Look for such things as ball bearing drive shafts, sturdy, lightweight metal or graphite frames, interchangeable spools, smooth line rollers and, above all, precision drags. It is imperative when you are fighting a solid 2 to 3 pound bass that the drag on the spinning reel moves smoothly without any jerkiness. It doesn't take much for a fish in this weight range to pop 6 to 8 pound monofilament with one good surge.

As holds true with all fishing tackle, purchase the best spinning reel you can afford. Models in this class are built to last and will prove to be highly dependable. Keep that spinning outfit alongside your baitcasting gear and you are now prepared to challenge a full spectrum of bassin' opportunities.

Use That Drag!

One of the most integral but often overlooked dimensions of serious bassin' is the proper use of the reel drag. Top-level guides and pros understand the importance of this device. With big stakes on the line, the loss of a single fish can mean the difference between a paycheck and heartbreak for the pro, or a satisfied customer to the guide.

Types of Reel Drags

The baitcasting reel has perhaps the most sophisticated drag system, consisting of a series of washers sandwiched together. With the prominent "star wheel," the angler is able to make fairly precise settings with even the most modestly priced models. As a rule, the baitcasting reel's drag mechanism offers a wider range of settings and perhaps more precision than the spinners. This is due to the larger washers that comprise the drag system in the casting reels.

Spinning reels are available with either front-loaded or stern drags. Spinners with front-loaded drags usually have larger washers than those with the stern knobs. There is simply more room available in this front portion of the reel to place the bigger washers. The larger surface area of these washers may serve to dissipate heat and friction a little better than stern drags. Still, many pros prefer the easy access of the stern knob for making quick adjustments in playing out the fish.

Using the Drag

There are a couple of key things to keep in mind when using the drag to fight bass. To begin with, set your drag when you get to the lake in the morning. These devices are somewhat sensitive to extreme cold and heat. It will be better to test the drag in the environment where you are fishing rather than in the warmer confines of your home.

Next, keep in mind that drag tension can vary during the day due to changes in climate or after repeatedly catching fish. Check the drag and make adjustments as needed throughout the day.

If you are using a light leader with a Carolina rig, for instance, make sure to set the drag to correspond to the breaking test of the leader, not the primary line. Your main line may be 12 pound test, but the leader is only 6 pound diameter. The drag should be calibrated for the lighter leader.

On this note, it is often difficult to get a proper response from the reel drag when using light monofilament. For example, when split-shottin' with 6 pound line, the drag has to be set fairly tight; otherwise there is too much slippage on the initial set. On the other hand, if the drag is set too tight, you may snap the light weight mono on the hook set. There are a couple of ways around this problem.

First, you can quickly disengage the anti-reverse switch on a spinning reel while holding onto the handle with your other hand. Then carefully reel backwards to pay out line instead of relying upon the drag. This is a delicate procedure termed "back-reeling." Many pros prefer to do this with light mono rather than worrying about a drag not working smoothly.

Another option is to use a spinning reel with one of the auxiliary drag levers. These will allow you to quickly give the bass line—or, if you need to, to tighten the tension—by easily flicking the lever either right or left. (Be sure to study this feature carefully to make sure you remember which side tightens and which loosens the tension.) When the level is repositioned in the center, the main drag mechanism goes back into effect.

The problem becomes a little more tricky with a baitcasting reel when you use light line. The best advice is to quickly turn the star drag backwards to loosen the tension. You can also apply thumb pressure intermittently on the spool if the bass starts to run the line out too easily with the star wheel backed off.

Drag Maintenance

When you are finished using your reels, turn the drag down to its loosest setting. This will keep the washers from sticking together which creates an unevenness in the drag. Most manufacturers recommend not using any lubricant on the drag washers. They are designed to perform without any outside compounds added to the mechanism. However, if the drag seems uneven or "jerky" when you pull out line, have the reel serviced and the washers replaced.

Trick Retrieves

Recreational bass fishermen frequently get caught in a rut by being less than imaginative when it comes to retrieves. The serious basser, on the other hand, realizes that the manner in which a lure is brought back to the boat may critically affect the strike-inducing potential of the bait. Put another way, how you retrieve your lure can be an integral component to the pattern the bass are keying in on.

We want to discuss the three primary types of baits found in bassin' arsenals and examine some of the different ways they can be retrieved to increase success.

Worms

Neophyte bassers probably make their most frequent errors while tossing plastic worms. Veteran guides may often watch their own clients simply cast and wind when wormin'. They emphasize that 99 percent of the time the biggest mistake made in using this lure is working it too fast. It was designed as a S-L-O-W-moving bait.

Even after slowing down the retrieve, there are some interesting things that can still be utilized while wormin'. For example, whether split-shottin' or slow-crawling with a Texas rig, occasionally stop and pause during the retrieve for a prolonged period—maybe as much as 30 seconds. Sometimes the bass will stop to carefully scrutinize the worm. After a delay in the retrieve, the fish may actually decide to attack the "dead" bait.

Another ploy to try when crawling a Texas-rigged worm is to instantly stop winding the moment the bait makes contact with some type of structure. Then, give the reel handle a quick and sharp 1/4 to 1/2 turn, using your wrist. The worm will violently jump off the rock, brush, or tree branch. This tactic, known as "chirping," can often generate unexpected strikes.

Crankplugs

Rather than simply chuckin' and windin' at a steady pace, stop intermittently through the retrieve. Then start up again. This stop-and-go procedure often produces strikes as the plug remains motionless with bass actually bumping into the lure.

Similarly, learn to use a much S-L-O-W-E-R retrieve in colder water with crankplugs. During the wintertime, bass will indeed attack a crankbait. Remember they are in a more lethargic feeding mode. Employ a steady yet significantly slower grind than you would during the warmer months.

Use your rod tip to induce more erratic action from your crankplugs. An errant baitfish or crawdad doesn't swim in either a straight line or in a single motion. Try to make your plugs dance and dart more by adding intermittent rhythmic twitches of the rod tip during the retrieve. Finally, perhaps the most important thing is to maintain constant bottom contact.

Spinners

With spinnerbaits, use similar variations on the retrieve such as the "stop-and-go," and the "rod-tip twitch." However, you must maintain a fairly tight line throughout the retrieve so there is enough resistance to make the blades turn.

On this note, be more precise in letting the spinner drop for longer periods during the retrieve. Learn to fish the "fall." Slow the retrieve down so the lure drops into a potential pocket of cover with the blade barely turning. As the spinnerbait helicopters down, be prepared for strikes on the fall. Be sure to always cast past the target and pull the spinnerbait by the target. Try to "bump" the structure with the lure. This simple strategy will result in more strikes by the end of the day!

Finally, consider winding your spinnerbaits barely below the surface. This is an interesting alternative to fishing a buzzbait. The spinner produces less commotion in a more subtle presentation. Again, maintain a moderately slow yet steady grind to keep the blades turning.

Be creative with all your retrieves. New patterns may emerge by making subtle adjustments in the way you wind your lures back to the boat.

Pick the Right Hook

Ironically, with all their hi-tech gear, many serious bass fishermen often overlook one of the most integral links between themselves and the fish—their hooks. Mike and Ron and other veteran bassers who make a living from this sport clearly recognize the importance of this element of

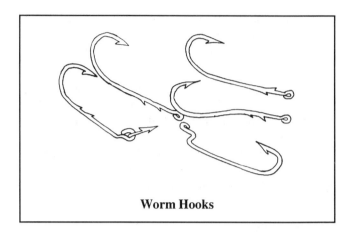

Worm Hooks

their tackle repertoire. Considerable forethought is given to the proper selection and use of the "right" hook for a particular lure or technique.

Let's examine then the basic categories of baits used by serious bassers and how they match the hooks to these lures.

Plastic Worms

It is estimated that more bass are caught on plastic worms than on all other baits combined. Of all the lures used in professional bassin' circles, the worm is probably the one most likely to be given serious consideration as to proper hook selection. This is due to the fact that this bait requires that the angler rig the hook into the worm itself. Regardless of the method—Texas-style, split-shotting, doodling, or the Carolina rig—the angler must pick the right hook to fit the worm.

As far as plastic worm hook designs are concerned, selection depends a great deal on personal preference. Some anglers like the simple Southern sprout design exemplified by the straight-shank Eagle Claw 95XBL. Other pros recommend a worm hook with the bend more offset, such as Gamakatsu or V.M.C. offset models.

Some hook manufacturers believe that more radical designs involving modification of the shaft and the bend generate greater penetration and solid hook sets.

A recent trend has been to focus more upon hook sharpness rather than emphasizing shaft and bend configurations. Japanese companies such as Gamakatsu and V.M.C. have pioneered the way, introducing needle-sharp, thin wire worm hooks in assorted sizes and colors. These are especially good for fishing soft plastics finesse style. An American manufacturer, Eagle Claw, has followed with their Laser Sharp line of plastic worm hooks.

It pays to be experimental when it comes to picking the right worm hook. You will find that one design will probably not suffice for all the assorted worms in your tackle box.

Another consideration in selecting the proper hook is the texture of the bait and the test line used. If the worm is one of the popular hand-poured models, it will be made from very soft plastic. A heavier gauge wire or forged hook will have a tendency to tear the soft plastic. More importantly, the bulkier hook will often offset the delicate symmetry and balance of these little "sissy baits," impairing their overall effectiveness.

Depending upon the technique and terrain, the angler will also have to match test line with hook style. For instance, split-shotters will typically use 6 to 8 pound test monofilament with 4 inch worms. Because of excessive line stretch, it may be difficult to get a good hook set with a heavy-duty worm hook. A fine wire or smaller diameter forged hook will team better with the light lines.

When slow-crawling a 4 inch worm through thick cover, the serious basser may scale up to 10 to 15 pound test line. If we use a lightweight worm hook with this heavier mono, there is a good possibility that you will straighten the hook out on a strong set. A thicker gauge wire or forged worm hook would be more suitable for the heavier monofilament.

Finally, it is also imperative to closely pair the right size hook with the right length of worm. Guides frequently find that their clients will want to switch plastic worms while using the same size hook. That tiny #2 hook used for 4 inch long hand-poured baits is simply too small for a longer 6 inch worm. There are no short cuts here—the hook must be changed along with the bait. You will need a hook closer to a 2/0 size to match with the six inch worm. A good guide will quickly have his customers make this subtle adjustment.

A hook that is too small will restrict proper penetration, and the worm will have a tendency to bunch up around it. Similarly, a hook that is too large will again impair the symmetry and balance of the bait, creating an unnatural silhouette underwater.

Crankbaits and Surface Plugs

In contrast to plastic worms, these lures come with factory stocked treble hooks right out of the package. Nevertheless, the conscientious pro may do certain things with the hooks on these reaction baits to enhance their fish-catching qualities.

First, there is the question of sharpness. All of these treble hooks, regardless of brand or style, should be pre-sharpened by the angler. Don't expect needle-sharp perfection directly out of the box. As a rule, bronze wire trebles will make a better point than nickel-plated or cadmium models. If the bite is exceptionally tough or the fish seem to be throwing the hooks, consider switching to a bronze treble.

Next, think about matching the color of the treble hooks to the forage bait the lure is intended to represent. For example, team bronze trebles, not silver-colored cadmium hooks, with a crawdad pattern crankbait.

The actual size of the treble hook is another important factor to consider with reaction lures. Many pros and guides feel that the lure manufacturers have a tendency to market their baits with hooks that are too small and too dull.

There are also a few other tricks that are worth noting when it comes to using the correct treble hook. Frequently, the angler will have to cast these crankbaits and surface plugs into potentially dangerous territory loaded with snags and similar obstructions. It is possible to make these lures more weedless, and actually increase hook-setting potential with some easy modifications done in the field.

Take a pair of dikes and completely clip off one of the three hooks on the trebles found on crankplugs. This will form double hooks. Now with only two points the front hook will have a tendency to ride closer to the belly of the lure making it fairly weedless. The rear double hook will also be less prone to snagging.

Another option is to remove the rear treble completely from the crankbait. Most lures will still ride properly with the single treble and are much more weedless, especially in shallow water. Amazingly, not that many more fish will be lost with only the single treble hook.

We replace lure hooks with V.M.C. and sometimes one size larger than the one that comes from the factory. After replacement with the larger size hooks you need to check the plug to make sure the increased size does not deaden the action of the lure.

Spinnerbaits

These lures pose still another problem when it comes to hook selection because the hook is actually built into the bait. The secret here is to closely examine the spinnerbait hook. You will find that some styles use hooks made out of medium gauge wire or forged bronze while others feature nickel-plated hooks.

This becomes an issue of strength versus flexibility and penetration. The nickel-plated hooks are generally stronger than the bronze wire or forged models. These are teamed with heavier wire frames for the spinnerbait. This type of spinner is perfect for the stump infested waters of the South using 10 to 20 pound test line.

Mike and Ron, in contrast, prefer a lighter wire frame that gives the spinnerbait more action. These models will commonly have the nickel hooks that seem to give the best penetration with 8 to 15 pound mono. Be sure to choose a spinnerbait that has a medium to light wire arm to maximize blade vibration, a good swivel that turns freely,

Cranking a Weed Line

a strong wide-gap hook, and a skirt whose strands do not stick together. The skirt must "breathe" or pulsate freely.

Jigs

Like spinnerbaits, lead head jigs have the hooks molded into the lure. Here again, there are subtle differences in the type of hooks used with the assorted jigs on the market today.

Lead heads with fine diameter hooks are effective for deep-water jigging using lighter 6 to 12 pound test line. Penetration is critical, working these lures in deeper water. The fine wire bronze hooks can be sharpened to maximize the chances of sticking bass at greater depths.

However, lighter gauge jig hooks are somewhat risky for, say, shallow water pitchin' or flippin' using 15 to 30 pound mono. The stress of the heavy line pulling against the fine diameter wire may bend the hook. A larger trophy bass could be lost by not switching to a jig with a heavier gauge forged hook.

Spoons

These rather simple lures also require some forethought in matching them with the right hook. Perhaps the most overwhelmingly common problem is that the factory stocked hooks are not nearly sharp enough out of the package. The serious basser working a spoon will typically be fishing deep with considerable line stretch. This excessive stretch is especially reduced with Berkley Trilene XT monofilament. To keep fish on the trebles coming up from deep water will require maximum sharpness in the hooks.

Also, the manufacturers invariably seem to sell these lures with treble hooks that are too small. Spoons do have a propensity to hang up and some bassers are reluctant to switch to larger trebles. The fact remains that fish in deep water are hard to bring in and a larger hook gives more "bite" on the set. Larger trebles also penetrate into a greater area of the bass' mouth.

An interesting alternative is to replace factory stock treble hooks with either single long-shank Siwash or short-shank live bait hooks used for saltwater species. These single hooks can be honed to perfection. They snag less and increase the fluttering action of the spoon. You may actually find that you get better penetration and leverage in setting up with a single hook on deep-water bass than with a treble. It is also more difficult for the fish to shake a single hook than a treble. However, keep in mind that you will also catch more fish on the outside of the mouth if the bass are just "nudging" the spoon when you stay with stock treble hooks.

Subtle Baits

The recent wave of minuscule offerings such as darter worms, tube lures, grubs, reapers, and the like have also necessitated a close scrutiny of the various hooks used with these baits. The dominant concern has to be with the *sharpness* of the hook. "Strikes" with these lures—if you can call them that—often take the form of nothing more than dull pressure. A good sense of feel, combined with fast reflexes and sharp hooks, is essential to mastering this kind of bite.

For the most part fine bronze wire hooks molded into tiny 1/16 to 1/8 ounce lead heads are the favored way to rig these soft plastic baits. Be careful to match the hook size with these little lead heads. Some will have a greater gap between the point and the shank. This helps to provide solid penetration. A tiny darter or p-head jig with too large a hook gap will overshadow the lure. This in turn affects the balance, symmetry, and overall action of the subtle bait.

These lures are made to either seductively fall or swim underwater. It is thus important that they are matched with lead heads that do not impede this action. The nickel-plated, forged, or cadmium hooks used with other jig heads usually will be far too heavy and bulky to team with these subtle baits.

Sharpening Hooks

As a final note, not enough can be said with regard to the importance of sharpening hooks. Whether it is a worm hook, a lead head, or the treble on a crankplug, do not assume it has been pre-sharpened at the factory.

Carry either a whetstone or a hook file with you when on the water. An alternative is to use one of the new battery operated honing devices. Routinely examine the hooks on all your lures after repeated casts throughout the day. Check for potential fatiguing as a result of pulling the hook out of snags. Inspect the point. Sharpen it if it has become dull.

If you are uncertain as to whether a hook can be saved, replace it. Don't take a chance on having a hook fail you when you need that last "kicker" fish or you set up on that bass of a lifetime!

The Luhr Jensen Hook File. Luhr Jensen markets miniature files specifically designed for sharpening hooks. Mike and Ron prefer these manual devices as the best overall tool for triangulating a hook point to needle-like perfection. These files are made from steel compounds that will shave down the metal of even the strongest forged hooks. It will usually take only one to three passes of the file over the point to bring the hook to razor sharpness.

When to Sharpen. Many hook manufacturers, including V.M.C., Eagle Claw Laser, and Gamakatsu, market hooks that require little if any sharpening. These hooks have enjoyed considerable success, particularly with hard-core, plastic worm fishermen. Still, many pros prefer to take a moment to resharpen even these more expensive models to absolutely guarantee precision points. Generally, if you can take the point of the hook and stick your fingernail with it using minimal pressure on the point, the hook is sharp enough. If not, then take the time to sharpen it.

Similarly, it doesn't take much bottom contact or impact with obstructions to dull a fishing hook. Routinely examine the hook in your bait. If in doubt, sharpen the hook. If still in doubt, replace it with a new hook.

Be aware that too much of a good thing can impair any worm or treble hook. This is especially true for many of the pre-sharpened models. The points on these hooks are frequently so finely honed that additional sharpening may actually dull the edge. Use the simple thumbnail test to ascertain proper sharpness.

What's Your Line?

With money on the line, Mike and Ron clearly understand that the monofilament, not the rod, reel, or lure, is the most critical link between the fish and the angler.

From the start, it is essential to invest in premium grade mono. After spending a considerable sum of money on a boat, tackle, and the cost of incidental transportation, don't make the mistake of purchasing cheap, bulk mono. Granted, it may seem attractive to own a big spool with thousands of yards of monofilament priced so inexpensively, but this line is usually not suitable for serious level bassin'.

Premium mono is typically sold in 250 to 1,000 yard spools. The larger the quantity, the better the price break. In contrast to the inexpensive bulk line, the premium spread has three features that contribute to its higher cost: uniformity, knot strength, and abrasion resistance.

Higher quality line is uniform in diameter and breaking strength throughout the spool. With cheaper mono, there can be intermittent spots where the breaking test varies. Similarly, premium line has excellent knot strength. Whenever you tie on a lure, the breaking strength of the monofilament is reduced to some degree at the knot. With the better grade lines, this decrease in knot strength is minimized.

Finally, premium mono is produced with materials and compounds that enhance its resistance to weathering and chipping. To successfully fish for bass, you must often cast your lures into cover that can play havoc on the external surface of the line. A slight chip or crack can translate into a lost fish. This effect is diminished with a top quality monofilament.

Line should also be matched for specific situations. For example, if you will be flippin' or pitchin' baits into thick brush, you will need a line with limited stretch and, more importantly, super abrasion resistance. Many manufacturers now market extra tough monofilament designed precisely for these conditions. You may also want to consider a high-optic fluorescent line for flippin' that will be easier to monitor for the most subtle strikes.

Anglers who prefer to "finesse" their fish with such strategies as split-shottin', doodlin', shakin' darter heads, or throwing tiny tube baits prefer a softer, thin-diameter monofilament to work highly pressured waters. In this situation, the minuscule baits will "swim" better with the more supple mono. There is a trade-off. There will be somewhat greater line stretch with many of the new ultrafine lines that makes hook sets at greater depths a little tougher.

On this note, serious bassers either working deep structure with jigs or spoons, or those tossing crankplugs, spinnerbaits, and top-water lures should opt for a line with minimal stretch and greater abrasion resistance. This is recommended whether you are fishing with a baitcaster or a spinning reel. This type of mono is somewhat stiffer than that used for the finesse game so it might not lie on the spinning reel spool as nicely. Still, you must minimize stretch as well as wear and tear on the monofilament while fishing with this assortment of baits to insure solid hook sets.

After investing in quality line, remember to routinely inspect it while in the field for nicks and similar rough spots. If in doubt about its reliability, cut off about 12 inches of mono and re-tie.

It is equally important to re-spool with fresh line on a routine basis. Do not expect even the most expensive mono to last all season long trip after trip. Monofilament line is not totally impervious to weathering. Anticipate a modest amount of deterioration. Buy the best line you can afford and change it frequently to insure success. Mike and Ron use Berkley Trilene XT, XL, Big Game, Ultrathin, and Select. Each has a different use for specific conditions and styles of bass fishing.

Serious Eyewear—The Polarized Lens

One of the most overlooked pieces of equipment in the serious bass fisherman's repertoire are superior sunglasses. Over the years we have talked about the need for anglers to invest in good sunglasses as perhaps the ultimate fish-finding device. But above and beyond this, keep in mind that eyes also need the protection from ultraviolet (UV) light quality sunglasses can provide. Not all sunglasses provide these features.

We have looked at a number of different sunglasses in search of the ultimate product that would feature the following characteristics: superior polarization, light weight, scratch resistance, and affordability. After considerable experimentation, we believe we have found the ultimate fishing sunglasses in the product line made by Costa Del Mar of Florida.

Bass anglers need to have superior polarization in a lens. Polarization blocks the nasty horizontal reflected light we call glare. This greatly increases your ability to see below the surface of the water and thus to spot key targets.

So, check out the sunglasses you own now. If they are not polarized—no matter how expensive or fashionable they are—they aren't what you need for fishing. Pick a pair that will help you on the water. Polarization is the only effective method for removing dangerous and irritating glare.

We like Costa Del Mar because it specializes in polarized protective eyewear specifically designed for fishermen. The lenses are optically correct, hard coated for scratch resistance, and provide the ultimate in glare reduction. In addition to being fashionable, these models are also exceptionally light weight, durable and suitable for serious tournament angling and guiding where sunglasses may be worn from 10 to 18 hours per day.

These sunglasses also come in a variety of lens colors which filter out varying amounts of glare and light for a variety of situations. Select the color that works best under the conditions you will be fishing.

Color	Percent Light Transmission	Fishing Conditions
light gray	21 %	maximum glare moderate sunlight
dark gray	10%	maximum glare intense sunlight
light amber	29%	maximum glare sight fishing low light, haze or fog
dark amber	12%	(same as light amber)
light vermilion	21%	under maximum glare provides visual acuity enhances color
dark vermilion	10%	(same as light vermilion)

Think about how many times you have tried to follow your cast, pick up your lure as it hits the water, or tried to "sight" fish in the shallows while flippin' or pitchin' to bass? If you take this sport seriously, then why not develop a repertoire of different lens colors for such critical conditions as low light, intense sun, glare, fog or haze.

Quality, *polarized* sunglasses are an additional essential addition to the L.C.R.s, paper graphs and flashers you utilize to locate fish. These glasses also help to protect your eyes under extreme climatic conditions. The investment is well worth it!

A Serious Tackle Box

Time is money when it comes to serious bass fishing. Professional guides and tournament anglers realize that it is essential to organize the tools of your trade in a systematic way. You want to make certain that the right rod, reel, and line are readily accessible when it comes time to cast to prime targets.

How often have you had to scramble around in the boat through your gear to find the right lure? A well-organized tackle box can save the serious fisherman many valuable minutes. Working from a well-planned box, the angler can put the proper bait out on the water with the least amount of wasted time.

The Right Box

In the past, it was common for the guide or tournament angler to load his boat with numerous tackle boxes, to accommodate the different lure categories. Many pros now try to consolidate their tackle into a single box. This eliminates confusion, extra weight, and "lure overload." The theory is that it is better to fish with a narrow range of baits that you have confidence in then to carry six "war chests" full of lures.

Other anglers prefer to develop individual smaller tackle boxes for each lake they fish regularly. This simplifies picking the appropriate range of lures each time you go out. Your specific lake box is basically ready to go after you refill the stock levels up following the previous outing.

8 Pounder on a Double-Tail Jig

Once you decide upon the best box design for your needs, here are a few tips that will help in organizing it.

Soft Plastic Baits. Plastic worms, grubs, reapers, and lizards can be placed into small plastic zip-lock bags. Take a marking pen and describe the baits on the outside of the bags. The soft plastic lures are easily stored by layering the bags on top of each other. Fish attractants can be added to the bags and color bleeding is eliminated by keeping all the patterns segregated. This method works better than storing these lures in tackle box trays. You can also keep the bag out of the box within quick reach as you work with the "hot" soft plastic bait of the day.

Worm Hooks and Sinkers. Similarly, a lot of valuable box space can be salvaged by storing the plastic worm hooks in empty 35 mm film canisters. These containers are relatively waterproof. Each size of hook can be labeled by marking the canister lid.

Bullet sinkers can also be stored in the empty film containers. A small multi-compartment plastic box will serve the same purpose. Keep the painted slide sinkers separate from the unpainted weights. This will minimize the enamel from peeling off while stored in either the mini-box or 35 mm canisters.

Reaction Baits. Crankbaits can be hung vertically in special lure racks in some boxes or laid in either the trays or compartments of other models. A simple system is to divide the plugs by shape, diving depth, and color.

Consolidate large-lip alphabet crankbaits by shallow-to-deep divers. Then separate the various lures in each depth category by coloration. For example, keep the shallow-diving shad-colored plugs apart from those in the same color pattern that dive deeper.

Follow a similar procedure for spinnerbaits. Break down your "blades" by whether they are single or tandem, their head weight, and their skirt color.

Jigs can be separated primarily by the size of the lead head and the color of the skirting material. It might also help to keep plastic, vinyl, live rubber, and bucktail skirts segregated from each other in the box.

Jars of pork rind can be stashed in the bottom of a multi-tray box or in the individual compartments in a satchel style box. Use your marking pen, and write on the lid of each jar the type of pork rind it contains.

Spoons are the most basic of your lures to organize. Put narrow spoons with minimal action in one compartment, wide-bodied models that flutter more in the other. Your spoon supply can also be subdivided by overall weight of the different types.

Finally, keep a compact assortment of top-water offerings handy, separated by the diverse designs: prop baits, buzzers, floating minnows, stick baits, poppers, and chuggers.

This comprises the basic blueprint for systematically organizing a single tackle box. Working from one solitary box will eliminate a lot of confusion. It will also help the serious bass fisherman to make limited, yet precise choices in the shortest amount of time.

Serious Seasons

Serious Seasons

Freshwater bass are indeed the number one most sought after gamefish in the United States. Fortunately for those of us who pursue this widespread group of species, we can find bass in lakes, ponds, rivers, and streams throughout the year.

Unfortunately, however, these little green fish can be highly temperamental particularly with regard to seasonal patterns. Our success as serious bassers can thus depend greatly upon how well we are able to interpret and respond to seasonal changes, especially weather and temperature.

Beating the Elements

Serious bass fishermen must routinely contend with a wide range of climatic conditions. Too often, recreational bassers won't even attempt to fish in extreme weather. The veteran pro, however, has learned how to beat the elements. Regardless of whether it seems too hot or cold, too windy or raining, the accomplished serious basser finds ways to deal with the environment.

What are some of the key ploys the seasoned pros utilize to maximize their chances while fishing under adverse conditions?

Heat

Excessively hot days can be perhaps the most potentially dangerous situation under which to stalk bass. Apart from the fact that the fishing can be tough, the sun can become a subtle killer.

To begin with, anglers traveling to hot locales with little experience in this weather should try to gradually "acclimate" themselves. Most fishermen from the North and South, for example, who fish tournaments at Lake Mead, must be prepared to encounter summer temperatures reaching over 115 degrees!

Some anglers actually drive their rigs across country with the windows rolled up and the air conditioner off. This presumably helps them to become acclimated to the sweltering temperatures of a desert lake. The best advice is to take it easy on the water, making sure you are physiologically protected.

Above all, it is important to rehydrate frequently. The body is like an automobile radiator that needs water in extreme heat. Fishermen caught up in the fervor of a tournament are often remiss at doing this. Force yourself to drink fluids regularly through the fishing day. Avoid sweet sugary drinks. Use electrolyte drinks, or better yet, stay with water. Sports physiologists conclude that there is no better substitute for plain water to rehydrate the body in hot weather. Without this replenishment of fluid, heat stroke can be a real possibility.

Next, dress cool but use protection. The first inclination is to strip down into shorts and short sleeves. That's fine, but use a sunscreen. This will protect you against ultraviolet rays and the potential for skin cancer. Look for sun blocks with an aloe base if your eyes seem to react to the chemicals in some of these compounds and tear excessively. Don't make the mistake of exposing a lot of bare skin the first day or a dangerous, painful sunburn may result, especially if you've been out of the sun lately. As for actually developing a fishing strategy in the heat, there are a few basic approaches that will work on most lakes. Be prepared to encounter a typical "AM/PM" pattern. Light penetration is minimal at early dawn and the bass will often move into shallow water to feed. This is an opportune time to work top-water lures. As the sun directly bears down on the water, the fish and bait will move off the bank into deeper environments. They may return again later in the day.

By midday, some of the best activity is at the deeper thermoclines. On many lakes, for example, it is not uncommon to catch bass in 2 feet of water at day break, then at 50 foot depths by noon.

When fishing the "dark water," a variety of presentations are frequently effective. A jig, deep-diving crank-plug, or spinnerbait pulled in the deeper strike zones will often work. At other times, an array of more "finesse" tactics will generate strikes from reluctant hot weather bass. Scale down to 6 to 8 pound test line and fish smaller

Beating the Elements

4 inch worms on Texas rigs, or split-shot worms, grubs, and reapers along these ledges. Bottom contact is critical, often requiring at least 3/16 ounces of weight or more. Also, always be prepared for "pressure bites" as the fish lazily mouths the soft plastic bait drifted along the bottom.

All through the day look for areas that may provide a modicum of shade and sanctuary for the fish. Steep rocky walls, moss beds, tree-lined banks, the far backs of coves, and underneath docks and piers will often hold fish even in the midday heat.

The same tactics described for fishing the outside drop-offs will work in these shady areas. Another interesting option is to pitch a smaller, 1/4 to 1/2 ounce spoon. Most recreational bassers think of a spoon as a cold weather lure. If there are concentrations of baitfish holding in the shade of a steep wall or a boat dock, the erratic flash of a fluttering spoon may often trigger a vicious strike.

Cold

Serious bassers must similarly prepare themselves for the cold with regard to their apparel. The most important thing is to keep the extremities warm. Hands and feet can experience frost bite. There are gloves that are designed especially for cold weather angling. Some models, for example, have some or all of the fingertips open to allow for greater feeling and sensitivity when casting and handling the line. Other manufacturers market gloves made from neoprene rubber offering maximum protection for a high speed run across the lake.

Similarly, heavyweight thermal socks will serve to keep the feet warm. Avoid wearing the low-cut sneakers you liked in the summer. Consider switching to a higher cut arctic-pac style boot with a smooth outer sole. These boots have felt liners for additional warmth. The smooth rubber bottoms will not tear up the carpet in your boat like the lug soles found in conventional hiking or hunting boots.

With regard to outer wear, the trick is to layer your garments. If you know it is going to be cold, start with thermal underwear and add layers of clothing as appropriate. You can add a shirt, vest, scarf, and a heavier jacket. As the temperature increases during the day, remove one layer at a time for optimum comfort.

Finally, don't forget headgear. The baseball cap you used in the summer will probably not offer enough protection from chilling temperatures. Wear a knitted stocking cap, a hunting hat with ear flaps, or perhaps a woven ski mask. If you prefer, keep the traditional baseball cap with you to wear when the day warms up.

There are two general rules for bassin' in cold weather: fish slow, and fish vertical. With dropping water temperatures, the fish's metabolism can become slower and a sluggish feeding pattern may result. Bass do not want to expend too much energy to attack a bait. A slow-down approach is necessary.

Anything from crawling a worm to plowing a pork frog along the bottom can be productive, as long as you work it S-L-O-W-L-Y. Even a crankplug with a wide, side-to-side tracking pattern can be surprisingly effective with a slow retrieve.

Not only will the fish usually not move too fast to strike their prey, they will also not move too far. This is why a vertical presentation is so integral to mastering the cold water bite. Lures such as spoons, tail-spinners, and tiny darter or p-head jig-and-worm combinations are deadly worked in a vertical manner. Don't overlook worms or jigs doodled straight up and down or spinnerbaits "yo-yoed" off the bottom. Here again, a meticulous, slow presentation is the key.

It is also important to emphasize that this slow-vertical rule of thumb is not etched in stone. For instance, winter bass will sometimes suspend down the center of deep coves or on outside points. To adequately reach these strike zones, the best method may be to use a slow retrieve with one of the magnum-size deep-diving crankplugs.

Similarly, many serious bassers firmly believe that a small contingency of fish will invariably move up into the shallow water sometime during even the coldest days. Hard-core flippin' specialists have proven this point by nailing quality kicker fish near the bank in sub-50 degree water. It is also not that unusual to see a bass bushwhack a surface plug in the dead of winter as the midday sun warms the shallows.

Perhaps the most important feature of becoming a successful basser in cold weather is to *remain alert*. You must approach the lake on a chilly day figuring that strikes may be far and few between. However, if you maintain a high level of concentration, and are alert to taking advantage of the opportunity when it occurs, it won't take that many strikes to round out a limit.

Wind

Fishing in the wind can be an aggravating experience. Unlike the physical preparation needed to counteract heat and cold, dealing with the wind is usually more sporadic as a sudden blow cuts across the lake.

The onset of wind can often signal an actual increase in bass feeding activity. The wind may push baitfish near the bank or into the backs of coves. The bass will follow and may be easier to target in more concentrated areas.

The wind will also serve to break up surface clarity. This may make the fish a little less wary when it comes to attacking an artificial lure. Wind and ensuing wave action serve to oxygenate the water. This can also intensify feeding, particularly in the warm summer months.

Shrewd fishermen learn to use the wind to their advantage. They will look for so-called "mud lines" near the bank or along submerged points where baitfish will school. This is prime water to toss a crankplug or spinnerbait as you look for more aggressive fish in the stirred up water.

Although it is more comfortable to fish the lee side of the lake, an island or point, the windward side may produce the best action. Once again, this is where the surface water has been broken up and the baitfish may have been pushed into this zone.

Casting may be more difficult in the wind, but there are some remedies. Most of today's modern baitcasting reels have magnetic brakes that serve to minimize backlash. Throwing lures into the wind increases the potential for spool overruns. Simply turn up the magnetic setting and settle for a shorter cast but minimal backlash. If problems persist, opt for an open-face spinning reel that has a casting distance not excessively affected by the wind.

Bass will frequently annihilate soft plastic worms, grubs, and reapers in the wind. Casting these lightweight baits can be difficult if the wind is pushing the boat quickly down the shore. One alternative is to set out an anchor and concentrate on a good fish-holding spot. You may actually do better with this strategy than to try to work a worm while piloting the trolling motor against the wind and waves.

One other option is worth mentioning. Sometimes it is best not to try to fight the wind with even the strongest trolling motors. Instead, maneuver the boat up wind, and calculate a drift pattern so your rig glides along the bank or an outside flat. You can fan cast a reaction bait such as a plug, spinnerbait, or jerkin' minnow as the boat bobs along in the waves. Drag a plastic worm or grub Texas-rigged or on a Carolina setup behind the boat as it drifts.

Rain

Like the wind, rain does not require any particular specialized preparation other than rain gear and mental acceptance. Depending upon frontal conditions, the rain can be a blessing or a curse to the day's bassin'.

A summer storm following a warm front can dramatically stimulate feeding activity, particularly near the bank. The fish may be in a fairly active feeding mode to begin with. The rain may start to oxygenate the water and wash terrestrial critters off the bank. This can lead to even more aggressive activity from warm water bass.

Under these conditions consider shifting gears and toss a reaction bait. A crankplug, spinnerbait, or some sort of surface lure may produce results more rapidly in the rain than the slower wormin' patterns.

A winter storm may also generate a modest increase in feeding activity if it isn't part of a severe cold front. Rain combined with a major cold front may shut off the bite. The remaining strikes you receive during the rest of the day may result only with an absolute slow-down presentation.

A slow-crawled worm or pig'n jig combination inched along the bottom are viable lines of attack with cold winter rain. Strikes will usually be limited, but you may catch some quality bass as angling pressure drastically declines with the storm.

Stick It Out!

Bassin' under severe weather conditions is definitely tough. The dedicated serious basser, however, is a highly adaptable creature. This is the time to draw upon your mental and physical resources to really challenge the fish. You will need a balance of persistence and determination combined with solid mechanics and common sense. The veteran professional knows this is the time to put into effect all that they have learned. Beating the elements in this manner separates this level of fishermen from the others who give into the weather.

Slow It Down!

There is an entire repertoire of lures and strategies that are potentially more effective if the serious basser intentionally disengages from the fast-is-best mode and slows down his retrieve. This is clearly the case out West where so many of our fish are tallied with specific slow-down strategies.

Serious bassers across the country may also find that this slow-down approach allows them to meticulously concentrate on prime targets even on big bodies of water when the fish seem to be quite selective and need that extra effort to get them to bite.

There are definitely times when S-L-O-W is best!

Chill Out for Wintertime Bass!

With the first major frost signaling the arrival of winter, many bass fishermen figure it is time to stow away the tackle and warm up their favorite television chair. Cold weather bassin' is unfortunately too often stereotyped as the most difficult climate for catching these warm water species. Weekend anglers often mistakenly presume that wintertime bass fishing is nearly impossible with chilly days and lethargic, if not dormant, fish. The truth is that this time of year can actually provide the basser with some remarkably good action, and on larger trophy-class fish besides! Pressure on many lakes significantly subsides once autumn hues begin to fade. Boating and water-skiing traffic is minimal and angler interest has dwindled. This is the time to refine your techniques for cold water bass and take advantage of much of this deserted water.

Many techniques that are effective in warmer conditions will also produce in colder temperatures. However, certain modifications are necessary to fool sluggish bass this time of year.

Think Slow!

For the most part, the various bass species exhibit a slower metabolism once the water temperature falls below the 60 degree mark. This is particularly true for both northern and Florida strain largemouths. Alabama spotted bass and smallmouths seem to remain slightly more active than their cousins as surface temperatures drop. Anglers should therefore consider using certain "slow down" tactics to lure these more lethargic winter fish into striking.

Plastic worm fishermen can parlay their expertise during this time of year, but the key is to dramatically *slow down the retrieve*. A traditional Texas-rigged worm can account for some stellar catches in the winter, particularly with longer, 8 to 10 inch models. One theory is that in the colder water the bass simply won't move very far to attack a bait, nor will they feed that frequently. Therefore, a magnum-sized worm slowly inched across the bottom may represent that one, sporadic meal a semi-dormant bass requires to sustain itself for a few days before actively feeding again.

Another versatile weapon for the cold water attack is the lead head jig. Serious bassers rely upon this lure to maintain constant contact with the bottom. Here again, the trick is to resist the temptation to "hop" the jig as is done in warmer months. Instead, try to simply "pull" the lure along the bottom with a very methodical, slow pace. Use either plastic or pork rind tipped jigs.

When you bump into some submerged rocks or brush, continue to slowly pull the lure through the obstructions. Don't hop it. The jig represents a crawdad that will normally slowly plod through the brush and rocks and this is how the jig should be retrieved.

In contrast to jig fishing the rest of the year, in winter always be prepared for a subtle pressure bite when the bass nudges the bait. Remember these wintertime fish are not typically that aggressive or interested in feeding. So, quite often the "strike" takes the form of what seems to be a kind of hesitant resistance.

Crankbait fishermen can also get into the act. Forget that rapid fire chuckin' and windin' you were doing in the warmer seasons. During the winter, bass will often suspend down the center of coves at 15 to 30 foot depths. In years past, it was practically impossible to reach these fish with conventional crankplugs. With the advent of the ultradeep diving bait, a new dimension in the winter bassin' game was opened up.

Again, it is important to reduce the speed of the retrieve in using these specially designed crankbaits. A modestly slow grind seems to work well in exploring the depths with these plugs in the winter. Interestingly, we have also found the "strike" to sometimes be a soft "bump" rather than a vicious pull when using ultradeep diving cranks in the colder months.

Surprisingly, shallow running crankbaits can also be utilized for locating bass in the winter. Throw a crankplug along riprap or the rocky face of a dam to quickly find fish. In the winter, the broken rock retains radiant heat. Bass will often move up into the shallow riprap to feed as the temperature warms.

Whether you fish the crankbait deep or shallow, reduce the speed of your retrieve in the colder months. Give these slow-moving bass a chance to catch up with the plug.

Fish Vertical

Because of the decrease in metabolism, bass will also tend to move more along a vertical plane for short distances. This makes sense when you think about it. The fish are in a slow-down state with a decreased appetite. They move in close proximity to a potential morsel of food to minimize precious energy expenditure. Plastic worms once again can be utilized for the vertical approach with the popular doodlin' method where finesse-size worms are shaken over deep structure. Shake the worm along a deep submerged ledge using smaller 4 inch models to doodle directly in front of lock-jawed bass, irritating them into striking.

Sometimes even the doodling tactic will have limited results at best on super "twitchy" fish. Smart bassers will often switch to a tandem hook worm. Instead of being Texas rigged with a sliding bullet sinker, the tandem hook worm has an open jig head in the front and a trailer or "stinger" hook in the rear (more on this rigging later). The heavier 1/4 to 1/2 ounce jig head stays close to the bottom when you vertically shake this style of worm. With the open hooks in the front, as well as the rear "stinger," many hookups are salvaged that would otherwise be lost on these deep winter bass.

The ever popular 3/4 ounce Hopkins Spoon can also be effective in a vertical presentation during the winter. Cold water bass won't typically jump up too far from the bottom to attack a bait. Too many anglers make the mistake of working a spoon with long exaggerated lifts and drops. Bass at this time of the year won't move very far. We like to "flip flop" the spoon a few inches around the bottom with short rod twitches.

You can also try fishing heavy jigs vertically over structure. In midwinter, the bass on deep rocky impoundments will retreat at times to depths over 45 feet. Fish unusually large 3/4 to 1 ounce lead head jigs and literally "bang" them on underwater rocks and boulders. The heavy lead head keeps the line in the deep strike zone. More importantly, the distinct sound of the jig banging against the rocks calls in these listless fish and often irritates them into striking.

Don't Forget the Shallows!

We want to emphasize again that not all the bass in a given impoundment retreat to greater depths in cold weather. To some degree, this deep migration pattern holds true for many lakes. However, don't overlook the possibility of finding some fish up in the shallows even in extremely cold weather.

Numerous winter trophies can actually be flipped near the bank in the extreme shallows when other anglers have ventured off to work the deeper territory. Anglers have a tendency to move away from this terrain in the winter. If there is abundant coverage and forage, there is no reason for the bass to leave—but you have to slow down and fish real deliberately.

Finesse Worm Setup and Doodlin'

Slow-moving jigs are excellent for this super cold water bite. Both plastic and pork rind trailers will work. The secret is to leave the lure in the water slightly longer than you normally would when flippin' in the warmer months. It often helps to quietly shake the jig after it hits the shallow bottom again in an effort to generate a strike from these lock-jawed bass.

Have Cold Weather Confidence

Professional bass fishermen learn to adapt to all sorts of conditions. Bass tournaments and guide trips are staged throughout the four seasons including the dead of winter.

Cold weather bassin' can be very rewarding in terms of both the quantity and quality of fish that are for the taking. One key ingredient to mastering the winter bite is to *slow* down in your different approaches. The bass will not often move too far to bushwhack a lure. Thus, precise presentations are needed. Lure selection should be equally well calculated with regard to the depths fished and the type of dominant forage baits you are trying to match.

Above all, maintaining a high level of confidence may be the single most important ingredient for successful winter bassin'! Fish can definitely be caught during this time of the year. You just have to believe it!

Blades for Early Spring

As the weather warms, we move away from cold water slow-down strategies and change our pace with spinnerbait fishing. Typically, spring bass fishing is the time of the year when the fish move up into the shallows with the commencement of the spawning ritual. Springtime is the perfect season to throw a practically weedless lure like the spinnerbait into these shallow haunts.

Bass usually take some time to make the transition from the colder environment of wintertime deep water to the warmer, spring shallows. Thus, the serious basser will broaden his strategy when using spinnerbaits during this time of year. The key will be to focus on the *depth* at which the fish are holding. Then select the right blade to challenge the bass at a particular stratum—from deep to shallow zones.

We can examine this transition of fish moving from deep to shallow water, starting with the end of winter, and how to select and use the correct spinnerbait for each emergent springtime condition. Let's begin by looking at the fish as they start their migration out of deep water.

The Deep Bite

It is common for bass to situate themselves at the ends of points, or the edge of drop-offs or "breaks," along sheer canyon walls, or deep inside an old river channel. Spinnerbaits will frequently work to get these semi-lethargic fish to bite in the early spring. The critical feature, however, will be to throw a blade that will make constant bottom contact.

The traditional safety pin-style spinnerbait will work at 15-25 foot depths, but it will require some modification for optimal performance. The trick is to shorten the wire arm to which the blade is attached. A "short-arm" spinnerbait like this will sink quickly. It is made to hug the bottom and works best with a large Colorado blade. The secret is to S-L-O-W-L-Y retrieve the spinner along the bottom letting it bump and plow through every inch of structure. The shorter wire arm, combined with the big Colorado blade, creates a pronounced "thumping" sound with a lot of flash at greater depths.

Bass in that semi-lethargic post winter-early spring mode will often strike at this slow-moving short-arm spinnerbait as they are holding tight in bottom structure. A variation along this same line of attack is to switch to the seldom-seen twin-spinner.

These spinnerbaits are a radical departure from the classic safety pin design. Instead of one wire arm, the

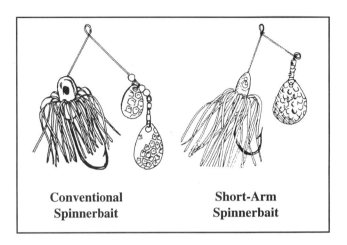

Conventional Spinnerbait　　**Short-Arm Spinnerbait**

twin-spin features two relatively short arms that give the lure the appearance of a menacing insect with feelers. Usually, two modest-size Indian blades are affixed to each of the twin-spinner arms.

Like the short-arm spinnerbait, the twin-spin excels as an early spring bottom-plodding lure. The twin blades create a tremendous amount of whirring sound plus vibration. The lure is fairly weedless and will also serve as a "fall" bait, if you pause on the retrieve and let it sink into submerged cover or off the edge of a drop-off. Look for many strikes to occur as the bulky twin-spin sort of "helicopters" down on the fall, with the two Indiana blades seductively whirling around.

Both the short-arm spinnerbait and the twin-spin seem to fish best in dark-colored vinyl skirts. When fishing the greater depths where these baits perform best, select skirts in purple, black or brown.

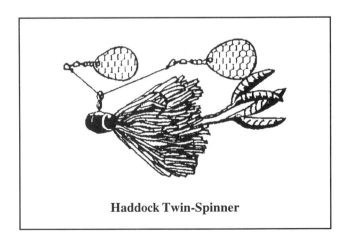

Haddock Twin-Spinner

Spinnerbaits in Deep-Water Conditions

Each of these spinnerbaits also matches well with either a standard size pork frog or split-tail eel as a trailer for springtime basin'. As for blade choices, in stained or muddy water common in spring conditions, use gold, brass or copper blades with the short-arm or twin-spin models. Hammered chrome blades are a favorite with these spinnerbaits in clearer, springtime water.

The Mid-Level Bite

During the early spring, the bass will frequently be on the move, working transition routes from deep to shallow water. Often the fish will be traveling, not so much on the bottom, but instead swimming in sub-surface strike zones, occasionally feeding on schools of bait.

In this situation, the traditional safety pin-style spinner will be effective. Run it through these mid-level zones in a manner similar to fishing a crankbait. Both single and tandem blade models will work, usually with some combination of Colorado or Indiana blades.

If the water is still exceptionally cold, stay with the new silicone, Lumaflex, R&M, or even the traditional vinyl skirts. The vinyl material seems to flare, or "breathe" best in sub-60 degree water. Today's modern spinnerbait skirts work all year long with no problem flaring or breathing irrespective of water temperatures. With regard to blade color, the gold, brass or copper models will continue to perform best in stained or muddy water. Hammered or smooth chrome finishes are more suitable for clearer water conditions.

In contrast to the rather stark, dark-colored skirts used with short-arm blades or twin-spinners, fish lighter shad patterns while probing mid-depths with these lures. Sil-

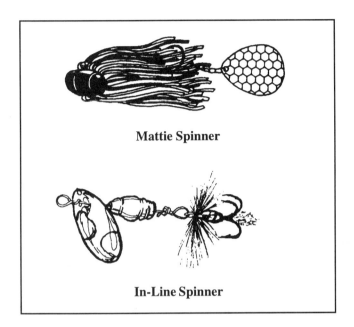

Mattie Spinner

In-Line Spinner

a white or yellow pattern, thrown on 4-6 pound test line with a spinning outfit, nails a lunker largemouth or bronzeback. It is the subtlety of these compact spinners that gives the bass something totally different to look at, often resembling a small, errant baitfish.

The Shallow Bite

Bass anglers will feel most comfortable throwing spinnerbaits into shallow shoreline cover during the early spring. If the fish have moved up into a pre-spawn pattern, a magnum willowleaf blade might produce that lunker of a lifetime.

ver, smoke, gray and white-colored skirts replicate the baitfish shade. Switch to basic chartreuse, or chartreuse/blue skirt patterns, if the water is exceptionally off-color.

There are also two other more obscure styles of spinnerbaits that may also be effective for this early spring, mid-depth action. The "mattie" is a tail-spinner composed of a simple lead head, a skirt, and a swivel with a blade extending back from the hook. This kind of spinnerbait can be thrown long distances, allowed to sink to a specific depth, then simply retrieved as you would a crankplug. Be aware that the mattie's jig-like construction with the open hook minimizes this lure's weedless quality.

One little trick worth noting with the "mattie" is to fish it with an intentional stop-and-go retrieve. On lethargic or suspended bass, in particular, a lot of strikes will occur as the lure is abruptly stopped, then allowed to sink. The strikes occur as you begin the retrieve again, with the bass presumably thinking that the injured prey is about to get away.

The other type of spinnerbait to use for this mid-depth approach really has its origins with the troutin' community. Simple in-line spinners such as the Shyster are most commonly found in trout fishermen's tackle boxes. They are small—ranging from 1/32 to 1/2 ounce—and usually feature a single treble hook.

There are times, however, when the bass are exceptionally spooky but are in a sub-surface cruising mode. We have seen many instances in our own guiding and tournament experiences where a tiny 1/8 in-line spinner in

Spring Lunkers

The willowleaf configuration generates a great amount of vibration. This type of blade also cuts through grass and weeds that may line the bank this time of year. It is remarkable that there does not appear to be any size in these jumbo willowleafs that will intimidate a trophy fish. More and more manufacturers are designing the big willowleaf spinnerbaits with not one—but two—extra large blades in tandem. This creates a wealth of flash, vibration, and often a "clanging" sound as the big blades slash their way through thick cover.

Using magnum willowleaf blades in the spring calls for stout tackle. This is a serious hawg huntin' bait, balanced perfectly with heavy action flippin' or poppin' rods and 15-20 pound line.

Speaking of flippin', it is also possible to occasionally flip bass in the early spring using spinnerbaits. As the fish move up into outside tule points or into the thicker portion of the reeds or brush, a carefully placed spinnerbait can sometimes generate explosive strikes from pre-spawn fish. The short-arm models we mentioned for exploring the deeper structure are also perfect for flippin'. Keep in mind that you want to use a spinnerbait in the 1/2 to 3/4 ounce range to penetrate through the thicker cover, scaling back to a 1/8 to 1/2 ounce model for working the reeds.

Expect to get hit as the lure falls vertically when flippin' a spinnerbait. You have to maintain a tight line or maintain a certain amount of drag to make the blade rotate. You can also quickly "pull" the blade out from the cover while flippin' at any time from when it breaks through the surface, all the way to when the lure hits the bottom. Don't be surprised to get bit right next to the boat, as the bass chases the spinner out from the structure.

Versatile Lures!

As you can see, spinnerbaits are highly versatile lures for the usually tough, but sometimes spectacular, early springtime action. Don't limit your potential by simply throwing the conventional safety pin style models. Try the short-arm, twin-spin, in-line and tail-spin designs as well. All of these various spinnerbaits have an application during the springtime.

Knowing that these lures may help you catch that early season trophy, be sure to examine the hooks on each spinnerbait carefully. You may have to take pliers and open up the gap between the point and the shank of the spinnerbait hook. On big bass, you will want to have a fairly wide gap in the hook to get maximum penetration when you set up on the fish.

Similarly, closely inspect the blades on all your different spinners. During the spring, early season run-offs will empty a lot of floating debris into the water, combined with the first bloom of aquatic vegetation. The blades must spin freely and should always be cleaned if they pick up any algae or weeds.

Spinnerbaits are simple lures to master. Keep them in fine working shape and fish them aggressively during this early spring trophy bass period!

Beat the Summertime Blues

With soaring summer temperatures and bright sunny days, catching bass can become difficult. The fish will invariably head toward more comfortable, deeper water following an initial morning feeding foray near the bank. The object then is to develop a repertoire of tactics that will allow you to probe these deep strike zones. Shrewd bass anglers will find the following methods useful in combating the "summertime blues."

Magnum Crankplugs

These lures have gained popularity in the last few years. Characterized by oversized diving lips, crankplugs in this genre can probe water that was previously impossible to reach with other hard plastic baits. Most manufacturers including Manns, Poe, Rapala, and Bomber, have each designed a series of these alphabet-style plugs to be fished at incremental depths. For example, on many deep lakes the bass will actually suspend down the center of coves in the summer. Before the advent of deep-diving baits, these fish would rarely ever get to see a lure. Once the bass are metered, select a crankbait that will swim at the appropriate depth, usually either 15, 20, or 30 feet. Make a long cast and drag the plug through these deep strike zones.

One tip worth mentioning is that these big crankbaits actually seem to dive deepest and swim better with lighter 8 to 12 pound test line. The trick is to quickly reel following the cast to get the plug to start its initial dive. Once it is down, back off and maintain a slow, steady retrieve.

Some serious bassers who are proponents of the magnum diving plugs, prefer to use a fairly stout and longer 7 to 7 1/2 foot rod. There are also specialized baitcasting reels with oversized handles and slower gear ratios designed for crankin' these jumbo plugs.

Be experimental and throw the oversized crankbaits on a variety of deep-water targets. Cast out over points,

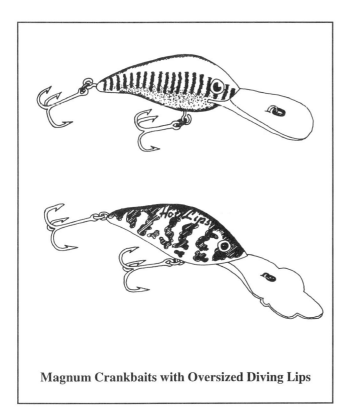

Magnum Crankbaits with Oversized Diving Lips

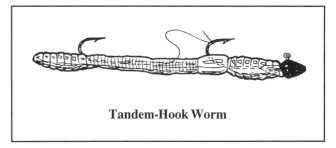

Tandem-Hook Worm

Work the tandem-hook worm by vertically shaking or hopping it over structure. A great proportion of fish will sort of gently "mouth" the tail portion of this lure. If you feel any unusual pressure on the line, gently swing and set. Remarkably, the little stinger hook will nail many bruiser bass sulking near the bottom.

Yo-yo Spinnerbaits

Normally we don't think of spinnerbaits as a true deep-water lure. During the summer, bass will frequently suspend in schools near clusters of baitfish. One strategy to get these fish to bite is to vertically drop a spinnerbait through the suspended schools.

Various spinnerbait designs will perform with this presentation. The basic safety-pin configuration is the most commonly used. Both single and tandem blade models will work. Another option is to try double-arm spinners for an extra slow fall. This double-arm design creates a lot of resistance in the water as the spinnerbait is allowed to slowly sink. For a quicker falling bait, switch to a single-blade tail-spinner. These are skirted jigs with a small spinning blade attached to the rear.

Once you have metered the bass, "yo-yo" spinnerbaits through the suspended fish. Watch for strikes on the initial drop as the blades "helicopter" down through the school. If you fail to get hit, throw the reel into gear and rhythmically lift-and-drop the spinnerbait repeatedly through the fish-holding area. The "yo-yoing" technique gives the lure the illusion of an erratic fluttering baitfish. Be alert for strikes to occur on the "drop" phase while yo-yoing the spinnerbait.

Bangin' Jigs

Summertime bass are not prone to move that far when they are holding in deep water. Tournament pros and deep-water guides have devised a method for enticing the fish to strike jigs when they are positioned on deep structure. Try using larger 1/2 to 1 ounce jig heads to maintain bottom contact. Drop these heavy jigs down to the bottom

against the riprap along the face of a dam, or through a grove of submerged trees. The protruding diving lip serves as a brush guard to some degree, making the big plugs fairly weedless.

Tandem-Hook Worms

Bass resting deep on the bottom can also pose a problem during the summer months. A plastic worm fished along the bottom can be a potent weapon on sluggish warm weather bass. However, it is often difficult to maintain good contact with the deep underwater terrain. As we mentioned earlier, one remedy is to use a vertical approach with a tandem-hook worm.

Start by lacing a small 3 to 4 inch worm on a 1/8 to 3/8 ounce jig head. Leave the hook exposed. Next, thread a smaller long-shank #4 to #6 Aberdeen or Carlisle hook into the tail portion of the worm. Tie a short 3 inch piece of 8 to 10 pound test mono to the open bend in the front jig hook. Connect the other end of the line to the trailer hook in the rear. Don't be concerned with the short leader joining the front and "stinger" hooks being left visible outside the worm. The bass will not be able to scrutinize it at these depths.

positioning themselves vertically over structure such as rock piles or decaying trees. Then bounce the lure, using exaggerated sharp twitches with the rod tip. This is termed "bangin' the jig." This technique has proven successful all the way down to 90 foot depths.

The bangin' technique keeps the heavy jig near the bottom at all times. Bass are attracted to the noise as the lead head "bangs" into rocks, brush, and similar deep structure. The fish will often strike the jig hard as their irritation levels rise with the noisy offering. (We'll talk about this strategy more in the chapter "Serious Jiggin'.")

Deep-Floating Baits

A final strategy is to use a Carolina rig to present soft plastic baits in deep water during the summer. Use a large 3/4 to 1 ounce sliding sinker, butted by a swivel or split ring. Add an 18 to 36 inch length of 6 pound test leader.

Now here's the secret. Tie a plastic swimming jig, grub, or worm to the lengthy leader. Lace the plastic lure onto a styrofoam floating jig head. Lures like the Gitzit, Haddock 18 Tail and Kreepy Krawler as well as the Spyder can be fished on a floating jig head, seductively suspended well off the bottom as it pulsates in the current. A Carolina rig with a heavy sliding sinker works best with these floating jig heads. The long 18 inch leader keeps the lure well off the bottom where the bass can easily see it.

This type of Carolina setup can be sensational for fishing deep clear lakes. The open hook on the styrofoam head permits quick, efficient hook sets at the 25 to 60 foot range. Surprisingly, there aren't that many obstructions that the open-hook rigging gets snagged on below 25 feet.

Carolina Rig with Floating Head

Hang in There!

Catching bass in the summertime is not impossible. It will, however, require patience and perseverance. Good electronics are necessary especially for pinpointing suspended schools of fish and bait. Continue to explore this deep-water environment. Put your lures where the bass live in the midday heat. You can beat the summertime blues!

Bassin' in Low Water Conditions

Sometimes during the summer or during a prolonged drought our favorite bass lakes may suffer a serious decline in water level. As many of the prime bass lakes have dropped to critical proportions, eliminating prime shoreline cover is necessary to insure a successful spawn. How greatly future generations of bass will be impacted remains to be seen.

Nevertheless, catch-and-release bassin' is still possible on these impoundments, posing a formidable challenge to even the most seasoned pros. Serious bassers will find that many of their favorite spots, once situated near the bank, are now high and dry, sometimes as much as 75 feet above the water. Many of the patented techniques that are effective when water levels are up will no longer work under these conditions.

Thus, anglers will have to re-orient themselves to a particular body of water in severe low water periods, adjusting their line of attack while working both shallow and deep.

Limited Shoreline Targets

The most obvious problem when bassin' in low water conditions is the distinct decline of prominent shoreline structure. Visible targets such as piers, docks, tules, boulders, trees and riprap are likely to be on high ground. The bank may assume a stark blankness, where everything basically looks the same.

Flippin' enthusiasts will be most affected by the low water. In the past, an accomplished flipper has been a dangerous tournament threat because he keep his baits in the shallow strike zone 95 percent of the time. The problem now becomes that without visible shoreline targets such as brush, rocks, and tules, where precisely is the new strike zone?

Many shallow water specialists adamantly believe that at least a small but significant number of bass will move up near the bank to feed each day. Presumably, these fish will be more active and, hence, prone to strike a well-positioned bait. For the most part, there should be no reason for this movement to completely cease solely because the complexion of the shoreline has changed with diminishing water levels.

We have found that a limited number of bass do remain near the bank on even the most drought-impacted reservoirs. However, the flippin' approach becomes a bad choice with the loss of visible structure. Instead, you will be able to cover more of this monotonous shoreline with a concise repertoire of fast-paced shallow water methods. Now is the time to move away from flippin' and canvass the bank with a mixture of pitchin', crankin', and rippin'.

Use the basic #11 Uncle Josh Pork Frog with a light 3/8 ounce live rubber jig to quickly pitch long strands of shoreline. Expect to get bit in the first 20 percent of the cast, often as the pig 'n jig sinks. Don't waste time working the lure back to the boat. You will have a lot of new territory near the bank to prospect. Keep moving with rapid-fire, short pitches.

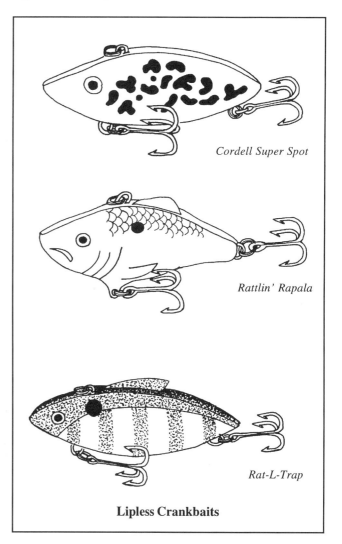

Cordell Super Spot

Rattlin' Rapala

Rat-L-Trap

Lipless Crankbaits

Switch to a plastic tail-swimming jig like the Haddock Kreepy Krawler, Yamamoto Hula Grub or Spider if you want to pick up the tempo even more. Another option will be to fish a large whip-tail grub such as the Mr. Twister or the Haddock Curl Tail models on a 1/8 ounce darter head. Soft plastic jigs and grubs are made to be fished fairly fast and can actually be retrieved similar to a crankplug.

On that note, shallow crankin' can be a potent method for quickly eliminating vast stretches of dead water. With this approach, it is imperative to carefully select those crankbaits that will properly swim through the shallow strike zones found off the bank.

Today's lure manufacturers have designed a series of plugs that are made to sample that first 1 to 6 feet of water. Examples of shallow runners include: Bagley's ET-2, Norman's Tiny-N, Crankbait Brand's Speed Trap plugs, and Rapala's Shallow Fat Rap and Shad Rap series.

Slab-shaped, "lipless" crankplugs such as the Rapala Rattlin' Rap and the Cordell Spot are ideally suited for this strategy. Lures in this genre can be cast a long distance. They can be retrieved either slow or fast, and will run through the shallow strike zones with minimal snagging.

Rippin' a floating minnow down long stretches of shoreline is another option for exploring the shallows on a lake where water is being drawn down. Using long, rhythmic twitches with the rod tip, serious bassers can

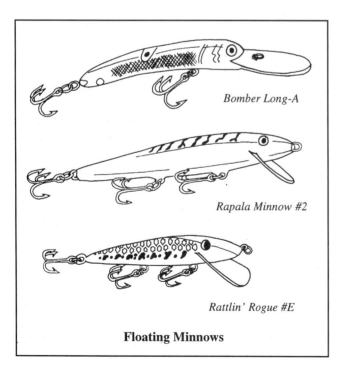

Bomber Long-A

Rapala Minnow #2

Rattlin' Rogue #E

Floating Minnows

"rip" a floating Rapala, Smithwick Rogue, or Jensen Minnow, quickly reaching that 4 to 8 foot layer off the bank.

These run-and-gun tactics allow you to quickly survey the new shoreline created by low water conditions, but don't overlook a more precise, concentrated approach utilizing your electronics.

When water levels drop, rely on your electronics to find isolated spots of broken rock, brush, or rubble scattered in 2 to 10 foot depths off the bank.

In low water periods, these small clusters of submerged brush or broken rock serve as a miniature "oasis" where bass can find sanctuary along an otherwise bleak shoreline. It is not uncommon to see lake locals "camping out" on one of these spots for long periods, waiting for bass to home in on this isolated shallow water structure.

In this situation a Texas-rigged worm, split-shotted reaper, or a slow-moving jig is perfect for thoroughly fishing a small shallow water "oasis" from all possible angles. We might also add that when lake water levels do rise, these little pieces of structure can become highly productive as transition areas where bass will hold while moving back and forth from deep to shallow depths.

Shift to Deep Water

With the limited amount of sanctuary available near the bank, schools of baitfish will migrate too deep, outside structure in a low water year. Although some bass will remain near the shoreline when water levels drop, invariably most of the fish concentrate in deeper strike zones.

In surveying a lake that has suffered a major draw down, one of the first places to look for bass is parallel to and outside long underwater points. Although a significant amount of the shallow portion of the point may now be out of water, the fish will usually continue to traverse it, simply situating themselves along the deeper edges.

Similarly, even the most gradual "break" or ledge may now hold concentrations of bass that no longer orient to the bank. Here again, the serious basser who is competent at reading his electronics will be able to locate these inclines or drop-offs and can focus his attack to the deeper water.

Subtle "humps" that might normally be nothing more than minor rises in the muddy bottom in high water years, may now assume a more important status in a drought-impacted lake. As the water levels drop, these muddy mounds may become small islands. Baitfish and crawdads may gravitate to the shallow slopes around these new formations and the bass will follow.

More prominent underwater structure like rock piles, creek channels, and artificial reefs may also play host to even greater numbers of bass in the lake's low water phase. Again, this is a result of the decline of the shoreline cover normally available in high water conditions.

The serious basser who has mastered the deep water structure game will typically have an easier time attacking a lake that is undergoing a dramatic loss of water compared to the shallow water enthusiast.

Some fishery studies indicate that many reservoirs have a resident population of deep, marauding largemouths. These fish remain in deep water through most of the year feeding on schools of threadfin shad. This phenomenon holds true for various lakes throughout the country.

Thus, the serious structure fishermen should be able to tap into this population of fish irrespective of lake water levels. Still, there are other schools of bass that may normally be more bank-oriented and might scatter out into deep water when lake levels drop severely.

In either case, there are some precise methods that will allow you to again explore significant amounts of "new" deep water without wasting a lot of valuable time. Serious bassers can select from a menu of deep-diving crankplugs, swimming jigs, Carolina rigs, metal spoons, or subtle baits to explore these strike zones.

A magnum-size crankplug will allow you to effectively reach deep outside structure down to about 20 to 30 feet. The advent of the oversize diving lip has served to take lures such as the Poe's 300-400 series,, Genuine Crankbait Hot Lips Express, Mann's Deep Hawg and Rapala Deep Runner Fat Rap into that 20(+) foot range where crankplugs were not normally seen.

Veteran guides and tournament pros working a lake suffering a major draw down of water will frequently throw one of these big plugs to explore all the major ledges, points, humps, creek channels, or emergent islands in a drought-impacted lake. Crankbaits with these oversize diving bills can be effective all season long and are excellent for locating a potential concentration of bass suspended off deeper structure.

Soft plastic swimming jigs like those mentioned for shallow water pitchin' can also be fished either fast or slow over deep structure. In contrast to the jumbo crankplugs, the jig can always be fished directly on the bottom as you probe water further off the bank.

Another ploy we have used on lakes that have had a lot of water drawn down is a Carolina rig. It is not uncommon for bass to become somewhat disoriented and sluggish in a reservoir where great amounts of water are let out in a short span of time. This is typical on many impoundments that store both drinking and irrigation water.

A grub or Do-Nothing Worm fished on a Carolina rig utilizing a 3/16 to 1 ounce sinker will make excellent bottom contact in deep water. Also, in contrast to split-shottin', the Carolina rig teamed with either the grub or Do-Nothing Worm can be retrieved somewhat faster, permitting you to sample more of the deep terrain. Similarly, a tandem-hooked worm or a 1/8 to 3/8 ounce lead head can be drifted or dragged, "hopping" over great expanses of deep, open water.

Bass will also sometimes suspend at deeper depths following a dramatic drop in water levels. This can be a kind of transition period whereby the fish are initially dislocated from shallower structure and are attempting to re-orient to their new, deep-water environment.

Deep-diving crankplugs, swimming jigs, and Carolina rigs with longer 6 to 7 foot length leaders will, to varying degrees, reach these suspended bass. Better alternatives include vertical spoonin', using tiny darter head worms, or grubs and lacing tube baits onto 1/8 to 1/4 ounce jig heads. These last three options can also be worked fairly fast through schools of suspended bass until you find a concentration of fish willing to bite.

The Confidence Factor

Perhaps the most important element affecting the serious basser's ability to catch fish in a low water condition is his confidence level. Anglers sometimes assume that because a body of water is smaller due to drought and draw downs, the bass will be easier to locate in more concentrated areas. Sometimes this is true. Other times the fish seem to be more scattered, more skittish, and overwhelmingly more difficult to find and catch than when the lake levels were higher. Be careful not to become too confident in the low-water period.

On the other hand, many anglers may feel absolutely lost in arriving at a lake, where most of the recognizable structure is now high and dry. Here a modicum of self-confidence in being able to fish subtle structure near the bank, as well as mastering the deep-water approach, is critical. Rest assured that there are still bass in these low-water lakes and they do have to eat some time.

Remain confident that you have a wide selection of strategies to choose from in attacking the low-water situation. Also, consider bringing a camera with you. Take photographs of all those prime pieces of structure that are now out of water. When the lake returns to its higher capacity, you will be armed with a wealth of subtle, secret spots that most fishermen will have forgotten!

When Bass Suspend

The one time bassin' can be most difficult is when the fish decide to suspend. This commonly occurs in the post-spawn spring, during the midsummer heat, and especially in the fall when lakes and reservoirs experience the turnover phenomenon. A bass suspended above the bottom is like a hovering helicopter that can't decide whether to land or take off. Fish in this condition can also be in a metabolic slow down and are highly lethargic feeders.

Bass may suspend in a particular body of water for a variety of other reasons. For example, a dramatic change in barometric pressure with an incoming storm can result in a suspended state. Similarly, major fluctuations in water levels exemplified by rapid increases or draw downs in a reservoir can force the fish to suspend. The introduction of chemical agents such as fertilizers or pesticides from run-off water can alter the pH balance of the impoundment. This too can put the fish out of "metabolic sync" and generate a suspended condition.

As we mentioned, bass will also frequently suspend during the turnover period following the first cold spell in the fall. This is when the recently chilled surface water settles to the bottom and is replaced by warmer bottom layers rising to the top.

Finally, throughout the year bass will follow migrating schools of baitfish that may stratify at temperate thermoclines somewhere between the surface and the bottom. The fish in this case may also be reluctant to strike a lure with the abundance of bait nearby.

When Bass Suspend

Whenever bass suspend, they become difficult, but not entirely impossible to catch. There are some specialized strategies shrewd anglers can employ that will assist them in presenting baits into these suspended strike zones.

Spoonin'

A vertical presentation with a spoon is perhaps the simplest tactic to try when bass suspend. After metering a concentration of fish with your electronics, it is possible to lower a spoon precisely to a particular depth where the bass are holding.

If the fish appear to be clustered around a mass of baitfish, an exaggerated lift-and-drop motion with the spoon will often be effective. In this situation the bass will probably be feeding on schools of shad minnows. As the spoon is raised up through the bait then allowed to settle again, it may often trigger strikes resembling a fleeing baitfish. A larger lure such as a 3/4 ounce Hopkins or a 5/8 ounce Haddock Structure Spoon will give off plenty of flash and vibration when used on actively feeding bass.

Smaller spoons like the 3/8 ounce Kastmaster or 1/4 ounce Hopkins No-EQL will be more potent when the bass are suspended but there is no sign of baitfish. These fish may be suffering a major case of "lockjaw," and are uninterested in attacking a lure. Using lighter monofilament and short rhythmic rod twitches, the angler can make these tiny spoons dart and dance through the suspended bass. This ploy will sometimes irritate the fish into attacking the offering.

Darters and P-heads

Serious bassers often use miniature 1/16 to 1/8 ounce lead head jigs on suspended fish. The lead heads are either rounded "p-heads" or arrowhead-shaped "darters." Thin 3 to 4 inch plastic worms or whip-tail grubs are laced onto the jig heads as a trailer.

Here again, by using light 6 to 8 pound test line, the angler can twitch the rod tip, making these little jigs swim erratically from side to side. Darters and p-heads can be worked in a vertical fashion, dropped directly below to the level where the bass are suspended. You can make longer casts to the bank and slowly "swim" the lures back through the deep strike zone. Occasionally pause allowing the jig to seductively flutter.

Always be prepared when using subtle baits like this for strikes to occur as the lure falls. Also the "strike" itself may not be pronounced. It will often take the form of nothing more than dull resistance on the end of the line.

Tube Baits

A variation similar to the darter or p-head jig is to use a hollow-bodied tube bait. Models such as the Gitzit or Berkley Power Tube should be rigged with a 1/16 to 1/8 ounce jig head. The trick is to push the tiny lead head up into the tube, forming a "soft-headed" bait. Next, inject the lure with an ample amount of your favorite fish attractant.

Tube baits rigged in this manner can be terrific on suspended bass. They can be fished either vertically or allowed to sashay down following a longer cast to the bank. As the tube slowly swims into the bass, a "vapor trail" of scent is emitted. This may help to excite otherwise lethargic feeders into striking the lure.

Deep-Diving Crankbaits

It is not uncommon for bass to suspend either in the dead of winter or during the peak summer periods. Deep-diving crankbaits are perfect under these conditions.

Crankbaits such as Mann's Deep 20(+) Hawg, Poe's 300-400 series, and the Rapala Deep Runner Fat Rap can be retrieved through the 20 foot barrier. As we noted, many guides and pros recommend using longer rods, baitcasting reels with oversized gears, and reasonably light 10 pound test mono to properly work these larger crankbaits at these depths.

Recreational bass fishermen may want to consider an easier option —trolling. This tactic is not permitted in most tournament situations. Nevertheless, the weekend angler may find it to be a real boon when the bass suspend in that 10-20 foot range. Be sure to let out enough line to get the big crankbait to dive deep. Also throttle down to a moderately slow trolling speed. Most of these jumbo-size plugs will plane to the surface if they are pulled too fast.

A variation on this theme is to use lead core line to take a wide range of crankbaits into deeper strata. The lead core line is usually associated with late season trout fishing, but it will definitely work with this kind of bassin'. The line actually has a lead core encased in dacron or similar material. Every 10 yard section is a different color.

Use a medium-heavy baitcasting outfit. Let out different increments of lead core line trolling your favorite crankbait or minnow plug tied to a 4-6 foot length of monofilament leader. Once the bass are located, note what "color" of line was last let out. On subsequent trolling runs, simply free spool enough lead core until you come to the color where the strike occurred. This will put you right back into the proper strike zone.

One final technique utilizing crankbaits is also worth mentioning. Lipless plugs like the Rat-L-Trap, Cordell Spot, or Rattlin' Rapala can be fished vertically over suspended bass. This ploy is seldom used by weekend bassers, although it is highly productive at times.

After metering the fish, lower a slab-shaped crankbait down to the level of activity. Quickly lift the rod up to the 12 o'clock position, then let the lure settle back down. This strategy is similar to vertical spoonin'. These plugs are designed to transmit tremendous sound waves under water. When they are "jerked" quickly in this manner, the vibrations are intense. This serves to call the bass in to investigate. Interestingly, most strikes occur as the lure is allowed to sink back down. Presumably, this action mimics a frightened, wounded baitfish.

Jerkin' Minnows

Along a similar line of attack, try jerkin' long floating minnows. This approach is especially deadly when the bass are suspended not much more than 6 to 8 feet below the surface.

Use larger floating Smithwick Rogue, Rapala, Bomber Long-A, Jensen Minnow, and AC Shiner minnow plugs. Make a fairly long cast. Then retrieve these lures using rhythmic downward sweeps of the rod tip to force them to dive well below the surface. Following each "rip" with the rod, quickly gather up the line to start the sequence again. The best sequence is a "jerk, jerk . . . pause." The speed of this sequence, however, can vary depending upon how aggressively the bass are feeding.

Strikes with the rippin' technique usually occur as the lure starts to float back up to the surface. This can be an effective way to cover a lot of territory when the bass are scattered but suspended slightly below the surface. The best strategy is to usually jerk these baits working parallel to the bank.

Spinnerbaits and Jigs

These lures are often overlooked as viable options to try on suspended fish. The secret is to learn to "swim" these baits through the precise strike zones, keeping them off the bottom.

A spinnerbait can be worked from the shoreline out into deeper water, using a slow retrieve to keep it down. An intriguing alternative is to use the spinner similar to a spoon in a vertical presentation. Simply let it fall into the school of suspended fish. Watch for strikes as it sinks. Then gently lift the rod and drop it as you would with a spoon. This is termed "yo-yoing." The whirling blades generate considerable vibration on the rod lift, then quietly flutter down on the drop. This too may resemble a frantic baitfish.

Plastic fork-tail jigs can also be retrieved in a similar fashion. Models like the Spyder, Yamamoto's Hula Grub, and Haddock's Kreepy Krawler are excellent jigs designed to "swim" through deep strike zones. Whether they are thrown towards the bank or yo-yoed vertically, the fluttering tails closely imitate shad minnows, or other indigenous baitfish.

Both spinnerbaits and plastic jigs can be worked to extraordinary depths. Bass suspended well below the 30 foot level can be reached with either of these lures if conventional spoonin' tactics fail to produce. Scale up in size, using blades or jigs in the 5/8 to 1 ounce range to reach these fish at the deeper levels.

Be Patient and Alert

Trying to coax suspended bass into striking a lure is usually a difficult proposition. It is important to remain patient and alert. Although you may see ample evidence of the fish on your electronics, strikes will often be far and few between. Don't necessarily expect a lot of activity.

When you fish for suspended bass, it is essential to make sure all the hooks on your baits have been pre-sharpened to perfection. You will need a quick and efficient hook set when these reluctant feeders decide to bite. Also maintain steady tension on the line as you carefully reel the bass to the surface. Avoid "pumping" the fish. This may often help dislodge the hook on bass brought up from deep water. As is often the case, some of the largest fish caught each season are those that are pried out of the suspended state!

Serious Structure

Serious Structure

If there is one word that seems to recurrently confuse the recreational bass fisherman, it has to be the term "structure." We don't have to unnecessarily complicate the meaning of this word. Put simply, "structure" is any place that has the potential to be a sanctuary where a bass can establish an ambush point to feed on prey. "Structure," in this sense of the term, may be shallow or deep, wherever bass are found.

Fishing Shoreline Structure

Why would bass gravitate to structure in the shallows? There are a number of reasons. To begin with, this is where you may find the water in many impoundments to be the warmest. Particularly in the early spring, prior or during the spawning period, this is the area where the females will commonly build their nests. As the shallows warm first with continued sunshine, the bass start to move up.

Even during the winter, the water near the bank will frequently warm up one or two degrees during the day with a little overhead sunlight. Because bass are cold-blooded creatures, they will move towards warmer comfort zones.

The shallows, because they are warmer, will commonly attract major forage baits towards the bank. Again, this may hold true on a particular lake, when the crawdads and shad minnows similarly migrate up into warmer water. Bass will usually follow the bait.

Shallow water can also become quite muddy or stained. This cuts down on light intensity which in turn draws the bass towards the more comfortable territory.

The water near the bank typically has most of the available structure on lakes and reservoirs. Brush piles, trees, moss beds, rocks, riprap, docks, bridges, and tules or reeds are examples of shallow water structure that will provide sanctuary for bass.

Lastly, there is also another phenomenon that occurs on crowded impoundments that may also attract bass to the shallows—water-skiing! When ski traffic is heavy, the wake from the boats often both churns up and oxygenates the water as it is pushed into the shoreline. In the warmer months, baitfish will head to this kind of water because the turbidity cuts down light intensity, combined with a rich source of oxygen. Once again, the bass will follow a migration path to the bank in this situation.

Great Shoreline Targets!

Recreational bass fishermen should thus try to develop their initial skills by mastering the proper ways to attack shoreline structure. Anglers often have a tendency to overlook some of the intricate subtleties that should be considered before throwing at these obvious targets. For example, is there a special side, angle, or time of day that will work best when firing off a cast towards a bridge, riprap, pier, or dock?

Structure like this can offer some of the finest fish-holding terrain on a given lake or river. There is a real "science" of sorts that top-level guides and pros employ to make the most out of fishing this form of man-made cover.

You will find, for example, that there are certain times of the year when bass relate more to one of these areas than to another. There are also distinct presentations that are appropriate for fishing each of these shoreline structures. Again, this can vary with the seasons.

Finally, there are certain key lures that are most effective in designing a strategy for fishing bridges, riprap, piers and docks.

Bridges

Bass find sanctuary throughout the year underneath bridges and along support pilings. Bridges provide a respite for fish during scorching summer heat. Smart bassers recurrently fish underneath this structure when the midday mercury soars. The water surface temperatures are obviously cooler under the bridge. The shade provided by the overhead structure cuts down aggravating intense light penetration and creates a comfort zone for the bass.

Bridges afford great sanctuary on a year-round basis. Pillars, for example, are basic structure for the fish to relate to. Bass can simply move up or down the piling anytime of the day. These concrete or wood support pillars are the main focal point of making a presentation in approaching the bridge. Even during the winter, the sun will warm the pilings and this additional heat attracts all types of aquatic life ranging from phytoplankton and insects to schools of shad minnows.

Position your boat so you can make some initial casts parallel to the pilings. Use either a spinnerbait or crank-plug to survey the water along these pillars and change plugs or spinners to match the depth of the water under the bridge. Try some shallow running lures to check for fish just below the surface. A 1/4 to 3/8 ounce spinnerbait, a lipless slab-style crankbait, and one of the latest ultrashallow running plugs are excellent lures to throw initially in this situation.

Next, switch to deep-diving lures and probe the base of the pilings. These might include heavier spinners or oversized alphabet-style crankplugs that can track at depths up to 20 feet. Consider pitchin' a shiny spoon down the bridge pillars. There are times when a buzzbait retrieved along the pilings can produce explosive results in the summer shade.

Crankplugs and spinnerbaits can be potent under bridges all season long. If the water temperatures are particularly cold, try a slow-moving lure. During the winter, for instance, a Fat Gitzit that gently falls vertically down the edge of the bridge pillar may generate a lot of action. This kind of slow-falling lure is excellent around bridges when the bass seem to be highly selective in their feeding.

Another option that is often effective for bridge bassin' is using small jigs and grubs. The important thing is to think *LIGHT*. Fish miniature 1/8 ounce darter jigs with plastic grub trailers or compact 1/4 ounce pig'n jig combos. The object is to have these lures seductively glide down the side of the bridge pilings, keeping the bait as close to the pillars as possible. The smaller lures will fall S-L-O-W-L-Y into the narrow strike zones found around the pillars.

Riprap

Another tactic is to carefully work shallow riprap. Like bridge pilings, these broken, jagged rocks, also retain radiant heat from the sun during the colder times.

Toss either a crankbait or a jig (usually pork) for fishing riprap. A primary technique is to crank parallel to the rocky bank in order to locate the fish. Don't necessarily expect to catch a great volume of bass by crankin' the rocks. The plug allows you to move quickly and determine if the fish are on this structure. However, quite frequently, the fish that are caught in this manner may be larger, solitary bass suspended off the riprap.

Once you catch a bass or two along the riprap, change to a pig'n jig. This is typically a #11 size pork frog with a live rubber 3/16 jig. Slowly and methodically bounce the pork among the scattered rocks, looking for otherwise lethargic fish nestled in the riprap feeding on slow-moving crawdads. Although jigs are frequently lost along the sharp rocky bottom, the effort is well worth it, especially during the chilly days of winter and early spring.

Piers and Docks

Fishing piers and boat docks along lakes and rivers frequently harbor excellent populations of bass. Here again, these structures are fishable all year long. In the wintertime, start on the end of the dock or pier concentrating your efforts on the sunny side of the float. Work a basic deep-to-shallow pattern. As the seasons shift, fish your baits further toward the bank and preferably parallel to the edge of the dock. By summertime, it is not uncommon to find bass directly under the pier or the boat moorings. Both structures shelter fish by providing shady haunts and ambush points during hot summer days.

Don't overlook flippin' a jig, worm, grub, or a shiny spoon along these targets. At times the bass will be holding extremely tight to the pilings and under structure. Move in close and make a gentle flip, allowing the lure to slowly fall along the wood or concrete foundation.

In the winter, try pitchin' a pork frog slowly along the piers or docks that face the warming sun. Another alternative is to use a fairly heavy spinnerbait with a shorter wire arm and a large single Colorado blade to thump along the end of this structure.

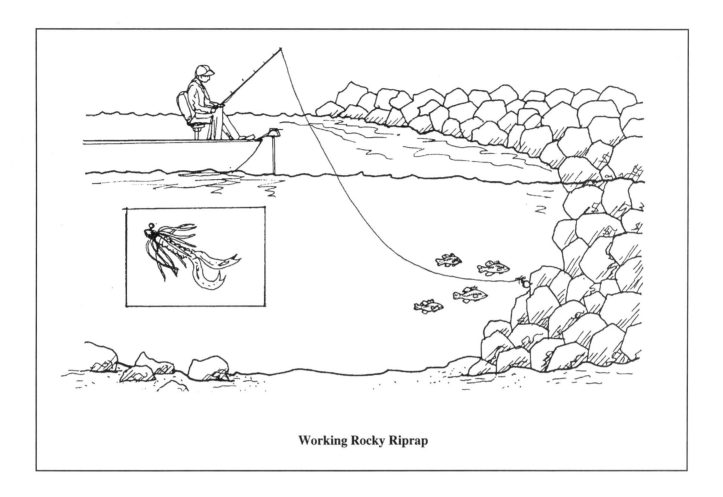

Working Rocky Riprap

As the water warms in the spring, consider adding a slow-falling tube bait, a plastic worm, or a tadpole-like slinkee to your tackle collection. Work these soft plastic lures on a 1/8 ounce darter head fished with a light spinning outfit.

Quite often, bass will also race out from underneath this structure to bushwhack a top-water plug, a buzzbait, or a soft plastic "Sluggo" during the warmer months. Make long, delicate casts with these surface baits into the shallow pockets where the docks or piers meet the bank.

The very ends of these floating structures should also be explored during the height of the summer. Spend a little more time working the ends of these docks in the summer because they often lead to deeper water. Bass will move up along this route from deep to shallow water following a path along the docks. As fall approaches, fish the shallow area under and alongside these piers.

The object is to develop a well thought out game plan for attacking bridges, riprap, docks and piers. Although this shoreline structure is readily visible and seemingly easy to fish, the guides and pros who utilize it work it methodically. We might add that any type of viable shoreline target is a real bonus on deep, clear lakes with stark shallow structure. So especially on conditions like this, boat positioning, proper lure selection, and seasonal patterns are important variables to take into account when fishing these prime targets.

Fishing Weeds: Ultimate "Soft Structure"[1]

Aquatic plants like cattails, pepper grass, hydrilla, milfoil, tules, bulrushes and reeds provide significant cover for largemouth bass in lakes, ponds, and river systems across the country. This type of vegetation can grow in massive proportions, sometimes lining the shore for miles. The problem thus facing the serious basser becomes how to read the "weeds" in order to key in on the best fish-holding areas.

[1] Portions of this section previously appeared in *Bassmaster Magazine*

Reading the Weeds

Whether you are fishing on a lake or pond, some of the most effective places to try are the subtle points formed by weeds. Look for depressions or points in the tules or an area that has a hump forming a point before you start casting.

Frequently, this vegetation grows along the sides and on the top of sloping submerged outcroppings. The tules, reeds, or grasses may not resemble a point like one formed from visible rock. Instead, it may appear to be nothing more than a cluster of scattered plants growing off the bank.

Tules or reeds found growing along these points often provide the bare amount of cover for larger bass moving up from deeper water. Invariably, some of the largest fish of the season are caught by anglers fishing these tule points casting not only uphill and downhill, but also working baits in a cross-point fashion.

Portions of a bank that have a mat-like cover of dead decaying reeds lying in front of live plants can also provide excellent shelter for the bass all through the year. In the warmer months, the mat provides shade from the midday sun. In colder periods, largemouths will be under the dead reeds. The decaying plants will act as an insulation blanket, retaining a modicum of warm water in the shallows.

Learning to discern the best potential cover in a river can be more perplexing. The river bank may appear to be a monotonous, seemingly endless line of tules or reeds. At first glance, all the cover may appear to be the same.

Start by looking for the identical types of terrain that you would key in on in a lake: tule points and matted reeds. Largemouth bass will also seek sanctuary in this kind of cover in a river. Next, be on the lookout for converging currents, exemplified by little eddies formed outside the weeds. Bass will hold tight to the plants lying near the backwash, waiting to ambush baitfish or crawdads caught in the whirlpool.

Similarly, certain stretches of a river system may have greater moving current than other areas. Working the tules and reeds while fishing "the current" can be highly productive. Here too, largemouths will hold tight to the weeds, ready to pounce on a prime morsel of bait as it sweeps by in the drift.

Typically, many anglers will avoid fishing the current since it takes considerably more effort and a high level of concentration. Instead, they may elect to work the tule banks where water flow is minimized. These calmer stretches are often "dead water," no matter how tempting the vegetation looks. Very little bait is being pushed past the plants along banks like these and hence few bass are found.

On the other hand, these are other areas that form backwater sloughs or even miniature lakes off the main river channel. "Pretty water" pockets may also be heavily lined with tule growth. Frequently, these backwaters may be relatively unproductive in the warmer months. As river water levels drop in the summer, there may be limited flow into these pretty water areas. Oxygen levels decrease and the water often turns stagnate.

In the winter, however, the water trapped in these pockets can be considerably warmer than that in the main river. Largemouth bass will root in tight to the reeds and tules that surround these pockets. Concentrate particularly on the plants that are found near the opening of the "pretty water." Bass migrating from the river into one of these tule pockets will often take up residence in the plants that line the bank near the mouth of the passage. Bait will similarly travel along this same route from the main river. Tules and reeds in this portion of the backwater are one of the first places where bait may be intercepted.

The actual structure and color of the plants may also provide the serious basser with some clue as to where to make a cast. Focus on the round tules instead of the flat reeds. For some reason, on many shorelines in both rivers and lakes the round plants hold more bass.

Certain plant coloration may also signal a potential fish-holding stretch. For instance, look for green-colored plants when you're working aquatic vegetation. The green color signifies deeper water to which bass are frequently attracted.

Working the Weeds

Accomplished anglers will modify their tactics for fishing the weeds. The most obvious strategy is to attack this terrain with shallow water flippin'. Expert flippers note that one of the benefits of this presentation is that it keeps the bait in the strike zone 90 percent of the time. This is a critical reason why this method is so potent for probing tules and reeds.

With so much "sameness" to this plant life, even the most adept basser recognizes that considerable ground will have to be explored to take fish from this kind of cover. Hence, the regimented short and quick underhand cast utilized in flippin' is perfectly matched for covering the weeds in an efficient manner.

Without question, the most prevalent lure used with this presentation is the basic pig'n jig combination. There is probably no better replica of an errant crawdad falling into the tules than the size, silhouette, and texture created with a live rubber jig and a pork frog.

However, in contrast to flippin' in heavily wooded cover or dense brush, working the weeds requires a slightly softer touch. To begin with, usually you will not need a jig heavier than 1/4 to 3/8 ounces in weight. It is not difficult for the pork to penetrate the upright plants. The lighter jig head yields a sensuous slow fall with the bait.

If you are flippin' pork into a heavy mat of dead reeds consider switching from the traditional Uncle Josh #11 Pork Frog to a #3 or #4 split-tail eel. The sleek-looking pork eel is prefect for slipping through the narrow openings formed on top of the mat.

It pays to be experimental when flippin' in this type of vegetation. Besides the pig'n jig combination, a variety of other plastic baits should be dropped into the tules or reeds. We'll talk more about these options in the chapter "Serious Flippin'."

It is also important to mention that sometimes in lakes the bass will not be lying directly in the thickest portion of the weeds. Instead they will be situated a few feet from the reeds cruising parallel to the bank. In this situation, the serious basser may make the mistake of motoring his boat to close to the plants in order to start flippin'.

A better strategy may be to begin to fish the tules and reeds with medium length pitches, working the bait all the way back to the boat. Many times anglers inadvertently spook the bass by driving over the outside of the weeds to flip the interior of the vegetation. After not getting bit, they may falsely assume the bank is "dead" when in reality the fish are a few feet off the tules or reeds.

Start by pitchin' the outside water. If the bite shuts off, as it sometimes will with changes in the weather, shift to flippin' and move your rig closer to the weeds.

In rivers, pitchin' will also be effective for floating downstream and rapidly firing off casts across the current. Position your boat parallel to the bank using your trolling motor for proper alignment. Lead head jigs laced with either pork rind or plastic trailers are your best bet for keeping the lure from being swept away too fast. Pay close attention to your line, keeping fairly tight tension. Any sudden interruption in the drift may mean a bass has hit the lure.

Besides the more conventional flippin' or pitchin' approaches, there are other methods applicable for fishing the weeds. For example in lakes and rivers where current is minimal, a plastic worm or grub presented on a Carolina or split-shot rig can be potent. Cover considerable terrain by casting the small plastic baits parallel to the plants. This rig often produces spectacular results when the bass are especially skittish or the water near the tules and reeds is exceptionally clear. As the worm or grub sashays down behind the sinker or shot, the fish may rush out from the weeds to attack the delicate bait.

Other anglers will use a spinnerbait with tandem willow leaf blades to work this type of vegetation. A 3/8 to 1/2 ounce spinner will fall relatively quickly with the blades rotating. A spinnerbait can be rapidly pitched or even flipped with short casts to cover a lot of the tule bank. The narrow width of the willowleaf blades and the tight rotation pattern also help to keep this lure from hanging up in the plants.

Spoons are also worth trying at times, especially if there are schools of shad nestled into the tules. Heavier spoons used for the traditional deep-water approach will usually spook the fish when utilized as a flippin' or pitchin' bait. Switch to lighter models with greater fluttering action. The Johnson Silver Minnow still leads the field for this type of presentation. It is relatively weedless and can be softly dropped right into the plants. Add a white pork frog or eel as a trailer to simulate a shad minnow fleeing in the weeds.

Other spoons like the Johnson Sprite, Krocadile, Rapala, or Kastmaster will also have a slow enough fall and fluttering action for pitchin' or flippin' in this sort of cover. It is best to remove the stock treble hook and replace it with a single weedless hook for fishing this vegetation.

Reaction baits should also be considered for fishing the weeds. A shallow running crankbait can be extremely effective for rapidly covering long expansive tule banks. Slab-shaped lures in particular such as the Cordell Spot, Rat-L-Trap, or Rattlin' Rapala perform best by casting parallel to the bank a few feet from the plants.

Top-water enthusiasts should be willing to make at least a few cursory casts to tule-lined banks any time of the year. If the bass are holding shallow to this cover, a surface plug placed near the bank may trigger strikes even in the colder months. As with crankbaits, it will be more efficient to work top-water baits as much as possible parallel to the tules or reeds.

We stumbled across another interesting strategy while fishing this vegetation. A buzzbait fished parallel to a tule bank can often be a terrific change of pace. Sometimes the bass seem highly reluctant to really attack the buzzer,

Pitchin' a Jig into Tules and Reeds

making short passes at the lure without eating it. In this situation, have a second outfit rigged with a short 3 to 5 inch long floating minnow. Make a follow-up cast to where the fish was seen, gently twitching the minnow along the tules. A vicious strike may result.

It appears that when the bass are lying tight to these plants, the buzzbait creates enough commotion to get the fish to move out from inside the tules. The ensuing cast with the small floating minnow often proves too much for the bass to pass up since curiosity was aroused with the buzzer.

Like all styles of bassin', learning to fish the weeds requires a certain amount of dedication and perseverance. This form of cover is a lot less obvious to decipher compared to "hard" structure like docks, trees, rock piles, and riprap. Nevertheless, be both persistent and creative in attacking shoreline lined with this plant life.

Besides approaching the weeds with conventional bassin' gear, try float tubing, fly-rodding, or walking the bank. Sometimes these alternative methods are equally productive. Whatever your fancy, you may find that some of the best bass bonanzas will be recorded while fishing the "weeds"!

Backwater Structure

Some of the most intriguing places to fish are the diverse sloughs, irrigation canals, and drainage inlets found coast to coast. These waters are commonly rich in nutrients and aquatic vegetation and usually devoid of major boat traffic. They provide ample sanctuary for catfish, panfish, and forage baits. This can also be prime bassin' territory if you learn how to read this type of structure.

There are definite, though sometimes subtle distinctions in the types of backwaters you may fish. For example, some such as those found along the lower Colorado River in California and Arizona are offshoots of the major river channel. As you drift down the Colorado, you will see numerous little indentations along the shoreline. These small "cuts" may be nothing more than a hollowed out portion of the bank or even be the entrance to longer, more mysterious passages. These may lead to a hidden lake an acre or more in size which locals term "pretty water."

In contrast, canals and culverts like those built in the Gulf States pose different problems. Fishing this maze of irrigation and drainage waters can be a formidable challenge. Many of these man-made conduits crisscross the countryside, starting from the ocean and penetrating many miles into the interior. Serious bass fishermen may actually find their lures being attacked by saltwater species such as sea trout, snook, and baby tarpon as they fish the waters nearest to the coast. As they reverse direction, and salinity decreases, populations of brim, carp, bowfin, and largemouth bass replace the marine predators.

Current is another feature that distinguishes the different sloughs and canals. For those that are found adjacent to a river channel, water movement can play a major role in the location of bass and baitfish. The flow usually gradually declines the further back from the river you travel. Sometimes the major pattern for catching bass in this environment is to look for the less turbulent water. Other times, the fish can only be found feeding in the current.

In some situations, the existence of current is more sporadic. A relatively quiet, slow-moving drainage ditch, for example, can suddenly change in complexion with run-off water rushing into it from a recent storm. Similarly, water movement in these irrigation canals can vary on a weekly basis. If the farmers need more irrigation water, the dams are opened and the current rips. If the need is diminished, the canals become more stagnant.

Vegetation is another variable affecting the make-up of a backwater fishery. For example, in the South, bass will relate to hydrilla, seeking shelter in this dominant water plant. In the West, river fishermen must learn to read the subtle differences between the bamboo and tules that line the banks along many of their waterways.

As water clarity varies in different impoundments, a similar condition occurs in sloughs and canals. In some backwaters, the effect of rushing current keeps the water fairly clear. This in turn makes the bass extremely spooky and difficult to fool. Other inlets display distinctively stained or off-colored water due to a variety of factors. The actual mineral content of the bottom soil can create a specific color to the water. Likewise, run-offs from fertilized farmlands may affect water clarity in these sloughs.

Along with variations in water coloration, pH levels can also fluctuate dramatically along this kind of waterway. Again, this is due to nitrates, phosphates, and other chemicals washing into the backwaters. This is yet another factor the bass angler may have to consider in learning to pattern fish in these waters.

Moving Water

Current can play a pivotal role in finding backwater bass. In warmer months, the area in the waterway with the greatest flow can be highly oxygenated. It may also be the coolest water in the canal or slough. Bass will gravitate to this water despite the turbulence.

Morsels of food consisting of baitfish, crawdads, and larger insects or amphibians can become trapped in the current. As occurs with trout and other river-bred species, the bass will rely upon the current as a feeding tube. They will typically face into the moving water, lazily waiting to ambush prey as it drifts helplessly by.

Plastic worms, lizards, snakes, grubs, jigs, spinnerbaits, and even crankplugs can be effectively fished in the current through the whirlpools and eddies. It is important to maintain a tight line. The current can quickly push the lure along. If there is excessive slack in the line, it will be difficult to get a strong hook set.

Not all backwater currents hold bass. To begin with, if irrigation dams upstream are letting in vast amounts of water, the flow may be too swift for the fish to stabilize themselves. Similarly, if a significant volume of colder water is being pushed through the canal or slough, the fish may relocate further back into the quieter pockets, seeking a warmer refuge.

One of the most critical places to fish in this type of eco-system is where the current from the main river channel converges with the stiller water leading into a cut. Be on the lookout for a grass bed, brush, or some rocks near the entrance to the cut. This is where the baitfish will hide. Bass will come into this area leading into the backwater to feed. The fish will lie right on the edge of the current, next to an eddy or someplace where the current slows down.

Trying to fish current may be a little more difficult in slow-flowing canals or culverts. Even here, cooler and more richly oxygenated water can be found in the form of the irrigation run-off. Moving water will hold fish in the canal system in the heat of summer. Moving water may also be cooler water, and that's where your baitfish will congregate.

Hydrilla Points

Veteran bassers who fish canals, sloughs, and culverts learn to look for subtle variations in the waterway that may be prime fish-holding structure. Hydrilla and similar aquatic vegetation may be one key form of structure in this type of eco-system. Bass prefer hydrilla over almost any other type of vegetation that you find. During the summer months, it offers oxygen and cover and it also holds a lot of bait. Food sources in the form of minnows, insects, amphibians, etc. will be with the hydrilla, and other plant life. Oxygen levels may also be higher around the vegetation.

An important target in fishing the sloughs and canals is to look for places where the hydrilla form a point. Usually this point will lead to deeper water, creating an access way that the bass may traverse in their daily movements. The hydrilla point can start from the bank and grow out into the canal or may be found more in the center where there is often prominent weed growth.

Water clarity is another critical variable to finding fish in these waterways. Some canals have muddy, chocolate-colored water. Others have greener, stained water with evidence of an algae bloom. Frequently, the better bass in a canal system are found in the somewhat cleaner, clearer water. This is because in canals off-colored water usually has a higher salt content. Largemouth bass and other freshwater species will gravitate to water where the salinity is dramatically reduced. On the other hand, you may be able to find more indigenous coastal species such as red fish, sea trout, and baby tarpon in the canals with more off-colored water.

Exceptionally dirty water in certain parts of the country may also signal something much more detrimental to the delicate ecosystem of the canal. This could be a result of herbicide or pesticide spraying with resulting run-off. Avoid those areas where the adjacent weed growth has been subject to heavy spraying. Usually when shoreline reeds, tules, and aquatic vegetation are killed by spraying, the bass move away from the area.

However, wherever you find cleaner water emptying into a canal, the largemouths will probably be nearby. The runoff water from culverts and irrigation ditches, particularly following a rain storm, can be rich in oxygen. Similarly, during the summer heat, this flowing water can be much cooler than that found in the more stagnant main channel of the canal. Baitfish, brim, and largemouth bass will look for this cooler, more oxygenated water.

Canal Bassin'

There are basically two types of lures to use for canal bassin': top-water plugs and soft plastics. As a rough rule of thumb, throw a lot of surface lures from spring through fall. Buzzers, prop plugs, chuggers, poppers, jerkin' minnows, and cigar-shaped stick baits will all work. Then, switch to plastic worms, grubs, lizards, and jigs from winter through early spring.

In the warmest months, the bass will move up shallow along the edges of the canals and stay there. Top-water is the name of the game and you can toss a surface bait all day long! In many canals, the baitfish that are prominent are small brim, shiners, and shad. If you use a top-water plug it imitates this main forage especially since they are not in the weeds, not traveling, and not roaming around. The bass pick up summer habitat and stay there from right after the spawn until September or October until the vegetation stops growing.

When colder weather does set in, canal largemouths bury into the matted tules, into the thickest portion of the hydrilla and moss, or into the deepest holes found in the waterway. These are the areas where the fish can find warmth and sanctuary.

A slower moving offering is more suitable for these conditions. Use your electric trolling motors to gently glide down the canals pitchin' plastic worms or grubs to these cold weather targets.

Interestingly, not many serious canal bassers prefer to flip this kind of water despite the endless array of shallow shoreline cover. This is probably due to the fact that there are often so many weeds that grow bank to bank that the fish are not necessarily uptight. On the average, these canals are shallow—5 to 7 feet deep. Sunlight penetrates the shallow shoreline vegetation, so the bass frequently don't need to be oriented to the bank. They can be situated right in the middle of the canal.

Largemouths will also often push baitfish up against the bank during the night and will still be there in the early dawn on many canals. Then, once the sun comes up work the deeper middle sections of the canal channel where light penetration is reduced.

There is no need to finesse these bass with super light line. The canal fish are particularly aggressive and not too hook shy. A standard baitcasting reel spooled with 10 to 15 pound test mono will perform nicely with both the surface plugs and the soft plastic baits. Larger worms in 6 to 8 inch patterns are also recommended over smaller 4 inch "sissy baits" when fishing canals.

Live bait enthusiasts can also partake of some excellent action along these canals working from the shore or from a boat. The bass will eagerly attack live shiners, small bluegill, nightcrawlers, waterdogs, crawdads and, sometimes, live crickets. The shiners, minnow, and bluegill can be caught directly in the canal then stored in live bait buckets. 'Crawlers, crickets and 'dads are sold in local tackle shops.

A Year-Round Fishery

Most canals, sloughs and culverts that host a largemouth bass population provide solid bassin' throughout the year for both boaters and bank walkers. Other species such as crappie, bluegill, gar, carp, bowfin, mudfish, tilapia, oscars, and catfish may also be on tap.

On a more somber note, the future of these canals and sloughs of this magnificent fishery rests on proper land management and control of hazardous run-off. Every effort must be made to insure that dangerous pollutants are kept from entering this type of fragile ecosystem.

Fishermen must voice their concern when sections of a canal are sealed off and water becomes diverted solely for agricultural interest downstream. This creates a potential pocket of "dead" water, low in oxygen, with an imminent die off of the major gamefish in that sector a real possibility.

Understanding Deep Structure

Structure, as we have mentioned, is often depicted as being either "shallow" or "deep." Most bass anglers quickly learn to identify the former as they work along the banks. Brush piles, moss beds, tule banks, downed timber, riprap, logs, boulders, piers and docks, bridges and dam faces are examples of shallow water shoreline structure that were discussed.

Most bass fishermen know the advantages of fishing this type of cover. The full arsenal of bassin' lures will invariably produce at one time or another when cast into these shallow haunts. Crankplugs, jigs, worms, grubs, surface baits, and even spoons pitched up along the bank can be used for working shoreline structure.

We can't always depend upon finding in shallow water either great concentrations of bass or fish that are willing to bite. Perhaps the single most important variable in locating bass is finding forage baitfish, particularly shad minnows. There can be a variety of reasons for these schools of bait to migrate a considerable distance off the bank. Intensified light penetration, heavy boat traffic, changes in barometric pressure, differences in pH factors, or dramatic temperature drops can all induce the shad to move to deeper comfort zones. When the bait moves, count on the bass to follow.

As the bass venture further off the bank, many otherwise accomplished shoreline fishermen lose confidence, simply because they can no longer see their targets above the surface of the water. The boulders, tree stumps, riprap,

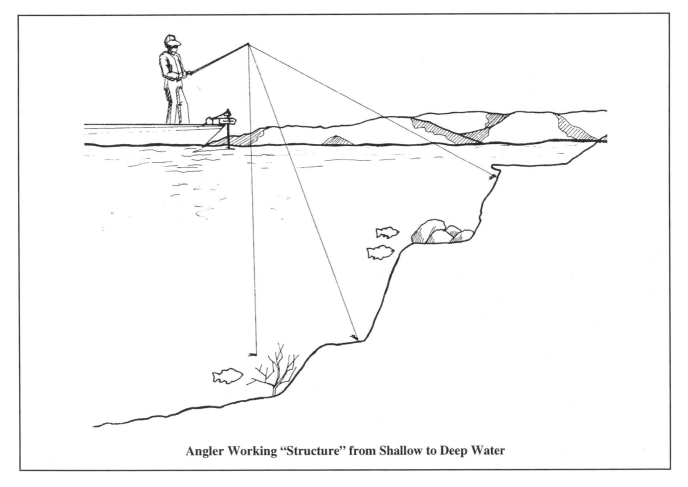

Angler Working "Structure" from Shallow to Deep Water

and lily pads that they were once throwing to have been replaced by more obscure forms of *deep structure*. While sitting out in 20 to 50 foot depths, the angler may be hovering over a completely different underwater world with a very subtle topography.

At these levels, "structure" assumes different forms. There are the more obvious submerged rock piles, trees, boulders, and brush that show up on today's modern electronic fish locating devices. The underwater picture becomes a little more complex and puzzling when this more conspicuous submerged cover is missing.

Now the serious basser must look for baitfish along less discernible structure such as ledges, drop-offs, breaks, reefs, submerged roadbeds, river channels, and underwater springs. A much greater understanding of electronics is needed. There also has to be a change in mental posture regarding both locating and fishing deep structure.

To begin with, the angler must approach the water off the bank with an open attitude. That is, try not to assume anything. Let your electronics help you explore the bottom terrain. Simply try to envision structure as anything that deviates from a smooth bottom." In this way, the most subtle variations become potential deep fish-holding areas.

On some lakes, particularly older impoundments and man-made reservoirs, the habitat is sparse near the bank to begin with. Hence, bass will locate near almost anything that represents that deviation from the smooth muddy bottom. Deep structure fishermen will thus key in on such things as a minor "break" in the terrain that lies off the shore. For instance monitor your flasher, L.C.R., or graph unit on a 15 foot deep flat as you work outside a particular bank. When you sense that the bottom is fairly bland and without distinctive features, look for that one subtle 1 to 5 foot drop-off that offsets this smooth mud. Bass will congregate along this gentle incline. Realize that it may be the only available structure in the immediate area from which the bass can establish an ambush point. When you find a little break, focus on it even further to find a point, some rubble, or brush along its length. This is where the bass will find a security spot.

Novice bass fishermen often maintain an air of skepticism when they begin to motor out to those 30 to 60 foot depths sometimes hundreds of yards offshore. The problem, of course, is that without understanding the bottom, all this water seems to look the same. The first thing to do is to monitor the baitfish activity with your electronics. The worst condition is to graph shad that are balled up out in the middle of nowhere without any adjacent structure.

Suspended schools like these only occasionally have hungry bass nearby. A more optimal situation is to have the bait located on some form of structure, for example, along an incline, drop-off, or rock pile where bass are more likely to be found.

Deep Structure Basics

There are a number of rudimentary tactics that serious bassers can practice to maximize their chances of both finding and catching fish on deep structure.

One common mistake is not utilizing electronics to the fullest extent. Keep an eye on your instruments. Motor around extensively in order to pinpoint deep structure fish. Have the meter running at full speed and use marker buoys to delineate the subtle drop-offs or "breaks." Once you are satisfied with your boat position, employ a strategy like doodlin', spoonin', or a similar vertical approach in an initial attempt to induce these fish to bite.

Another problem that may confront the angler accustomed to pitching baits along the bank is maintaining contact with the underwater terrain. Deep structure fish locate near the bottom. Therefore, it is imperative to use lures and presentations that *slowly* pass through this strike zone. Once again, we emphasize *slowly* since most of the bass at these depths typically react in a somewhat more hesitant manner when striking a lure than they would if they were bushwhacking a bait in the shallows.

You might also consider fishing small 4 inch worms on an open-hook darter head. Shake and twitch the little 1/8 ounce jig to make the worm dance from side to side. Darter head fishing is a sensational way to slowly present a bait along rock piles, reefs, staircase-like ledges, and even above deep submerged tree tops. Use these darters with both spinning or baitcasting outfits. We prefer to stay with lighter 6 to 8 pound monofilament. The fine diameter line imparts considerably more erratic action to this little jig in contrast to heavier mono used for more traditional worm fishing. Novice deep structure fishermen can learn to effectively fish darters in a short period of time.

If the bass are holding on even deeper structure, switch to the Carolina rig to maintain better contact. The key is to use a sinker heavy enough to plod along the bottom. Many bass fishermen have shied away from using anything larger than a crimped 1/8 ounce split-shot with this method. (This variation of the basic Carolina rig is commonly termed "split shottin'.")

However often at the 30 to 50 foot level with increased current and wind action, the smaller lead shot will simply not keep the little worms or grubs down along the bottom.

In this situation, use a much more prominent 3/16 to 5/8 ounce sliding bullet weight rigged Carolina style. Pinch a small BB-sized shot onto the 6 pound test mono about 18 inches above the worm hook for the bullet weight to butt itself against. After the cast is made, the grub or worm is slowly reeled in with no additional action imparted into the retrieve. The Carolina setup is also a relatively simple strategy to master.

At times more traditional reaction lures can also be employed to seek out deep structure fish. Certainly, with the advent of first 20 foot and now 30 foot diving plugs, the angler may find some of the more aggressive bass at depths never before invaded by crankbaits. By the same token, heavier 1/2 to one ounce spinnerbaits, lead head jigs and, of course, an array of vertical spoons can all take a number of deep structure fish once they are located. Although the emphasis recently has been on using soft plastic lures for structure bassin', don't underestimate the potential of these other baits to perform quite well in deep water.

More Deep Structure Talk

Once the angler has located fish off the bank, and tried some of the basic deep-water tactics, there are a few other ploys that may assist him or her in getting more strikes. For some reason, many dedicated bass fishermen seem to be reluctant to use an anchor. Some anglers prefer constant "stand up" fishing and feel that anchoring up to a location may dull their overall energy level and effectiveness. Interestingly enough, we have found in our own experiences that budding structure fishermen sometimes perform consistently better with the boat anchored over the target spot. In doing this, the angler does not have to fight wave and wind action that is frequently more intensified off the bank.

Also, delicate and precise presentations can be made meticulously working the bait over the structure. This is especially true if the serious basser no longer has to worry about the trolling motor and boat position. A greater level of concentration can be placed on the cast and retrieve through the deep strike zones.

It is also imperative to develop a minimal working knowledge of your electronics. Regardless of whether you prefer a paper graph, flasher, or liquid crystal recorder, you must have some confidence that these instruments will indeed locate structure. However, sometimes bass anglers rely too much on their electronics to find individual bass at great depths. Often their instruments are either not sophisticated enough, not hooked up properly, or the fisherman's eyes are simply not trained to detect the fish on the bottom. All is not lost. Concentrate more on locating schools of baitfish and the basic ledges and drop-offs that should traditionally hold fish. Sometimes, even the best instruments will not clearly pick up bass nestled right on the mud. Have confidence in the spot you select and try at least a few casts in a seemingly good section of structure.

Finally, don't go totally overboard with the deep-water attack. Remember, even in the coldest days of

25' Deep Structure (11 to 14 lbs.)

winter when the fish are located deep, there can always be a sporadic movement back up into the shallows. If some bass fishermen are guilty of being too oriented to the bank, then some structure fishermen may be equally at fault for staying too long out in deep-water. Bass are not sedentary creatures by nature. They follow the forage bait which in itself often moves unpredictably. The sign of a competent serious basser is being able to quickly adapt and readjust a game plan to respond to prevailing conditions.

Fishing deep structure is an essential approach that complements a strong shallow water game plan. Be experimental in investigating the opportunities that lie off the bank. Develop the skills to master a few of the deep-water presentations. Fish them with confidence and then expand your repertoire of deep-water strategies. As our water becomes more pressured by shoreline fishermen, deep structure bassin' will become an integral component of the serious basser's bag of tricks!

Drifting and Dragging

Two rather unusual tactics for fishing deep structure are "drifting" and "dragging." Both of these methods have become popular in bassin' circles for fishing deep while surveying large expanses of open water, often in foul weather, with maximum efficiency.

Drifting

The main feature separating the drifting strategy from dragging is the lack of reliance on an electric trolling motor. Often the winds that whip across big barren lakes can generate considerable swells, waves, and chop. These are tough conditions in which to try to power a fully loaded bass boat with an electric trolling motor.

The serious basser can instead set up different drift patterns in which their boats will be pushed across the water aided solely by the wind. A typical drift pattern, for example, could be working the shallow flats in a large cove. Using the larger outboard engine, you could motor your rig to the far, lee side of the cove. After positioning the boat parallel to the bank, you can then allow the wind to gently push you across the cove. Once you reach the other shore, start up the big motor, drive back to the leeward side and begin another drift.

A considerable amount of territory can be covered by wind-drifting in this fashion. Similar drift patterns might be established between two points, down a rocky dam, over submerged trees, or along an old creek channel. Drifting allows the bassmaster to concentrate more upon

the baits bouncing along the bottom than having to fight the elements while maneuvering the trolling motor.

There is a multitude of different lures that are highly adaptable for drifting. By far, the simplest to utilize are soft plastic baits.

The standard Texas-rigged worm bounced on the bottom with a 3/16 to 5/8 ounce bullet weight makes a perfect drift bait. The heavier sinkers are often necessary to maintain solid bottom contact, particularly with a fast drift or in deep water.

It is important to note that worm fishing on the drift is different from using this bait from a more stationary casting platform. For one thing, be ready to drop the rod and actually give the bass some slack when you feel the first "tick" in the line. Sometimes, the worm is plodding so fast along the bottom with the drift the fish can hardly stay up with it. Hence, give the bass a moment to eat the bait.

Also, because the drift is moving the worm for you, it is best to embed the hook barely through the outer layer of plastic. "Skin-hooking" the worm like this will make it somewhat less weedless. However, a quick efficient hook set is more possible with this ploy.

The Carolina rig is another excellent combination to try with the drifting strategy. Use anywhere from a 1/4 to 1 ounce bullet weight or oval egg sinker butted against a swivel. Attach an 18 to 36 inch length of leader line tied to a worm hook.

The heavier sinkers will provide for adequate bottom contact with even the fastest drift in the deepest water. A plastic worm, curl-tail grub, or feather-like reaper can be drifted with this Carolina setup. These baits will, to some degree, float up off the bottom. This can be a deadly combination when drifted over submerged weed beds or rock piles.

You may also want to switch to a specially designed styrofoam floating jig head for deeper water drifting. Lace on Garland's Spider or Haddock's squid-like 18-Tail to the floating head and drift these baits well above the bottom.

Another variation on this theme is to use Jack Chancellor's patented Do-Nothing Worms. These bland-looking baits are not used enough across the country. We prefer a simple smoke-colored Do-Nothing worm drifted in the most inclement weather to consistently nail quality fish while other anglers are fighting the wind.

Draggin' this bait, the dying, fluttering action simulates the way shad move in deep water. The turbulence created by matching it with larger sinkers and a Carolina rig and plowing it along the bottom also helps to attract bass.

There are other lures besides the soft plastics that also have some intriguing applications when used as drift baits. Heavier 5/8 to 1 ounce slab-shaped spoons, for example, such as the Hopkins #075 or Haddock's Jig'N Spoon models can be vertically "yo-yoed" over deep ledges as the boat drifts along.

Frequently, it is almost impossible to maintain good boat position over these offshore "breaks" in the wind while using a spoon. With the drifting technique, simply let the spoon sink to the bottom and then give it a few pronounced lift-and-drop motions with the rod. As the boat drifts along, let out more scope in your monofilament to maintain good bottom contact with the spoon. At some point, you will find that you cannot let out much more line and still have control of the lure. Quickly reel up, vertically drop the spoon below the boat again, and start the spoon-drift all over.

Other more traditional reaction baits such as crank-plugs, spinners, or surface lures can also be tried with the faster drifts. Anglers working from either the front or back seat of the boat can make a series of rapid-fire casts to either open water or shoreline cover while the rig is being pushed in the wind.

With these kinds of lures, one of the latest high speed baitcasting reels can be a real boon. A baitcaster with at least a 6:1 gear ratio will help you fire off casts and retrieve your lures quickly, keeping pace with a fast-moving drift pattern.

Finally, not all bass fishermen prefer to use lures when the winds kick up on a lake. Live bait enthusiasts have been employing the drifting tactic for years for catching bass in rough water. Nightcrawlers, mudsuckers, shiners, waterdogs, and other indigenous baitfish can be drifted along the bottom with a 1/8 to 1/2 ounce lead shot crimped 12 to 18 inches above the bait. Here again, as with plastic worm drifting, be prepared to give the bass a modest amount of slack line and a chance to eat the bait.

Dragging

Dragging, in contrast to drifting, relies upon the electric trolling motor to maintain more precise boat position. The angler basically keeps the trolling motor on heading the boat up wind while dragging a lure on or near the bottom.

In competitive-style bassin', the dragging method is not considered to be the same as trolling which is usually illegal for most tournaments. As long as the contestant makes intermittent casts while dragging over a long stretch of water, technically speaking, he is not trolling.

Both the Texas-style worm and the Carolina rig will work equally well for dragging baits over deep underwater terrain. However, most bassers prefer to add a modicum of rod tip action to the soft plastic lures while moving with the trolling motor.

One variation is to rig a 4 to 6 inch long worm Texas-style, behind a 3/16 ounce slide sinker. Drop the worm either straight below the boat or make a cast away from your rig. Once the bait hits the bottom, throw the reel into gear, pick up the slack line, and rhythmically shake the rod tip.

As the boat glides along, this modified doodlin' approach, sometimes termed "doodle-slidin'," will often trigger strikes on lethargic deep-water bass. It has been a consistent winner on many deep lakes.

It is not necessary to give the fish any slack before setting the hook with the doodle-slide. Whereas the worm may be moving quickly on the drift, the boat operator governs the speed of the bait while dragging.

Some anglers opt to drag worms laced onto an open-hook lead head. Tiny 1/8 to 1/4 ounce darter or p-head shaped jigs are often used instead of a Texas setup. The rationale is that there are very few obstructions in these deep reservoirs so why not use an open hook for maximum setting power.

Recently, however, some pros are finding that the specially rigged worm with tandem-open hooks we mentioned previously may be an even better alternative for deep-water draggin'. These baits are relatively simple to construct.

Select any 4 to 6 inch worm that you have confidence in. Thread it onto a 1/8 to 1/4 ounce lead head. Next, tie a short 2 to 3 inch long piece of 10 to 12 pound test monofilament to the center of the open jig head. Then tie the other end of this line to a #2 to #6 long-shank hook. (Some pros simply use a plastic worm hook while others prefer a Carlisle or Aberdeen style.) This rear hook forms the "stinger" for this lure.

As the tandem-hook worm is dragged along the bottom, use your rod tip to add a "twitching" motion. Many bass will be nailed with the rear stinger. Shake the tandem-hook worm vigorously. Do it in a manner similar to doodlin'. Your trolling motor will do much of the work for you all the way down to 50 feet. Drag and bounce this bait through broken rocks. Always be prepared for a pressure bite while draggin' these worms.

Draggin'

This unusual worm accounts for numerous deep-water fish that may otherwise be missed with more conventional rigging methods. The rear stinger hook is the secret!

Plastic fork-tail jigs such as Haddock's Kreepy Krawler, Garland's Spider, or Yamamoto's Hula Grub are also frequently used as drag baits. Drag them where there is sloping terrain and small rocks with the points gently tapering off the bank.

On these lakes you can actually see the bass near the bottom with your graph. Free-spool a heavy 3/4 to 1 ounce jig with swimming plastic tails and just troll-motor this bait above the bottom in 25 to 60 foot depths. Let the jig bump over the bottom and swim above the structure. If

there is a fish down there it will usually eat the bait on the drag. We find that we actually catch more bass with dragging if we use hardly any rod tip action. Just let the troll motor do all the work.

Twin-spinners are another "sleeper" lure to use with the dragging method. These are basically lead head jigs with vinyl or live rubber skirts and two wire arms with spinner blades that extend out from the bait. With the blades spread apart, the twin-spinner appears rather insect-like with prominent "feelers."

These lures are perfect for making good bottom contact, particularly in the colder months. As the twin-spinner is slowly dragged across the bottom, the whirling blades may call in otherwise sluggish bass to investigate. Add a pork rind trailer for an even more sensuous-looking drag bait.

A final tactic worth trying has been used extensively for saltwater species, but rarely in serious bassin' ranks for highly sensitive Alabama spotted bass. Invariably, the spots will follow migrating schools of threadfin shad down to 90 foot depths. A small #5 or #7-S floating Rapala minnow worked at these extreme depths can be a phenomenal bait for deep-water spots.

You have to use a special dropper setup to get a small floating Rapala down to the 50 to 90 foot range. Tie your main line to a three way swivel. Then tie on about 12 inches of leader to one of the swivel eyelets. Tie on a 1 to 2 ounce spoon sinker to the other end of the leader. Next, add an 18 to 24 inch length of leader to the remaining eyelet and tie the tiny Rapala onto it.

The heavy sinker takes the floating minnow down quickly. The Rapala then suspends 18 to 24 inches above the sinker, floating well off the bottom. Using your trolling motor, simply drag this floating minnow rig over areas showing fish and bait activity, occasionally giving the lure a quick twitch with the rod tip.

It is indeed an extraordinary sight to see bass taken on this combination at such depths. Teamed with the dragging strategy, the floating minnow rig permits the angler to cover great amounts of water while maintaining excellent bottom contact with the heavy sinker.

Although driftin' and draggin' have become staple methods for serious bassers fishing deep Western lakes, these techniques will work anywhere the angler has to confront wind, depth, and large expanses of water. You will find that largemouths, smallmouths, and spotted bass can equally be taken by drifting or dragging lures along the bottom, practically anywhere in the United States.

However, don't become lazy when employing these two tactics. Each still requires proper bait selection, perfectly balanced tackle, precise hooking, and a high level of concentration to make them perform under adverse conditions. Drifting and dragging are valuable additions to the serious bass fisherman's arsenal of techniques.

Vertical Bassin'

Fishing deep structure for bass with a vertical presentation is one of the more difficult approaches for the recreational angler to master. Most fishermen learn to stalk their quarry with some form of horizontal retrieve.

Whether tossing a worm to a shoreline target or winding a crankplug in open water, it seems more natural to bring the lure back in along a horizontal plane.

There are certain situations when a precise vertical line of attack is quite productive. Here then is the basic how, when, and where of vertical bassin'.

When

During periods of extremes in water temperature, bass will often situate themselves in compact areas, hugging to the bottom. The dead of winter and the hot dog days of summer are major times to concentrate on the vertical strategy. The water may be either too cold or too warm to stimulate the fish into an aggressive feeding mode.

Similarly, there are occasions following major climatic changes, fluctuating water levels, or turnover phases when the bass suspend in tight schools and again are not too interested in attacking a bait. Here too, a vertical presentation may trigger strikes from semi-active fish when more traditional tactics fail.

Where

There are certain topographical features in a particular body of water that may be conducive to a vertical approach. Obvious places to work a lure straight up and down include submerged points, ledges, sheer rocky walls, and the face of a dam.

Don't overlook more subtle structure such as a gentle "hump" that may arise off an otherwise bland muddy bottom. This type of terrain is typical of many reservoirs. Bass often cluster around the hump and are prime targets for the vertical bait.

How

A virtual smorgasbord of lures will work when presented in a vertical fashion. Let's first review some of the obvious baits then focus on the more obscure lures suitable for the vertical attack.

Spoons

When most bass fishermen think of vertical fishing, the most common bait that comes to mind is the spoon. These are relatively simple lures but there is a certain methodology required to make the spoon perform.

First, if the bass seem to be on an active feeding pattern, try a narrow-bodied spoon that will sink fast and put you immediately into the school or structure. The Hopkin's #075 and Haddock Jig'N Spoon are fast-sinking models.

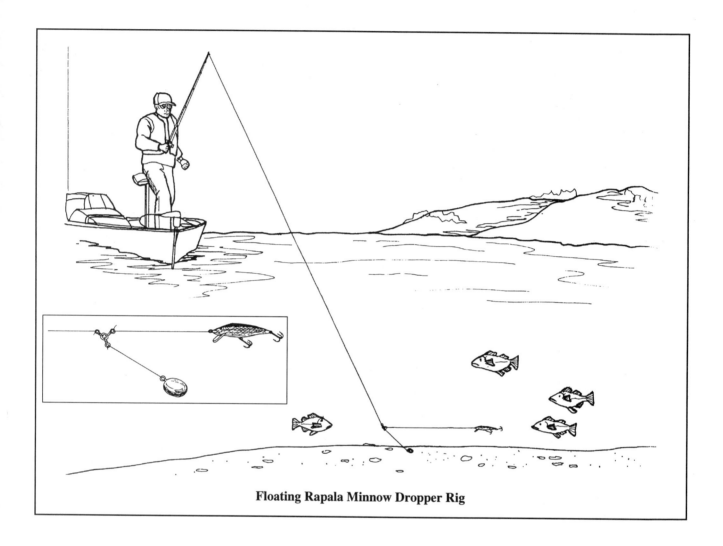

Floating Rapala Minnow Dropper Rig

If the fish appear to be lethargic, a slow-sinking, wide-bodied spoon may be more effective. The Haddock Structure Spoon and Johnson Sprite exemplify this type of fluttering bait. It pays to be experimental until you determine which sort of spoon design the bass prefer during a given outing. Always be prepared for strikes to occur on the "sink" as you free-spool the spoon to the bottom.

Novice bass anglers often make the mistake of employing an excessively pronounced lift-and-drop motion with the rod tip to make the spoon rise and fall. Typically, the angler lifts the rod up to the 12 o'clock position then lets it drop parallel to the water. This forces the spoon to erratically "jump" up off the bottom then slowly flutter back down. This tactic may often work with more aggressive bass.

If the fish seem to be sluggish, a less exaggerated rod tip sequence may be more productive. Using quick, short,

rod lifts with the wrist, make the spoon rise and fall no more than 12 inches from the bottom. The trick is to have the spoon kind of flip-flop on or slightly above the bottom, mimicking a slow-dying baitfish.

It is also important to keep in mind that this facet of the vertical approach can be effective all year long. Spoonin' is sometimes falsely regarded as primarily a cold water, wintertime tactic. The fact is vertical spoonin' will work throughout the year and especially whenever the bass are gathered tight around schools of bait. (We'll elaborate upon this tactic in a later chapter.)

Worms

Plastic worms can be utilized as vertical lures in a number of ways. One of the most popular techniques in recent years has been to "doodle" this bait.

Vertical Spoonin'

Using either 6 or 8 pound test monofilament, thread on a 3/16 ounce bullet weight. Next rig a 3 to 4 inch long plastic Berkley Finesse Power Worm, Texas style. Usually, either the straight or paddle tail design works best for vertical doodlin'.

The object is to lower the small worm directly over bass that are holding on a rocky ledge or drop-off. Then shake or "doodle" the worm with short rhythmic rod twitches. This makes the bait dart and dance along the bottom. Bass that are normally not interested in feeding may strike the doodle worm out of sheer aggravation.

Always be alert for pressure bites as the fish gently mouths the worm while vertical doodlin'. If you feel any form of dull resistance or pressure on the end of the line—you know the drill—swing and set!

Like spoonin', doodlin' is a vertical strategy that has year-round application. The key is to stay with super light lines and tiny worms and to maintain a high level of concentration.

Darters and p-heads are small 1/16 to 1/8 ounce lead heads with either 2 to 4 inch plastic worms or grubs laced onto the open hook. The arrowhead-shaped darter practically "darts" from side to side on the fall or when twitched with the rod tip. The round p-head jig sinks in more of a straight line.

Both of these minuscule worm-and-jig combos are terrific for the vertical game. If you are fishing in deep water with minimal obstructions, the open-hook configuration will stick a lot of bass that might otherwise be missed with the doodle worm setup.

As with doodlin', expect many pressure bites with darters and p-heads. Pay attention to any unexpected tension on the end of the line. Also look for a subtle "tick" as the light mono suddenly jumps or moves off to one side.

This is a sign that a bass has inhaled the lure and is swimming off with the bait.

Tubes

Hollow-bodied tube baits such as the Berkley Power Tube are perfectly suited for vertical bassin'. This is especially true when the fish are in a slow-down state.

These lures perform best when they are custom rigged. Many anglers thread the tube onto a small darter or p-head so the jig head rests outside the bait. Most pros prefer to actually slide the tiny jig up inside the tube then carefully push the hook eyelet through the soft plastic.

This internal rigging makes the tube bait both glide and swim in a tight circle with the lightest flick of the rod tip. It also creates a "soft head" that the bass may hold onto longer in contrast to exposed lead.

In a vertical capacity, tube baits should be fished similarly to a darter or p-head. However, these lures have a certain amount of buoyancy, particularly in underwater currents. This feature, combined with the slow-falling action of the internal rigging, makes the tube bait a great weapon for suspended fish.

After metering bass suspended off the bottom, drop the Power Tube directly over the fish. The lure gently darts back and forth as it sinks. Watch for strikes! After you throw the reel into gear, give the rod a short twitch. Let the tube sashay back down a few inches. Pressure bites are the norm with this type of lure.

Blades

Spinnerbaits are usually overlooked as a possible vertical bait. There are times when these lures produce remarkable results compared to the basic parade of worms, tubes, spoons, and jigs.

Both tandem- and single-blade spinnerbaits will work on a vertical drop. For fishing deeper water, use a spinner with the larger rounded Colorado blade. These will give off a lot of vibration in addition to considerable flash. The basic color combination is white skirt with nickel blades to mimic a school of shad.

For the vertical attack, fish the spinnerbait as you would a jig. Either lower it to the bottom or through schools of suspended fish. Use a long lift of the rod tip sort of ripping the blades up through the strike zone. Then, maintaining a fairly tight line, let the spinnerbait fall a few feet, dropping the rod parallel to the water.

Surprisingly, the bass will hit the lure both on the lift as the blades are rapidly whirling or on the drop as the bait softly "helicopters" on the fall. It is imperative to keep a taut line with this bulky bait to feel not only the strike but to also keep the blades turning at all times.

Crankplugs

It has been only in recent years that the pros have leaked out the secret of using a crankbait in a vertical manner. Not all plugs will work, however. You will need one of the flat-sided, slab-shaped lures like the Cordell Spot, Rat-L-Trap, or Rattlin' Rapala for this presentation.

Look for schools of suspended fish. Once located, let one of these crankbaits sink directly into and somewhat below the school. Lift the rod in a long sweeping motion to "rip" the plug through the fish. Then let the slab-bait slowly flutter back down a few feet.

Continue this fast rip-and-drop motion for a few moments. If nothing happens, then *quickly* retrieve the plug back to the surface. As you would expect, be ready for a bass to bushwhack the lure on its upward ascent once you start to wind it in.

Patience, Alertness, Contact!

The three critical ingredients to mastering the vertical approach are: 1) have patience, 2) continue to remain alert through slow feeding periods, and 3) always try to maintain good contact when working directly on the bottom.

Vertical bassin' is usually practiced when the fish are in a sluggish feeding mode. When strikes are far and few between, this is when we have a tendency to relax and lose both our concentration and proper contact with the strike zone.

Develop a level of confidence with the vertical game. Learn to present your lures "up and down" all through the year. Remember when the bass are not interested in moving too far or too fast to attack a bait, it may be time to switch to the vertical structure attack.

Serious Finessin'

Serious Finessin'

Much has been written in recent years about "finesse" bassin'. The finesse school uses light, spider web-like monofilament, soft rods, small reels and, especially, an army of minuscule, soft plastic lures.

Specialized finesse strategies such as doodlin', driftin', shakin', split-shottin', line-feelin' as well as fishing darters and tubes have been developed and refined. Now they are recognized as viable and potent methods across the United States and particularly whenever the bass are finicky and the angling pressure great.

It Started Out West

Bass anglers from the South and Midwest may initially be confounded by the starkness of deep clear lakes commonly encountered in the West. Fishermen accustomed to structure such as fallen timber, lily pads, hydrilla, and moss beds in other parts of the United States will find they must use different techniques on such lakes. These impoundments have sparse vegetation and, for the most part, monotonous, hard, muddy bottoms.

Thus there are not that many places for the bass to hide in lakes like these. That's the good news. The bad news is that extreme water clarity, often combined with heavy angling pressure, low fish populations and intense recreational boat traffic, makes bass found in such waters particularly wary and quite hook shy.

Ron and Mike have consequently had to devise numerous intricate methods to use on deep clear reservoirs. These tactics involve utilizing the "finesse" element of this sport. They are the foundation for catching fish in these lakes as well as getting bass to bite during extreme cold fronts and other tough fishing conditions.

The Finesse Game

This style of bass fishing requires considerable forethought and planning when it comes to proper tackle selection. To begin with, the angler has to "think light" in terms of lines, lures and, to some degree, rods and reels.

Because these waters are so clear, it is necessary to dramatically scale down in line diameter. The bass can be quite spooky. Most pros will be using superthin 6 to 8 pound monofilament when fishing these impoundments. The fish will definitely have a tendency to shy away from the heavier lines even if they are matched with one of the array of finesse baits.

Most of these lures are made out of soft plastic and range in length from 2 to 5 inches. Soft "plastics" in this genre include tiny worms and grubs, feather-like reapers, hollow tube baits, and miniature swimming jigs. These finesse lures work for two specific reasons. On one hand, they most closely replicate both the size and the silhouette of the major forage bait found in Western impoundments—threadfin shad and small crawdads. Recent studies revealed that the average size of natural prey found in the stomachs of bass rarely exceeded 3 inches in length.

These tiny plastic lures also excel for another reason. Teamed with the gossamer mono, small baits like hand-poured worms, whip-tail grubs, or reapers swim quite well, mimicking natural forage. Heavier monofilament in 10-20 pound test definitely inhibits the subtle action of these minuscule offerings.

Split-Shottin': The Next Generation

As we noted, both guides and tournament anglers alike have designed certain strategies to use on highly pressured reservoirs. Slow-crawlin' or "stitchin'" a worm is one favorite. The unique doodlin' method is another. Vertically bangin' jigs and fishing tiny darter heads can be equally effective. Of all the finesse tactics none compares to split-shottin'.

Interestingly, this technique has been utilized for decades. It is nothing more than a simplified version of the Carolina rig. A lead split is crimped about 12-30 inches above some sort of soft plastic lure. The bait then seductively trails behind the shot as it rises and falls along the bottom.

In recent years, however, split-shottin' has received considerable attention. Quite frequently a majority of the fish caught in tournaments are tallied primarily with the split-shot method. Split-shottin' is now a staple in many bassin' war chests. Like other patented methods such as flippin' or pitchin', it too has evolved into a "science."

We want to look at the finer dimensions of the split-shot approach. We'll focus on the lines, rods, reels, sinkers, hooks and, finally, the revolutionary new baits being used with this method.

Monofilament

Split-shot aficionados are adamant about the need to fish one of today's premium grade monofilament lines. Most of the soft plastic lures used with this approach are not much more than 3-5 inches in length. These baits—which include worms, reapers, grubs, and imitation crawdads—must be teamed with light mono to enhance their precise swimming actions.

Most split-shottin' today is practiced with 4-8 pound test line. Small diameter monofilament like this can have tremendous stretch and lack of uniformity in the less expensive grades. It is thus imperative to select a line with a relatively small diameter and minimal stretch, combined with great abrasion resistance and knot strength. Many split-shot experts concur that the line is the most critical link between themselves and the fish—not the rod, reel, or even the lure.

Rods and Reels

The overwhelming majority of split-shotters prefers to use a spinning rod and reel. It's easy to understand why. A split-shot rig can be cumbersome to cast, especially with plastic baits dangling 18-30 inches below the lead shot. A spinning outfit is easier to use, particularly if a two-handed cast is employed for maximum distance.

Originally, many anglers started split-shottin' with relatively stiff single-piece 5 1/2 to 6 foot spinning rods. However, in recent years, many of the pros have found that the stiffer rod often inhibits the feel of the tiny baits. More importantly, using a medium heavy or heavy blank can result in many broken lines when setting the hook on 4-6 pound monofilament.

Instead, there is a new wave of 6-7 foot rods designed with this tactic in mind. Many are custom made, while others are modified graphite, Kevlar, or boron versions of rods originally designed for trout fishing. Some of the longer 6 1/2 to 7 foot models are sold in two-piece blanks. Most fishermen agree that a two-piece rod is somewhat weaker than a single-piece blank. In split-shotting this is not a problem, especially when setting the hook using such light monofilament. Many experts actually prefer the slightly softer rod often found in the two-piece models.

Most split-shotters use a lightweight spinning reel. The lightest models have graphite cases and match well with the space-age composite rod blanks. Also the fine diameter lines seem to spool particularly well with the spinning reels, resulting in considerably long casts necessary to fool hook-shy fish. A precision reel drag is a necessity.

Whippier 6-7 foot medium-light to medium action baitcasting rods can also perform quite well with this tactic. Originally, many split-shot addicts fished almost exclusively with spinning combos. Lately many of the pros have begun to switch to casting outfits for a variety of reasons.

First, the newer baitcasting reels are now quite lightweight, with fast revolving spools and hi-speed gears. They will accommodate considerable amounts of small diameter 4-8 pound test monofilament. Also, the better models are designed so the gossamer line won't inadvertently go behind the reel spool. This was a problem common to baitcasting reels of the past when they were filled with thin monofilament.

Today's compact baitcasting reels have ultra-smooth star drag systems. This can be a real boon in playing out a trophy size bass that will often succumb to a miniature split-shot bait. The star drag on the better quality baitcasters permits the angler to put considerable pressure on the fish, keeping the tension carefully set slightly below the breaking test of the fine diameter line.

Split-Shot Hooks

Most soft plastic lures utilized with this method are rigged weedless Texas-style. With a plastic worm hook embedded back into the bait, it is possible to practically cast this rig around every conceivable type of structure. It can be fished shallow near moss beds and hydrilla or deep along rocky ledges and submerged cover. The weedless rigging also serves to let the hook act as a keel. This maintains the delicate symmetry needed to insure the proper, slow-swimming action from the little baits.

Unlike conventional worm fishing, split-shotters may find certain problems persist in using this basic Texas rigging. Invariably, you may go to set up on the bass only to miss the fish because of poor hook penetration. The problem is with the light monofilament, combined with a soft-tip rod. There is basically not enough power to drive the hook through the plastic and into the bass' mouth with this type of specialized split-shot outfit.

Veteran split-shotters remedy this problem by "skin-hooking" their lures. While still using a weedless Texas rig, the trick is to implant the hook point barely under the plastic "skin" of the bait. To do this, it is necessary to have the hook embedded off to one side of the lure instead of down the center of the bait.

Obviously, a small split-shot worm, grub, reaper, or similar offering will not be as weedless with this skin-hook ploy. Usually you can actually feel the hook point barely poking out from under the plastic. However, you will be able to quickly tear the hook out of the plastic and drive it into the fish's mouth by skin-hooking the bait. This can be effectively accomplished even with spider web-like 4-6 pound test line.

Often many so-called strikes with the split-shot method go undetected until it is too late and the bass expels the lure. We now all recognize this phenomenon as the "pressure bite." What happens is that the fish gently "mouths" the bait without much aggression. The "strike"—if you can call it that—may take the form of dull resistance on the end of the line.

This can be a nerve-wracking experience for expert and novice alike. One option is to rig the lure with an open hook instead of the weedless Texas configuration. Select a #1 to #8 long shank bronze baitholder hook (these are normally used for live bait fishing). Thread the worm, grub, reaper or other lure onto the hook, head first. Slide the bait up until the hook eyelet is covered, then push the barb through the plastic so it is exposed.

For the most part, the lure is no longer weedless. On deep lakes with bland muddy bottoms, there are limited obstructions for the bait to get hung up on. Now when the bass mouths the lure, it will practically hook itself with the open point.

This leads to another issue, hook sharpness. Numerous guides, teaching pros, and tournament anglers are adamant about the need for super sharp hooks. This is a high priority when it comes to split-shottin'.

Bass caught on this presentation tend to be quite acrobatic. Remember there is considerable line stretch and limited resistance in using such lightweight monofila-ment and matching rods. It is thus quite common for the fish to skyrocket to the surface, jump, shake its head and subsequently throw the small worm hooks typically used with these little lures.

Pre-sharpening all your hooks before using them with the split-shot technique is an excellent insurance policy. Another way to hedge your bets is to invest in the new ultra-sharp hooks. Many of the most accomplished split-shotters prefer to use hooks that are honed to needle-like perfection. The Eagle Claw Laser series, Gamakatsu, and V.M.C. hooks exemplify the latest in hook-sharpening technology. They are distinctively expensive but may be worth the investment when strikes are few and far between.

Even with this new generation of super sharp hooks, take the time to actually inspect each one before using it. It doesn't take much to dull this type of hook—in or out of the water. You might be amazed to find that you can actually find a few "duds" right in the factory boxes that must be re-sharpened before use.

Advanced split-shotters also emphasize the need to routinely check hooks after repeated casts. Many of these anglers now carry one of the new electronic honing devices in the boat with them. Hooks can thus be recurrently sharpened to insure the best penetration possible with this particular technique.

Sinkers

As was mentioned the most rudimentary way to set up a split-shot rig is to simply crimp the lead shot 12-30 inches above the chosen bait. Still it is important to select the proper size and type of shot for prevailing conditions.

To begin with, avoid buying so-called "reusable" split-shots. These are sold with little protruding "ears" that allow you to use your fingers to pinch the shot on and off the line. In reality, with superfine diameter mono, it may take pliers to crimp this style of shot tight enough so that it won't slip down the line. The ears also have a tendency to snag on brush and rocks.

Instead, use the old-fashioned round lead shot. If you are fishing 4-6 pound test near the shore in gin clear water and the fish are skittish, use a small BB-size shot. On the other hand, if you are working off the bank on deep structure in the 15-60 foot range, crimp on a fairly large split-shot.

Much split-shottin' is practiced at the deeper strike zones. In our own experiences, we have found that a larger shot helps to keep the bait near the bottom. Split-shottin' is not the easiest tactic to master. Novice anglers will find

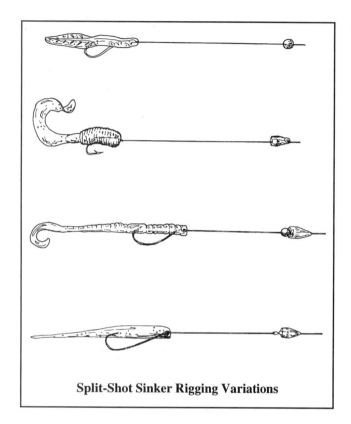

Split-Shot Sinker Rigging Variations

it helpful to have the larger shot bumping the bottom at all times. They will have more control over their lures and will be able to feel the subtle strikes more easily.

Another interesting alternative is to substitute a sliding bullet weight in place of the split-shot. Thread the bullet weight on the line and gently crimp it right at the tip of the cone with pliers. Some anglers may object that the monofilament is more subject to breaking as it rests inside the slide sinker. The fact of the matter is that this rarely occurs, especially if you are careful to crimp the bullet weight cleanly about an 1/8 inch below the tip.

Although a slide sinker crimped in this fashion does not look as neat and clean as the more rounded split-shot, it may actually work better for three reasons: 1) the bullet weight cartwheels less in the air as it is cast compared to the split-shot; 2) the bullet shape allows the bait to be more easily pulled through thick cover and other obstructions; and 3) these sinkers can be purchased in a wide range of weight all the way up to 1 ounce sizes. This allows the fisherman to maintain excellent bottom contact in the deepest water under the toughest conditions.

One another sinker option is worth consideration. This actually utilizes both the rounded shot and the bullet

weight in conjunction. It is relatively easy to assemble. Slide the bullet weight up on the line to where you want it to rest. Next crimp on the tiniest BB shot you can find directly under the bullet weight. Now when the bass strikes the bait and pulls the line the only resistance it feels is the little BB shot. The line slides through the bullet sinker as it rests on the bottom.

A final rigging ploy is known as the "California rig." This is a technically advanced split-shot setup. With this setup you thread a minuscule fluorescent pink bead butted up against a small bullet sinker. Then directly behind the lead a tiny rubber stopper is affixed. The bead serves as an attractant. The rubber sinker stop is adjustable so it can be moved up or down the main line allowing you to vary the leader length. With this rig, you feel practically no resistance except the stop when the bass pulls on the bait. The bullet weight and plastic bead remain motionless as the lure slides through.

Regardless of which one of the four split-shot rigs you prefer, it is important to experiment with how high above the bait the sinker is placed. There are times, for example, where the fish seem to be some distance off the bottom. In this situation, it might be best to locate the sinker 24-30 inches above the lure. At other times, the bass are feeding right on the bottom. In this case, it is more effective to use a shorter leader, stationing the sinker 6-12 inches above the bait.

The length of the leader can also affect the speed at which the non-floating lure glides downward. If the bass seem to prefer a slow-falling offering, affix the sinker 18-30 inches above the soft plastic bait. If the fish tend to be more aggressive, shorten the leader to quicken the fall.

The sinker is probably the most overlooked component of the split-shot technique. It plays an integral part in the total presentation of the various finesse lures. Experiment with sinker style, overall weight, and the distance the sinker is spaced above the bait.

Split-Shot Baits

Worms. In the early stages of split-shottin', most bass fishermen used plastic worms with this rig. Initially, mass-produced models were the staple. Later, there was an explosive demand on the West Coast for custom-made, supersoft, hand-poured worms—most of which were sold for split-shottin'.

There are some specific guidelines that the recreational basser will find helpful in selecting the proper worm for this method. To begin with, pay attention to the shape of the worm's tail section. If the bass are sluggish and reluctant to strike, use a straight-tail pattern. Switch to a curl-tail worm if the fish seem to be more active.

Most split-shottin' is commonly practiced with shorter 3-4 inch long worms. Most of the indigenous forage that bass eat such as crawdads and minnows rarely exceed this length. This is one reason why split-shottin' is so deadly when the fish want a precise replica of natural prey.

Don't hesitate to use large plastic worms with this finesse presentation. There are times when the bass are clearly keyed onto a bigger, more prominent silhouette. Longer 5 to 8 inch worms can also be split-shotted in this situation. However, you may need to use a stiffer medium-heavy rod instead of the lighter action models to insure a solid hook set.

Finally, don't overpower the split-shot worm with an exceptionally large heavy-duty hook. Remember, these lures are meant to lazily swim up and down with this strategy. If the hook is too big or too heavy, the worm will sink rapidly, losing much of its seductive motion.

Reapers. Tournament anglers and guides on clear lakes and pressured water still rely upon the plastic worm as the primary lure for split-shottin'. They have also found a variety of other soft plastic baits to work quite well with this tactic. Second to the worm is an unusual bait known as the reaper.

The reaper was actually designed over 25 years ago. It is made to resemble either a leech or, as some anglers believe, a feather. Both hand-poured and injection-molded models are available primarily in a 2 inch length.

The reaper is perfect for the meticulous slow-down retrieve employed by most serious split-shotters. This particular lure has practically no built-in action whatsoever. Its potency would seem to be in the way it kind of glides through the water, mimicking a vulnerable, tiny shad minnow.

It is essential to use thinner wire worm hooks with this bait if you rig it Texas-style. A heavier hook normally used for larger 4-8 inch worms will offset the exact symmetry and balance needed with the reaper causing it to sink too fast or to spin. The hooks should be small, ranging from a #2-#1, in order to allow the reaper to slowly dart along on the retrieve.

Also, invariably the angler will experience some frustration in learning to split-shot the reaper. When teaching this technique, we have observed that normally the "bite" is either mushy pressure or a little "tick" in the line. Novice bassers may mistake this strike for a panfish or a trout. Don't be fooled! After you feel that initial tick or resistance, pause for a moment. Reel up any remaining slack line and be ready for a second, more vicious attack. This is termed "dead sticking" the bait.

Presumably what happens is that bass in an inactive feeding mode may initially make a weak pass at the reaper, not really being interested in eating the lure. Then as the reaper remains motionless for a moment, the fish

4" Power Worm

seems to sense that it has easily wounded the tiny morsel. After a second or two, it moves in for the final kill.

Slinkee. Long-time guide and lure manufacturer, Dave Mitchell, of Yucaipa, California, designed this unique split-shot bait. Mitchell's Sweetwater Tackle specializes in soft hand-poured plastic lures. While in the field, he noted that bass would often forage on small tadpoles.

After some initial experimentation, Mitchell perfected his Slinkee to imitate the length, shape, and erratic swimming action of these immature amphibians. This lure is highly suitable for the split-shot approach fished at a variety of depths. Use a #2-#1/0 worm hook, embedding the point under the plastic "skin".

You will find that the Slinkee is an excellent compromise between a worm and a reaper. It has the upper body thickness of a plastic worm and the tapered tail of the reaper. The Slinkee measures slightly over 3 inches in length, again closely matching natural prey.

Billy C-Dad. Bill Craig is another veteran tournament angler from Southern California. For years Craig witnessed many trophy largemouths and Alabama spotted bass annihilating live crawdads in the spring. He believed that a soft.plastic replica of a crayfish could be produced that would work in such shallow water conditions.

Craig teamed with hand-poured bait expert Mitchell and together they designed the Billy C-Dad. Many serious bassers now feel that this lure is about as close as you can get to duplicating the size, texture, and swimming movement of a real crawdad.

The Billy C-Dad is meant to be fished considerably faster than other split-shot offerings. We have found that the bass seem to strike the C-Dad within the first few seconds following the cast. The fish will either hit the bait on the fall or right after it is first lifted off the bottom at the start of the retrieve.

Split-shotters can thus use the Billy C-Dad to quickly cover a considerable amount of potential shoreline. This is about as close as you can get to a rapid-fire presentation with this technique. Toss the C-Dad near the bank. If you are not bit on the sink, retrieve the lure slowly for about 3 more feet. If the bass still fail to show an interest, wind up and fire off another cast.

The Billy C-Dad is a bulky lure and sometimes difficult to use with the split-shot method. However, the trick is to rig it with a #1/0 to #2/0 Keeper Hook, secured with the auxiliary barb implanted into the nose of the bait. It is imperative, because of the thickness of the C-Dad, that the lure is skin-hooked off to one side. This unique lure is marketed by Advanced Angler Technology.

Kreepy Krawler. This lure was the brain child of another West Coast tackle manufacturer, Bob Suekawa, of Haddock Lures in Torrance, California. Some years ago, Suekawa visited many bass tournaments in the West and documented which lures were accounting for the most limits. He found that many fish were being caught on both plastic jigs and pork rind-tipped pig'n jig combos.

Suekawa then created a bait that has a prominent soft plastic skirt at the head, a ribbed thorax midsection, and fluttering forked tail. The "Kreepy Krawler," as he christened this unique lure, is unlike all other plastic baits in that all three portions of the lure are fused together in the injection molding process instead of being molded in separate components.

Originally, most of us fished the Kreepy Krawler laced onto a lead jig head. Then split-shot enthusiasts got into the act. They found that the Kreepy Krawler was an extraordinary lure split-shotted at extreme depths—sometimes greater than 60 feet. Like the Billy C-Dad, the Krawler can be rigged Texas-style utilizing the Keeper Hook and skin-hooking the bait.

18 Tail. Suekawa took soft plastic design one step further with his unusual 18 Tail. This lure has a head and midsection consisting of segmented plastic spheres. Then the tail portion flares out with 18 waving miniature tentacles. The 18 Tail resembles half a worm or caterpillar fused with a squid-like tail section.

We have found that this lure is quite adaptable to the split-shot approach. It can be rigged with either a #1-#1/0 worm hook, Texas style, or with a floating jig head. The secret to split-shottin' the 18 Tail is to retrieve it ever so S-L-O-W-L-Y. With even the most minimal retrieve, the 18 tentacles begin to tantalizingly move in the water. This bait can be highly effective on the most lethargic feeders. "Dead stick" this bait, intermittently pausing through the retrieve.

Tube Baits. Hollow-bodied tube baits such as Berkley's Power Tube have been the rage in tournament circuits from coast to coast. Much of the time, "tubes" are fished on tiny 1/16-1/8 ounce lead heads.

However tube baits can be dynamite when teamed with the split-shot presentation. There are a number of ways the pros rig tubes for split-shottin'. Some have developed complicated hooking procedures involving wooden toothpicks to keep the hook properly stationed or using short-bodied tubes especially designed for split-shottin'.

Here is a rather simplified way to split-shot tubes that has routinely worked for my clients. Take either a long-

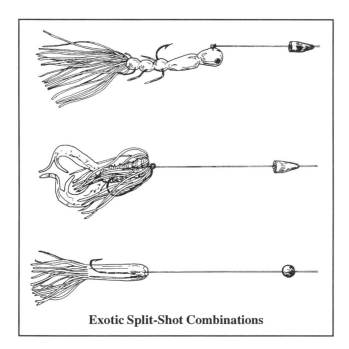

Exotic Split-Shot Combinations

shank Aberdeen or Carlisle style hook normally associated with live bait fishing. Both of these style hooks have prominent ringed eyes. Push the point of the hook through the head of the tube, drawing the hook into the hollow cavity until you get to the ringed eye. Any size tube will work.

Carefully pull the eye of the hook through the plastic in the head portion of the bait. As the eye passes through the nose, the plastic will reseal itself, closing the opening. The long-shank hook now rests completely inside the tube bait. Make sure the short bend in the hook lies outside the tube, hidden among the tentacles of the tail.

Granted, this is a strange-looking rig—but it works! When slowly split-shotted, this hollow bait will be eagerly pursued by the bass who will gingerly mouth it. Although the hook is exposed, the bend is so short and it is practicably weedless. When the bass compresses the tube as it mouths the lure, it will frequently hook itself on the sharp open hook.

Grubs. Single curl-tail grubs have also racked up high marks in the split-shot sweepstakes. Larger 5 inch models such as Berkley's Power Grub, Yamamoto, or Mr. Twister's Grub are popular split-shot favorites. Smaller 3 inch patterns including Twin T's Salty Grub are equally popular when the bass want a more compact bait.

Grubs can be split-shotted using a #2-#2/0 worm hook, Texas style. Skin hooking is again in order due to the thick bodied design of these lures.

Sometimes better results will be obtained by threading the grubs onto a long-shank baitholder hook, leaving the barb exposed. The two barbs on the shank of this style hook serve to secure the thick grub better than a conventional worm hook. The exposed point also results in many bass hooking themselves with even the slightest amount of pressure. Grubs fished in this manner are an excellent deep-water presentation where obstructions are minimal.

An All-Year Strategy

Serious bass fishermen should consider turning to the split-shot approach to fool fish on their pressured waters. It may take some initial practice to master this specialized method. The effort will be worth it. Split-shottin' is applicable all year long. It will work on all the major bass species in virtually every part of the country.

Split-shottin' is an integral weapon in our arsenal of tricks. The rigging and selection of split-shot baits outlined here is only the beginning. Undoubtedly other strategies and lures will be employed in the future. This method is open for experimentation. Nevertheless, the two most important points to remember with this technique can be summarized as: 1) be patient, alert, and try to S-L-O-W down; and 2) when in doubt, once again, swing and set!

Carolina Magic[1]

Like the split-shot setup, the Carolina rig is one of the most potent strategies the serious basser can employ when a slower presentation is in order. We have had to routinely rely upon this method to catch fish on deep clear lakes.

To review again, the Carolina rig in its traditional form is simple to construct. Take your main line and run it through a 1/4 to 1 ounce bullet weight, depending upon the depth you are fishing. Next, tie the line to a quality swivel so the sinker will slide no further. Add a section of leader varying from 18 inches to as much as the length of the rod. Tie your selected bait to the other end of the monofilament leader.

After you make the cast, the heavier bullet weight sinks quickly to the bottom. Your bait will then trail some distance behind the sinker. If your soft plastic lure is fairly buoyant, it will float the leader length up off the bottom. If not, it will have a tendency to rise and fall a shorter distance above the bottom as you slowly retrieve the rig.

It is the suspension of the bait above the bottom as well as the rising and falling action on the retrieve that make the Carolina rig so effective, particularly at greater depths

[1] Portions of this section previously appeared in *B.A.S.S. Times*

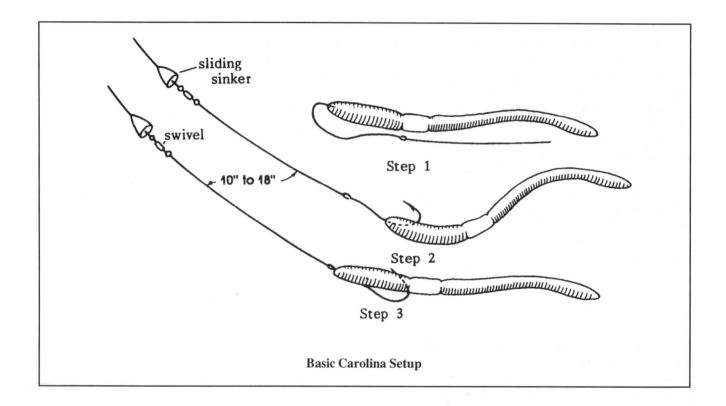

Basic Carolina Setup

over 20 feet. This motion apparently mimics the fluttering action of a dying shad minnow or the erratic maneuvering of an errant crayfish or similar prey.

The sinker is an integral component. Not only does it keep the bait in the deeper strike zones, it also creates a certain amount of curiosity as it leaves little "puffs" of churned up mud as it is dragged across the bottom.

Many anglers also thread on a fluorescent plastic or glass bead below the bullet weight then tie it to the swivel. The bead acts as an additional, colorful attractant, as well as generating a certain amount of "clacking" noise as it bangs up against the swivel and the bullet sinker.

Other Variations

There are two other variations of this basic Carolina rig we have used with considerable success when on deep, tough-to-fish impoundments.

On some river lakes there can be a significant amount of underwater current. The 1/4 to 1 ounce bullet weights may not be heavy enough to keep the rig on the bottom when the current is ripping. In this situation replace the bullet weight with an oval sliding egg sinker like those used for troutin' or catfishing. This kind of sinker is readily available in anywhere from 1/2 to 3 ounce sizes—

plenty of weight to keep the bait down in the fastest currents.

Another option is to eliminate either the swivel or the extra bead and to really simplify the setup. Tie on a basic Texas worm rig using the larger bullet sinker. Next, slide the lead weight up to about 36 to 48 inches above the bait. Then carefully crimp it onto the line using flat-nose pliers.

If done carefully, you will rarely impair even the lightest monofilament with the crimping. The bullet sinker crimped in this fashion will perhaps create a little more resistance on the line when the bass mouths the lure compared to a slider setup. We have used this simple rig extensively and we have rarely found fish that are so sensitive to the weight that they refuse to eat the bait.

Also, with this modified Carolina rig, the serious basser can easily slide the crimped sinker up and down the line, essentially adjusting the length of the leader. There are times when a particular deep structure pattern is contingent upon how far the bait is suspended above the bottom. This crimped sinker setup allows for quick adjustment without having to re-tie the leader.

On this note, with this simplified rig, you eliminate two extra knots where the swivel was attached to your main line and the leader.

Carolina Baits

An amazing repertoire of soft plastic lures will fish perfectly with the Carolina rig. Plastic worms are the most popular lure used with this setup. One of our other favorites to use with the Carolina rig is the 6 inch Power Lizard especially fished around all types of grass, humps, and stumps, particularly in the spring. With a Texas hooking, anywhere from tiny 2 inch long paddletails—so-called finesse or "sissy" baits—on up to 8 inch long "snakes" can also be dragged Carolina style.

Of course, we must not fail to mention that B.A.S.S. touring pro Jack Chancellor's famous tandem, open-hook Do-Nothing Worm teamed with the Carolina rig still produces limit catches across the country.

Other popular finesse lures, including 2 to 3 inch long leech-like reapers, curl-tail grubs, and soft plastic lizards or crawdad replicas, can all be effective on the Carolina rig when conditions dictate a slow, deep presentation.

Some other less obvious applications are also worth noting. Tube baits like the Gitzit and Berkley Power Tube can also be fished with the Carolina rig. With these lures, you can still hook them weedless, Texas-style. You can carefully thread the "tube" on the hook, pull the eye of the hook through the nose of the bait, and leave the point totally exposed.

There are usually minimal obstructions at greater depths. So, like the Do-Nothing Worm, a tube bait—or for that matter any worm, grub, reaper, or plastic 'dad—can be fished with an open hook on the Carolina rig.

Another intriguing innovation we mentioned earlier is to use a small styrofoam floating jig head we mentioned with the Carolina program. Lures such as Haddock's squid-like 18-Tail or the Spyder Jig look sensational on a floating jig head. Both of these lures can be rigged with the open-hook, non-weedless, styrofoam jig head. As they float up off the bottom, even the slightest motion makes the tail sections of these lures "pulsate." Strikes can be vicious on a suspended bait like this!

An All-Season Rig

The Carolina rig excels in a deep-water capacity over 20 feet. Technically, feel free to fish a Carolina-rigged bait at any depth where you desire optimal bottom contact with your sinker, while having the lure suspended to some degree above the weight.

This is a particularly effective strategy for covering large expanses of deep open water. You can wind drift with a Carolina rig or you can lazily drag it, guiding your movement with the trolling motor. Over a deep structure spot, fan cast with a Carolina rig, meticulously covering all the potential fish-holding terrain in a slow-down fashion.

The basic rig and the variations discussed here can be utilized all season long. Again, the key variable may be depth. During the summer doldrums, a Carolina rig can be your secret weapon when the bass head for deeper, cooler water. Similarly, in the winter, fish the Carolina rig all the way down to 90 feet as the bass move deep with schools of baitfish.

Above all, if you want to maximize your success with this specialized technique, you will have to be patient, alert, and willing to work S-L-O-W. Bass at deeper strike zones won't always attack with great vigor. Be ready for mushy "pressure" bites, then "swing and set" on any unnatural resistance.

Carolina magic works all year long, coast to coast!

Those Terrific Tubes!

It all started in the mid 1960s when a little-known lure manufacturer brought out the first bait constructed from a plastic tube. Back in those days, Bobby Garland was a fanatic when it came to crappie fishing. With the invention of his Mini Jig, many of these feisty panfish ended up on stringers throughout the West. Little did we know that this breakthrough in tubular lure design would usher in an entirely new dimension for professional bass fishing.

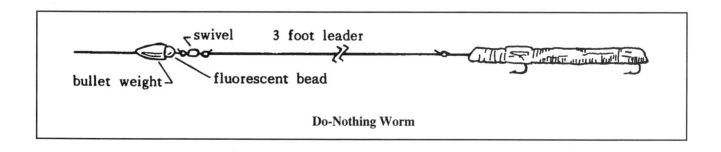

Do-Nothing Worm

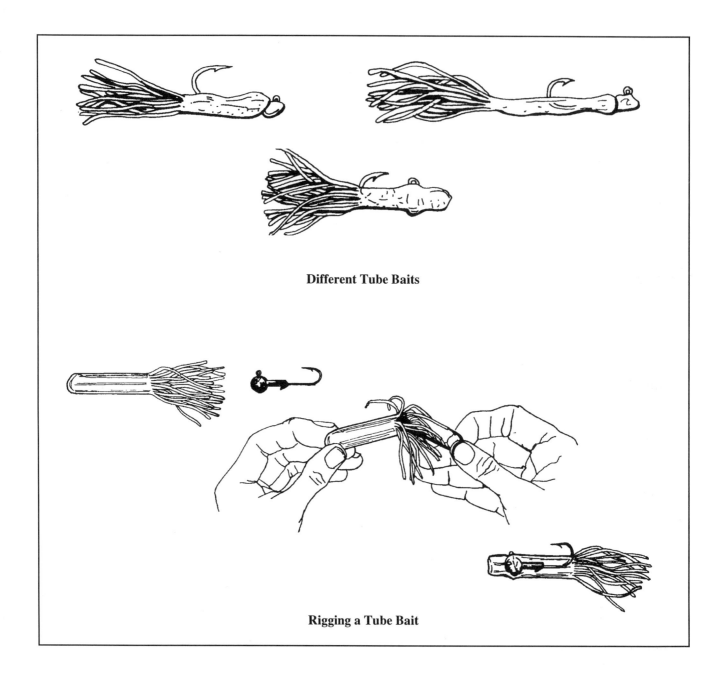

Different Tube Baits

Rigging a Tube Bait

In 1974, the first prototypes of what is now known as the Fat Gitzit evolved from the Mini Jig. For nearly 7 years, Garland fished and refined this secret bait until he was satisfied with its precise shape and action. In the early 1980s when the first Fat Gitzits hit the market, few serious bassers gave the lure much of a chance, especially in major tournaments.

Slowly but surely, Garland started to consistently bring bass to the weigh-ins. His fellow anglers began to take notice of the Utah pro's unique little baits and the light outfits he used to fish them.

Today the Gitzit and its various "offspring" remain some of the most versatile lures found in serious bassin' circles. From coast to coast, tournament bass fishermen and veteran guides have discovered the marvel of this minuscule bait. Here are some of the rather innovative techniques that these pros have developed for using the Gitzit and similar "tubes."

The Light Touch

This is perhaps the most common approach to fishing the Gitzit. We found that on clear Western lakes, this miniature offering will generate strikes when more conventional plastic baits failed to produce. The trick is to think "light." This means *fine diameter lines* and *small* jig heads.

Using primarily 6 to 8 pound test monofilament and spinning outfits, we usually fish tube baits on a 1/16 to 1/8 ounce lead head all year long. We take the front of the jig and push it up as far into the hollow cavity as possible. Then, we press down on the plastic so that the jig eye protrudes through the lure. This is the way most tournament bassers prefer to use the Gitzit. Note that because the lead head is seated up into the lure, it is necessary to cut off the bait and re-rig it every time you want to make a size or color change.

Some novices run the small jig through the nose of the bait, leaving the rounded lead head externally exposed. Although this makes for convenient replacement of the plastic body, the lure simply doesn't swim as well with this kind of setup.

This is the key to the Gitzit's success with the "light touch"—it's erratic and sensuous movements. After the cast is made, the lure slowly sinks with the tiny jig head, but darting from side to side. This action closely mimics the movements of a frantic baitfish or a crawdad. It is important to closely watch your line and be ready for a strike as the lure falls. Don't set the hook too hard. When you detect a strike, a nice smooth set is all that is needed.

Sometimes it pays to switch to a heavier 1/8 ounce head for depths over 25 feet or in windy conditions. The tube bait can be fished even deeper, all the way down to 60 feet. Yo-yo it with a 1/4 lead head inserted into the tube for this deep water action.

Bassers across the country have found the light touch to be a highly effective shallow water strategy. For instance, the coon-tail and hydrilla moss found in the South is prime tube bait territory. Fish the "tube" along the edges of this vegetation that borders deeper water. Similarly, this bait is excellent for fish suspended in the trees. Seek out the ones near deep water drop-offs especially during the summer months. Bass will often bushwhack a small, subtle lure like the Fat Gitzit as it glides through the hovering fish.

Wormin' the Tube

Interestingly, these small lures can also be used along the same line of attack as the plastic worm. There are actually specially designed jig heads that accommodate the bait when rigged Texas style. Out of the water, the Gitzit seems somewhat unassuming upon first glance. Gently crawled like a worm, the pulsating tentacles respond to the slightest rod twitch, bump, or change in current. This lure can be an intriguing option to a small 3 to 4 inch worm when it is retrieved diligently across the bottom.

The Gitzit also makes an excellent bait for the flippin' enthusiast. There are certain times when the bass spook easily with larger offers such as the pig'n jig or a 6 to 8 inch plastic worm. The Gitzit, with its compact silhouette, is a great alternative under these conditions.

Serious bassers adept at the shallow water game also recognize that sometimes a jig or plastic worm drops too quickly, moving past lethargic fish before they can hit the bait. Here again, a tube bait flipped into shoreline brush, trees, or similar riprap, can trigger strikes due to its super-slow falling action.

When flipping the tube baits, consider using slightly lighter monofilament than you would with a worm or a jig. A smaller diameter line in 10 to 15 pound test will allow the lure to swim better. Flip this miniature offering on a Texas rig with a pegged bullet weight, or use a 1/8 to 1/4 ounce jig head with a built-in stiff monofilament brush guard. Many flippers prefer to rig the Gitzit with the lead head outside the bait, with the monoguard running over the lure and tucked back into the tube. Watch for a slight "tick" in the line. This often signals a pick-up when flippin' with this little bait.

Tubes as Trailers

Tube baits also have utility as supplemental trailers for other lures. For example, some pros use Gitzits behind a spinnerbait. By putting the tube bait under the live rubber skirt you will find that the blades fall even more slowly. Another ploy is to simply remove the spinnerbait skirt, and slide the Fat Gitzit over the lead head portion of the lure. This has the effect of creating a "soft" spinnerbait.

Tube baits come in an awesome array of color schemes. Serious bassers can thus devise some unique spinner combinations using tube baits to give hook-shy bass something new to look at. Fat Gitzits also double as trailers behind top-water lures. They can be added to existing buzzer skirts as is done with spinnerbaits or used exclusively in place of vinyl or rubber skirts. This may also facilitate keeping the buzz bait closer to the surface with the extra bulk.

Some accomplished top-water specialists have found another interesting application for these tiny tubes. Many times a bass will "blow up" just below a big surface plug

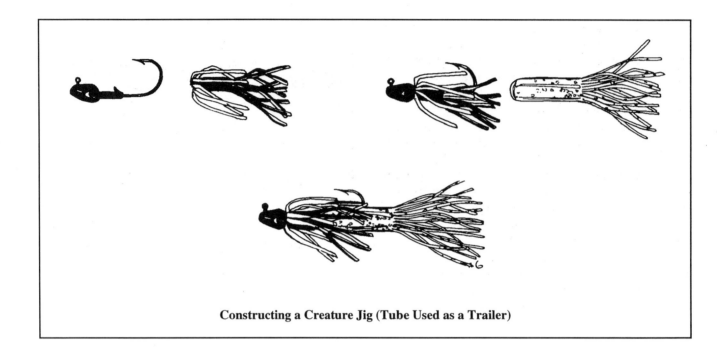

Constructing a Creature Jig (Tube Used as a Trailer)

such as a Zara Spook. Hollow-bodied tube baits can be dynamite on these otherwise-missed fish. After a bass makes a pass at the surface plug, quickly fire off another cast to the same spot. Only this time, toss a tube bait on a 1/16 ounce p-head. There is no trick to it. The fish will hit the Gitzit as it strikes the water or seconds after it starts to sink. Throw directly into the splash. If you don't get bit within a couple of feet—that bass probably isn't going to eat.

Tubular lures can also be good jig trailers. We have fished a "sleeper" bait called the "Creature". This is composed of a soft plastic Spyder skirt with a Gitzit threaded behind it. On many deep, clear-water lakes we have found this combination bait to be potent when the bass are in a non-aggressive mood. Expect the strikes with the Creature to be just like the Gitzit—subtle.

Plow the hollow-bodied Creature slowly down underwater ledges and along outside points. The slightest movement makes the mass of plastic tentacles undulate. This lure is an excellent alternative to the Gitzit when bottom contact is essential.

More Tube Tips

Here are a few more tricks we pass along to enhance your success with tube-style baits. First, try some of the other variations if the Gitzit isn't producing. The larger Jumbo Gitzit measures 5 1/4 inches long in contrast to the 3 3/4 inch length of the standard Gitzit. Fish this magnum-sized version if the bass are keying on a larger bait. Another possibility is the shorter 2 1/2 inch Gitzit. This smaller model works particularly well when the fish are extremely skittish, or when the bass are feeding on tiny, "pinhead" shad.

Next, consider using the 5 inch Skinny Squid as yet another option for tube bait fishing. This creation is perhaps the oddest of all the tubular lures. It fishes best with a 1/16 ounce jig head rigged externally through its nose section. The hollow portion of this bait is too narrow for an internal jig head. The Mini-Squid has fantastic action when a seductively slow presentation is in order. The thin, elongated body makes this lure practically sashay in the water.

A recent innovation is the magnum-size A.A.T. Caba Caba Tubes. Originally designed for saltwater fishing, the giant Cabas work like huge Gitzits on big Florida-strain largemouths accustomed to feeding on planted trout or similar large morsels. The Caba Caba Tubes can either be split-shotted or fished on a light jig head, internally rigged in the hollow cavity.

As for color selection, here's a simple rule of thumb. Light transparent tubes match closely with threadfin shad. Darker opaque patterns imitate crayfish. The "peppered" effect created by adding black glitter to such shades as clear, smoke, chartreuse, amber, or brown has long been the rage in the tournament circles. Rainbow trout colors have also garnered a select following. You can also custom color these baits with permanent markers to create even more unusual schemes.

Finally, we want to emphasize again the importance of taking advantage of the construction of these unique baits with regard to utilizing fish attractants. The hollow body is a natural receptacle for holding various liquid and solid scents. Since the Fat Gitzit and its cousins are fished so slowly, the attractants are practically "time-released" underwater. This leaves an aromatic "chum slick" often calling in bass from some distance.

Be adventurous with these diminutive lures. Fish them under a wide range of conditions. Don't let their simplicity fool you. Many tournaments are being won and lunkers weighed in by anglers experiencing the tube bait phenomena!

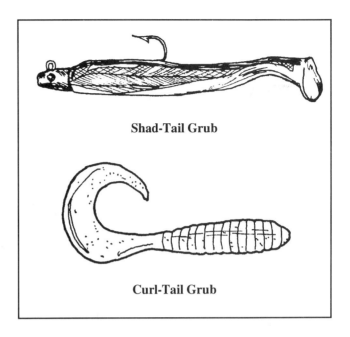

Shad-Tail Grub

Curl-Tail Grub

More Finesse Baits

Beyond worms and reapers there are a collection of lures that have tremendous application as finesse baits when teamed with light monofilament.

Curl-Tail Grubs

Large, single curl-tail grubs have been one of the hottest lures to hit both guiding and tournament circles in quite a while. This is a rather interesting phenomenon. Historically, this style of bait has been noticeably absent in many tackle boxes until recently. In contrast, grubs with simple straight or flatter tail portions have been used on a variety of bass species for some time across the country. Currently, the larger single curl-tail model has become the most potent bait in this genre. It is this prominent tail that seems to drive the bass wild all year long.

The beauty of this type of subtle lure is its incredible versatility. The most popular way to fish this bait is to simply swim it on a 1/8 to 1/4 ounce jig head with an open hook. On super clear impoundments where the bass spook easily, this rig allows you to back off your target and to make longer casts in the windiest weather. Fish this grub on 6 or 8 pound test line with a spinning rod. Work the bait deep—up to 60 feet. Concentrate on ledges, submerged brush, and especially the shadows and crevices formed by steep rocky banks. These are prime ambush points for largemouths, bronzebacks and spots as well as places

where shad will be found. Use these baits with 1/4 ounce jig heads at the deeper depths and then switching to 1/8 ounce for shallower water. You will be able to cover as much territory with this lead head and grub combination as you would with a crankplug.

Many times this bait has saved the day for us, especially on crowded lakes. Outfitted with a spinning rod and reel and 6 to 8 pound test, a raw novice can be quickly taught to catch his limits of bass with the sickle tail grubs. All he has to do is cast it out, let it settle a few feet, and retrieve it back in a slow, steady fashion.

Be especially alert with grub style lures for often the "strike" feels something like mushy pressure. This is a very critical feature to be aware of when fishing these baits or else many strikes will be missed. Other times you may see your line go slack or move slowly to the side as the bass inhales the grub and slowly swims with it. When in doubt, always swing and set. Keep constant tension on the retrieve to avoid unexpected slack and consequently having the fish throw the small jig hook.

Shad Tails

Another hot finesse bait is a tiny knob-tail, minnow-like soft plastic shad made by such companies as A.A. Worms, A.A.T. and Ambusher. This lure perhaps comes closest of all the soft plastic baits to replicating small threadfin shad. In contrast to other commercially injection-molded plastic baits, some of the most unique color schemes ever imagined can be found in soft plastics. These shads are designed on a very slim profile, again in an attempt to match the natural shad population.

You can fish the shad-tails in one of two ways. The most common is to work the lure on a 1/8 ounce p-head or darter jig with light, 6 pound test line. You can then use the bait like this for bass that are scattered at different depths, breezing through schools of shad. You can swim the shad-tail through suspended fish or yo-yo it vertically in deep water.

Along this line, one little feature that most bass fishermen miss with these lures is to fish them with an even smaller, minuscule, 1/16 ounce jig head. Upon first thought, some anglers might feel that such a super-light lead head would not be heavy enough to give the lure its characteristic throbbing tail action. However, interestingly, although the tail vibration is reduced with the ultralight head, what happens instead is that the entire torso of the bait shimmies from side to side. Sometimes this particular action generates strikes when the typical tail-shaking fails with a heavier jig head.

The other technique that has been a fairly well kept secret is to fish the shad-tail grubs Texas style. This presentation is often overlooked for this kind of finesse bait. This unconventional method really works though. It allows this knob-tail lure to sort of flip-flop on the bottom, simulating a dying shad. This little trick can be especially effective during the colder months in deep water. It is important to thread the hook Texas style along the top and bottom seams, otherwise the bait will rotate randomly.

Darters and P-heads

Frequently lunker class bass will suspend off the bottom. These fish may be in an active feeding mode or in a lockjaw state. In either case, try to swim a small 1/8 ounce dart-shaped or p-head style jig through the fish-holding

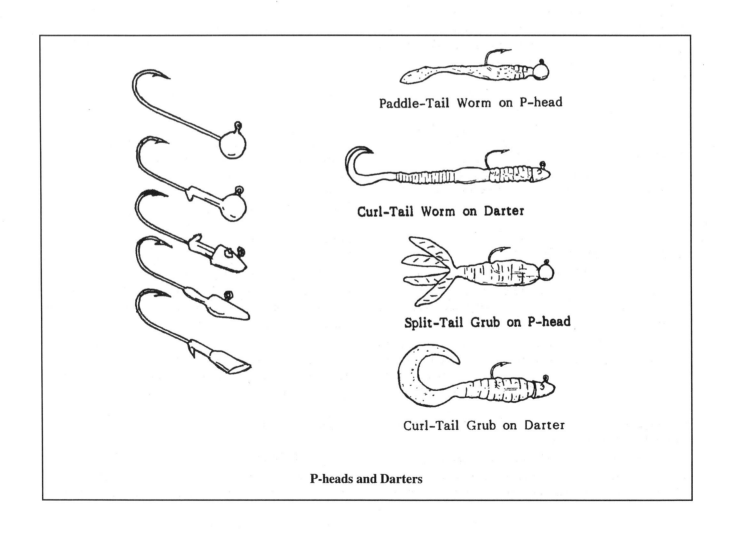

Paddle-Tail Worm on P-head

Curl-Tail Worm on Darter

Split-Tail Grub on P-head

Curl-Tail Grub on Darter

P-heads and Darters

area. Three to 4 inch plastic worms or small 3 to 5 inch curl-tail grubs can be laced onto the tiny jig heads. Shake the rod tip occasionally to make the little lures dance from side to side, imitating frantic, fleeing bait. The delicate symmetry of these lures is maximized by using light 6-8 pound test line—nothing heavier.

Crappie Jigs

There are certain ultralight baits designed originally for pan fishing that also account for unexpected strikes from bruiser-size largemouths. Smart bass anglers now carry a selection of tiny crappie jigs such as the Blakemore Roadrunner, Crappie John Finger Jig, the Mini-Jig, and Mini-Squid. If the shad population in the lake seems particularly small, these miniature baits are definitely worth trying. Quite frequently, the larger fish will not attack an offering until the lure precisely matches with the size of the indigenous baitfish.

Trout Lures

It is no mere coincidence that trout fishermen often hook a bass in lakes that have both species. As was noted with crappie jigs, small trout spinners and spoons may actually come closer to mimicking the overall size and natural movement of immature baitfish. Also, the more subtle "flash" from a small spoon or the gentle "hum" and vibration of a trout spinner may be the "quiet" presentation that stimulates big bass into striking. Veteran bass pros have had recurrent success throwing little yellow or white Roostertail, Shyster, and Bangtail spinners. Similar results have been recorded using traditional trout spoons like the Kastmaster or Johnson's Sprite for the deep-water approach.

More on Pressure Bites[2]

When a bass decides to attack a spinnerbait, top-water lure, or crankplug, there is little doubt that he means business. The strike is typically strong and distinctive with these kinds of reaction baits.

In recent years, a whole new wave of soft plastic lures has flooded the serious bassin' ranks. Little doodle worms, tiny tube baits, and feather-like reapers now are being seen at more and more lakes across the country. Specialized methods like stitchin', doodlin', split-shottin', driftin' and draggin' were especially designed to be used with these soft plastic offerings.

The problem is that in contrast to using hard-bodied lures where the strike is pronounced, it is often difficult to discern when a bass has eaten one of these soft-plastic

baits. Veteran guides and pros often describe this ambiguous kind of strike as a "pressure bite."

So then, what precisely is a pressure bite? We have found that in the seminars we conduct it is perhaps easiest to think of it as nothing more than the feeling of a dull resistance on the end of the line. If you are unable to distinguish this type of pattern, it will be hard to successfully compete on many deep clear Western lakes. During the winter, post-spawn, and midsummer periods, the fish frequently evidence this subtle feeding mode. You will definitely have to know when you are pressure-bit in order to put bass in the live wells under these conditions.

There are some specific strategies the serious basser can use to maximize his chances when the bass are on a pressure-bite pattern.

Use Quality Mono

Many of the methods previously described are effective primarily with light monofilament lines. Split-shotters commonly prefer 6 to 8 pound test mono, often scaling down to gossamer-thin 4 pound test for small, highly impacted impoundments. Many worm aficionados are also using 6 to 8 pound test, while some jig fishermen in the West have now resorted to the lighter 8 pound test mono. These pros claim that they get bit better on the deep clear lakes with fine diameter line.

When a bass gently mouths a plastic worm or jig, creating that sensation of "pressure," it is imperative to swiftly set up on the fish. Some lighter lines have considerable stretch. Using better quality mono minimizes this problem. This will result in better hook sets, especially at depths over 20 feet.

Watch Your Line

As simple as this sounds, it may help significantly to actually watch your line in using these soft plastic baits. Sometimes the bass will "peck" at this lure prior to holding onto it. This may be signalled by nothing more than a slight "tick" in the line.

If you can monitor this "tick" you can quickly gather in the slack line and prepare for the pressure phase of the attack. Some pros are strong proponents of using high viability fluorescent monofilament for this kind of light-line bassin'. With this more opulent mono, it is easier to detect that initial movement in the line.

Super Soft Baits

One theory widely held by many pros is that the bass will clearly hold onto a soft plastic worm, reaper, or grub

---

[2] Portions of this section previously appeared in *B.A.S.S. Times*

longer than one made from harder plastic. Many fishermen believe that during a tough bite. The advantage of a softer bait is that the bass will hold onto it longer. The softer plastic is more lifelike and feels like flesh in the bass' mouth.

Add Salt

Along a similar vein, many of the country's top pros feel that a soft plastic lure impregnated with salt will result in finicky bass holding the bait even longer. Supposedly the salt makes the offerings taste more like a real crawdad or baitfish. Thus when the bass are in a pressure mode, they should theoretically "mouth" the lure for some time before rejecting it.

Almost all hand-pour worm operations add salt to their baits as a routine procedure. Many injection-molding companies also market an extensive array of worms, grubs, jigs, and reapers loaded with salt.

Sharpen Those Hooks!

Once the angler has discerned that he is pressure bit, a quick hook set is in order. With the light lines and tiny baits, solid penetration is often difficult. This is commonly the case when the fish are holding in deep water.

It is thus critical to use needle-sharp hooks during a pressure bite. Pre-sharpen all worm hooks. Do the same with the hooks on darter heads used with small soft plastic grubs and worms. The bass can also pressure bite larger plastic swimming jigs and basic pork rind trailers. Make an effort to sharpen these hooks as well.

Hooking Tricks

Many pressure bites occur while fishing a plastic worm. The traditional Texas rig will not always work with the light monofilament fished deep with small plastic offerings. Two hooking tricks are particularly suitable with these baits when reacting to a pressure strike.

The first is termed "skin-hooking." Instead of embedding the hook into the center of the worm, gently slide the hook under the thin outer layer of plastic. When the hook rests under this thin layer or "skin" of the bait, it will not be as weedless as a center-hooked worm. The angler can quickly pull the hook free from the lure with the least amount of resistance. With quick reaction on the part of the fisherman and nearly instant penetration of the hook, many bass will be stuck with this skin-hook ploy if they are on the pressure pattern.

Another variation of this skin-hook technique works especially well with thick soft plastic baits and particularly with the slug-design models. Simply rig the bait Texas-style but actually push the hook all the way through the center of the lure. Then re-embed the point barely under the "skin" or surface layer of plastic. In the first method, the bait is skin-hooked with the hook off to the side of the lure. With this variation the bait is skin-hooked with the hook embedded in the center of the lure.

A third tactic is to disregard the Texas rigging altogether and instead switch to an open hook. Take a small #6 to #8 long-shank baitholder hook normally used for live nightcrawlers or crawdads. Run it through the head of the plastic worm or reaper, pushing the point out through the body of the bait. Granted, the lure now is not that weedless. Many bass will be nailed as the fish mouth the bait and practically impale themselves on the small open hook. This technique is terrific at depths over 25 feet where underwater obstructions are minimal.

Scented Baits

When the bass are on a pressure bite, it is to the angler's advantage to have the fish hold onto the lure as long as possible. The longer the bass mouths the bait, the more time the fisherman has to discern this unusual strike.

As was mentioned, the addition of salt to ultrasoft plastic lures seems to encourage the fish to hold onto the bait. Commercially marketed attractants can have a similar effect.

In our own experiences, particularly with the split-shot method, we like to apply scent to the outside of these worms, grubs, and reapers. Too many times the one of us

Adding Berkley Strike to Tube Bait

who was fishing with scent thoroughly trounced the other who had a "clean" bait. Usually this scenario occurs during a tough pressure bite.

Tubular lures such as the Gitzit and Berkley Power Tube are also excellent choices under conditions when the bass seem highly selective. Fill the hollow cavity of the "tubes" with fish attractant for an added effect. You may find that the bass will hold the bait for some time as the scent trickles out of the tube.

Learn the Lake

Another tip that will improve you catch ratio in a pressure bite pattern has nothing to do with mechanics or lure trickery. You will be more prone to react quickly to this situation with a fundamental knowledge of lake topography.

For example, if you learn a particular impoundment over repeated visits, you will come to know where the primary submerged structure is located. So, if you are then working soft plastics over a stretch of bottom that you intrinsically know is composed of hard mud, you won't have to think twice about instantly setting when you feel pressure on the end of the line. Prior knowledge of the underwater terrain tells you that there is nothing there to get snagged on—hence it must be a fish!

Be Alert!

Perhaps the best tip of all for catching bass during a pressure bite is to remain alert. When the fish are attacking the bait in such a subtle fashion, "strikes"—if you can call them that—may be far and few between. The veteran pro knows that this is the time to concentrate. It is also when novices tend to relax and opportunities are missed.

Remain "tuned in" to these soft plastic lures as they plod along the bottom. Be ready to set up on the most subtle resistance. "If in doubt . . . swing and set!"

Serious Hardware

Serious Hardware

Traditionally most fishermen begin bass fishing by throwing some type of hard bait. Spinners, crankplugs, spoons, buzzers, chuggers, poppers, and floating minnows are examples of the diverse kinds of "hardware" the serious basser stocks in his arsenal of lures.

In this chapter, we will examine some of the finer elements of chuckin' and windin' with serious "hardware."

Systematic Crankin' for Bass

Many recreational bass fishermen have a tendency to either oversimplify or overcomplicate the selection and use of crankplugs. On one hand, some anglers get into a rut by choosing the same plug trip after trip despite fluctuations in prevailing conditions. On the other hand, some novice bass fishermen become overwhelmed by all the crankplugs on the market. They don't know where to start when it comes to selecting the right lure from their tackle box.

There is a systematic way to develop a concise repertoire of crankplugs for your tackle arsenal. By dividing these lures in terms of diving depth, coloration, size, and action, you will be able to narrow your crankplug choice down to suit the conditions you are fishing.

Diving Depth

Perhaps the most integral component to crankplug design is the lip or "bill" of the line. This is the device that serves to drive the bait downward upon the retrieve to a prescribed depth. As a rule, crankplugs with short diving lips are made for shallow water conditions. Those with longer, more pronounced bills are designed to dive deep.

The object is to initially estimate the depth at which the bass seem to be holding. This information can be gleaned from a variety of sources. Using fish locators and similar electronic instruments, the angler can monitor both bait and bass activity. This will clearly give a strong indication where the fish are feeding.

Without electronics, the bass fisherman can rely upon past knowledge of prime spots on the lake, current reports from marina operators, or a basic understanding of bass movement based on seasonal patterns.

Once you select the depth to start fishing choose a plug that is correspondingly made to swim through that strike zone. For instance, companies like Rapala, Poe's, Rebel and Luhr Jensen market an entire family of lures designed to attack a lake from the shallowest to deepest water.

If the bass were determined to be in a sub-surface feeding mode, this is where a floating-diving minnow can be deadly. The Jensen Minnow, Rapala #9-13F, Smithwick Rogue, and Bomber Long-A are made to float at rest, then dive a few feet under the surface on the retrieve. As we mentioned, these particular lures are highly effective on a "jerk, jerk, pause" retrieve or with a constant "jerk" below the surface. The speed or cadence varies day to day as the aggressive feeding patterns of the fish change.

Another way to fish the so-called "jerk" baits in a sub-surface fashion is to make long sweeps with the rod to quickly drive the plug down. In between sweeps, these floater-divers will start to float to the surface. This is when you may expect strikes to occur. This is known as "rippin'."

If the bass are working slightly deeper, select a more traditional fat-body plug with a small diving lip. Luhr Jensen, Rapala, and Rebel all market special shallow divers. These plugs can be retrieved F-A-S-T since they run in a straight line. You can reverse speeds and use a

S-L-O-W grind with the shallow runners working a few feet below the surface.

As you move off the bank, it is often important that your plug makes good solid contact with the bottom. Luhr Jensen's Triple Deep series provides the basser with a concise choice of lures designed to hit the 10, 15, and 20 foot ranges.

Another intriguing alternative that allows the angler more latitude in depth selection is Luhr Jensen's Hot Lips Express series of plugs. These lures have specially designed diving lips that can be changed easily in the field to give you a wider span of depth control. The Hot Lips Express lures are capable of true 10 to 16 1/2 foot diving range, normally unheard of in a bait this size.

Coloration

The best dimension to key in on when it comes to selecting proper coloration in a crankplug is to try to match it for the dominant forage bait in the lake (remember "match the hatch"?) For example, use plugs in traditional crawdad patterns if crayfish are the major source of food for the bass population. If shad are the major forage, then a standard Tennessee shad color will usually be effective.

Consider other minor sources of forage bait in a particular lake. Plugs in corresponding panfish patterns may be the hot selection for matching perch, bluegill, or crappie. Similarly, frogs may be indigenous to the shoreline. Here a crankplug in the old favorite yellow-green color scheme may prove to be the sleeper.

When it comes to crankplug fishing, color selection can also be affected by climate and water conditions. A rough rule of thumb is to use dark-colored baits under dark skies or in stained water, lighter shades under bright sky or clear water.

It also pays to try newer color patterns that give the bass something dynamic to look at. Luhr Jensen's "clearwater flash," for example, can be dynamite in the Hot Lip Express plugs with its opulent prismatic reflection. This particular coloration closely resembles the rainbow-like hues of frantic shad minnows. Poe's white spook and Storm's phantom patterns are equally potent "sleeper" colors.

Other less popular metallic colors such as gold and solid chrome often produce erratic light refraction underwater. This can also serve to trigger strikes from bass when more traditional-colored plugs fail to produce.

Size

The size of the crankplug is usually selected with regard to the size and silhouette of the primary forage bait in the lake. If the crawdads are on the small size, then a more compact lure in the 2 5/8 to 3 5/8 inch length would be appropriate. Switch to plugs from 4 to 4 1/2 inches if the shad are large and mature.

When it comes to crankin' it pays to be experimental. The adage that "big baits catch big bass" often proves correct if you select a large plug looking for a trophy. However, there are times when lunker bass are so bombarded by big baits that a more compact plug revives interest as they strike the tinier morsel.

A recent concern in crankplug technology has been in designing a plug to closely match the natural silhouette of indigenous baits. Luhr Jensen's Fingerling Hi-Catch plugs are long thin-bodied lures made to replicate small baitfish in terms of size, action, color, and silhouette. These unique plugs come in a wide array of colors ranging from fingerling trout and shad minnow, to perch and baby bass fry. The largest models will dive up to 12 feet on the retrieve. Rapala's classic Shad Rap series, especially in the natural shad finish, similarly duplicates, in near-perfect fashion, the real baitfish.

Action

The most subtle dimension to crankplug selection is the action of the lure as it is retrieved under water. This is sometimes hard to determine without first trying the bait with a particular spinning or casting outfit.

You will find that some plugs track with a very "tight" side-to-side vibration, while others have a "wide" wobble. At times, the bass will definitely key in on one action over the other.

For a wide, slow side-to-side motion the Jensen Minnow, for example, is a good choice used with a rippin' or twitchin' retrieve. Similarly, the thin Fingerling Hi-Catch will also have a seductive "wobble" with a slow retrieve.

Fast retrieving a crankplug produces increased vibrations and tighter swimming action. The Luhr Jensen's Speed Trap, Hot Lips Express, and Triple Deep TD series of baits excel in this capacity when combined with modern high-speed baitcasting reels. The same holds true for Rapala Shad Raps and lipless baits like the Cordell Spot, Rat-L-Trap, and Rattlin' Rapala.

Again it is important to be flexible and try different plugs at the same depths to key in on the swimming action the bass prefer.

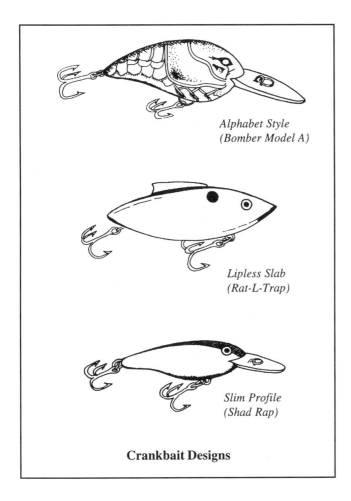

*Alphabet Style
(Bomber Model A)*

*Lipless Slab
(Rat-L-Trap)*

*Slim Profile
(Shad Rap)*

Crankbait Designs

Crankbait Landing[1]

Although the crankbait is one of the best fish locators a bass angler can own, frequently, even serious bassers find themselves losing fish on crankbaits once the bass is hooked. There are a few simple ploys that will help to maximize your chances of landing more fish on these plugs.

First, make certain all the hooks are pre-sharpened before you use the lure. Factory treble hooks are notoriously dull right out of the package. Sometimes it also helps to replace stock trebles with larger size hooks as long as the balance of the bait is not affected. Similarly, consider changing to nickel-plated treble hooks with bronze versions. The bronze treble usually can be honed to needle-like perfection.

Second, think about switching to a soft-tip rod. The medium-heavy graphite model you have been using for plastic worm fishing may be too powerful for crankin'.

With stiffer graphite blanks, the reaction of the rod to counter-pull on the line as the bass strikes the plug and pulls may inadvertently yank the plug from the fish's mouth. Softer tip rods made from either fiberglass or a graphite blank with a fiberglass tip section help to remedy this problem.

Once the hook is set, maintain steady constant pressure on the bass. Avoid erratic "pumping" retrieves to maintain solid hook penetration. The most dangerous time is when the bass starts to jump. Keep your rod low—maybe with the tip even in the water—to reduce the chances of the fish jumping and throwing the hook.

On this note, examine your drag—it may be too tight for crankin'. You will find that a somewhat looser-than-normal drag setting may actually serve to give you a better hook set with a crankplug. If the drag is set too tight, particularly with a stiffer rod, again the hooks may tear loose with the shortest run.

Also, another little tip is to keep the rod tip pointed towards the water and reel the line in slightly off to the side. This keeps the monofilament lying near the water surface. It then becomes difficult for a bass to skyrocket to the top and shake the treble hooks. The fish encounters too much resistance to become airborne due to the surface tension with the monofilament slapping against the water.

When you go to land a bass taken on a crankbait, a net is indispensable. It is important to gently lead the fish into the net. Once again the hooks may pull loose if you try to quickly turn the bass or drag it into the net. So often, the fish are barely hooked with this kind of lure.

Finally, if you prefer to "lip" the bass without the help of a landing net—be careful! This may be the most dangerous lure in your arsenal when it comes to landing a fish by hand. Make certain you keep your face—and your partner—out of the direct "line of release" should the hooks tear loose and the plug comes flying out of the water. It is critical to reach for the bass' lower lip once the fish is exhausted and near the bait. Grip the lip firmly, taking care to keep your hand away from the crankbait. Use surgical hemostats as a handy tool to quickly remove treble hooks without damaging your catch.

Top Secrets for Top-Water Bass

There is probably nothing more exciting than to watch a bass explode and literally inhale a surface plug. Many anglers have a tendency to treat top-water lures in simplistic terms. They buy the bait, take it out of the package, cast it, and retrieve it back in. There is a real art to consistently catching bass at the water line.

---

[1] Portions of this section previously appeared in *B.A.S.S. Times*

We will examine some of the secret ploys used by Mike and Ron to fool fish with top-water plugs. You will find that these tactics are relatively easy to incorporate into your repertoire. More importantly, the subtle tricks devised for throwing surface lures can be utilized on bassin' waters across the United States.

Cosmetic Secrets

Deciding which color top-water plug to throw should not be left to random selection. To some degree, Ron and Mike try to pick a color scheme that most closely replicates forage baits native to a particular impoundment. Lure manufacturers market such obvious color patterns as silver/glitter shad, frog, perch, baby bass, and rainbow trout to imitate natural prey.

However, there are situations when even the most seemingly appropriate color choice fails to produce. Now is the time to try more obscure shades.

For some years, we have found that more bland, less obvious coloration will often produce on highly pressured lakes. One secret pattern is a pale bone color. Many lure companies have discontinued bone-colored plugs. This is due to minimal consumer demand for this rather boring pattern. For some reason, a bone-colored top-water bait often generates strikes when conditions are tough. This tone is particularly effective with stickbaits, propbaits, chuggers, and poppers.

What if you can't find your favorite surface lure in bone? Using a pen knife or a car key, carefully scrape away much of the lure's original paint to produce a flat bone finish. The bone color seems to produce best when you leave a little of the chrome or silver paint on the bait to create a very slight scale effect.

Remember what we discussed earlier in "Match the Hatch"? Sometimes it pays to remove all the paint in order to produce a dull, non-lustrous appearance. Another option is to completely scrape only the underside of the bait. Maybe you have watched a bass make a roll on a solid chrome surface plug without eating it. Chrome is considered a good summer color. Scrape off the paint from the underbelly, leaving a plug that is half bright, half dull. When using poppers, chuggers, and stickbaits in this customized finish, strikes typically result from lethargic hot-weather fish.

The flash created from the solid chrome lure is sometimes too much for the bass to handle. By removing some of the paint, the brilliance of the bait is toned down but still rouses enough curiosity for the fish to eat the plug.

Some top-water experts have found another highly subtle color that works when the bass are super finicky — clear. In a strict sense, this is not really a color at all, but rather a lack of one. However, a surface plug with a clear see-through finish often produces stellar catches on sluggish fish. This unusual pattern is rarely thrown by recreational fishermen and seldom seen by the bass.

The effect of color on a top-water bait may also be seen in a few other secret tips used by the pros. Try adding a black lateral line and gill dot to a surface lure. The black spot in the gill area and the lateral line forming a dorsal vein make the surface lure look like a wounded shad. Add a red gill line to otherwise plain finish plugs with a red marking pen or fingernail polish. When bass are feeding on bluegill in summer, take advantage of the bright yellow underbelly of a frog-colored plug. Use the frog-colored top-water lure so the fish see that yellow bluegill-like belly as they come up underneath the bait.

Specialized Lures

The shape, design, or silhouette of a top-water plug can also be a significant factor to consider. Considerable territory can be covered quickly when casting a buzzbait. Not any buzzer will do. Select a buzzbait with prominent counter-rotating blades. Often the bass on crowded lakes become accustomed to the basic whirring sound and commotion of standard buzzer blades. By using a lure with two separate blades turning in opposite directions, evidently a distinct sound or vibration pattern is produced which excites the bass into attacking. Most novice bassers won't throw a buzzbait with this kind of blade configuration. They prefer to use a buzzer with a single blade instead.

Perhaps the best all-around buzzbait is a 1/4 ounce model that squeaks or makes a clacking sound from the noise and commotion generated from its particular blade design. In clear calm water a buzzer with subtle clear Lexon blade is often most effective.

At times, some unusually big surface lures can fool lunker-class Florida bass. Rather than tossing a conventional freshwater-size bait, try an extra large minnow plug designed primarily for saltwater species. Using stout, heavy-duty gear, rip, twitch, and jerk a 7 inch Bomber Magnum Long-A or a Rapala #18 floater in a similar length. Minnow-shaped lures in this genre are made to mimic either small carp or rainbow trout—prime morsels for jumbo Floridas.

The flip side of this strategy is to scale down in size and use a smaller floating minnow when the shad are only 3 inches long. Try tinier Rapalas and Rebel plugs which are more commonly associated with trout fishing. These can be terrific top-water lures when teamed with lighter 6 to 8 pound test mono. Twitch them along the surface when the shad are on the small side. Shorter surface minnows like these are distinctively absent in many of the best tackle arsenals.

Trick Top-Water Retrieves

Accomplished top-water fishermen use specific lures to create a certain action or effect while the baits are worked on or near the surface. For example, many anglers who throw a walking-type stickbait such as a Wood Walker or Zara Spook fail to work the lure in the tightest pockets. It is these areas bordered by branches, rocks, tules, or brush that trap bait and serve as prime ambush points.

Many bass fishermen are afraid to throw big baits into these traps. Even then, once inside the pockets, they have to try to work the lures behind the structure. The way to do this is with a modified retrieve. Most novice bassers learn to "walk the dog" by twitching the rod tip first to the left and then to the right with pauses in between. Instead, try pulling the bait to just one side, without pausing, in a rhythmic twitch-twitch-twitch motion. By doing this, large stickbaits will actually "walk" or veer off to the side, tucking behind structure nestled in the pocket.

Much has also been written about using a "drop bait" as a back-up to a larger top-water lure. A common practice is to first throw a big floating plug. If a bass blows up on the lure without getting hooked, fire off another cast with a slow-sinking plastic worm or tube bait.

Here's another potent one-two punch using a back-up system. If you are throwing buzzbaits and the bass seem to be making lazy passes at the lure without nailing it, make a follow-up cast with a small minnow plug. Slowly twitch the minnow barely below the surface with minimal splash. A vicious strike may result. It's as if the buzzer arouses the fish's interest, but not enough to trigger the strike. A compact floating minnow quietly swimming along the same path as the buzzbait may be too much for the bass to pass up.

Mike and Ron rely heavily upon these lightweight plastic and balsa minnows when the bass are up shallow in the spring. Here again, with these lures, the fish will commonly crash on the bait sometimes missing three sets of treble hooks. Rather than using a drop bait as a follow-up the trick is to let the minnow rest totally motionless following the strike. Wait for all of the ripples to clear. Then give the minnow one *single* twitch with the rod tip. One twitch is all it may take to generate a strike. Presum-

ably with this tactic, the bass senses it has wounded the baitfish as it lies still following the initial pass. That isolated twitch apparently resembles a fluttering minnow on its last death throws. The bass then zeroes in on the final kill.

As a final tip, let us pass along a valuable lesson. Like many anglers, we had a tendency to become too "trigger happy" when a bass hit our top-water baits. With the excitement of the splash, the sight of the fish, combined with the noise and commotion, the first inclination is to rear back and set up immediately. Unfortunately, too often the bass has only rolled on the lure and is long gone by the time you pull back on the rod.

We have cured this tendency when teaching beginning top-water fishermen with a relatively simple technique. After making a cast with a top-water plug, turn your head away from the line of sight as you retrieve the lure back in. Set the hook only when you *feel* the bass on the end of the line.

This is possibly the most critical secret to becoming proficient with a surface plug: set only when you *feel* resistance, not when you see the strike.

Be Experimental

These are only a few of the many strategies the top pros and guides use to trick surface-feeding bass. It is important to be flexible and somewhat experimental in this sport. Avoid getting into the rut of using stock lures and basic cast-and-retrieve approaches in top-water bassin'. Try innovative color schemes, customize your surface plugs, use a variety of retrieves, and impart unusual movements to these exciting lures. Explosive action may be the result!

Chuggers—A Forgotten Lure!

Many bass fishermen avoid tossing a full range of top-water lures feeling that some styles require too much work and too much patience. The chugger exemplifies this. Floating minnows, stickbaits, and assorted poppers receive plenty of action. For one reason or another, fewer anglers fish the chuggers.

The chugger design falls somewhere between a stick-bait such as the Heddon Zara Spook and a more distinctively cupped popper like the Rebel Pop-R. The interesting thing about using these lures is that some chuggers can actually combine the best features of both a stickbait and a popper. This makes the chugger a potentially unique, multi-purpose weapon in the serious basser's arsenal.

The simplest technique is to use the "chug" as a conventional popper. This is the classic approach and it works particularly well in still water. Cast the chugger out, wait for the concentric ripples to fade, then give the lure a quick "pop." Let the lure remain motionless for a few seconds then follow up with another "pop." Occasionally the bass will seem to casually "slap" at the lure without getting hooked. Patience is critical here. If the fish makes a pass at the bait but misses the hook, let the chugger remain totally motionless for a few seconds. Then give the "chug" a single little "pop." This often has the effect of totally aggravating the bass into making one final, and more vicious, attack. This tactic works particularly well around vegetation such as moss beds and tule banks.

On lakes with stark shoreline cover, many anglers prefer to use a somewhat faster popping action. In clear water, the chugger can be cast a long way on light monofilament. Immediately after the lure lands on the water, start a rhythmic popping retrieve with medium rod strokes. This creates a lot of splash, bubbles, and a gurgling sound. Quite often bass will skyrocket up from 30 foot depths in this clear water to annihilate this small surface lure.

A more conventional approach requiring a little practice is to "walk the dog" with a chugger. To do this, point the rod tip towards the water and pull the lure with short twitches. This has the effect of making the chugger dart from side to side generating a slight spray of water and subtle popping action. Some anglers prefer to walk the dog all the way back to the boat without stopping. Others believe it is best to intermittently pause a few seconds every few feet then resume the retrieve.

The walk-the-dog strategy has been instrumental in bringing in many trophy largemouths to the net when teamed with a large stickbait. There are times, especially under clear water conditions, when the bass are very skittish and a big lure will quickly spook them. A smaller chugger allows the basser to make long casts with a scaled-down top-water plug, resulting in a delicate landing as it hits the surface.

Chuggers are a rather simple yet versatile class of baits that can be fished with minimal practice. It is best to tie them directly to the line without using any additional snaps or split rings. Don't hesitate to throw the "chug" on light mono or under difficult conditions. Be experimental and try a variety of retrieves. Florida and northern-strain largemouths, smallmouths and Alabama spots will all strike this underrated surface plug. The chugger is a real sleeper and a welcome addition to any serious basser's tackle box!

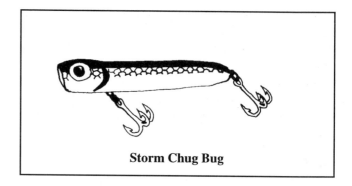

Storm Chug Bug

Doctor Your Crankbaits!

Most bass fishermen are inclined to use a crankplug right out of the box. Many of these baits are made with such a high level of sophistication that they are indeed quite fishable right off the shelf. However, Ron and Mike firmly believe that they can dramatically enhance the performance of crankbaits if they make specific modifications to the factory stock lures.

Coloring

Depending upon how creative you are, you can do anything from adding a subtle touch of color to repainting the entire plug. For example, take a fluorescent chartreuse marker or paint pen and apply a single stroke of color under the head portion of a crankbait. This little splash of chartreuse often helps the bass to see this type of plug as it travels through muddy water.

Sets of assorted colored paint pens are also available that are coded with the 26 major shades found in the Color-C-Lector chart. Instead of trying to find a plug that features both the primary and auxiliary colors as indicated by the meter, you can take an existing bait and quickly touch it up to match the Color-C-Lector reading.

As we mentioned earlier when talking about color and shade, the versatile black marking pen has been a staple in many tackle boxes of pros we fish with. For instance, one simple yet effective trick with the black marker is to add a prominent black spot to the area on a light-colored crankbait that represents where the gill covers would be on a threadfin shad minnow. Put the black "dot" on each side of the lure.

We have personally witnessed one angler outfishing another at a 5:1 difference using identical crankplugs with the exception of the addition of the mysterious black "dot." Some pros believe that the dot makes the lure more closely replicate a big shad minnow with similar natural coloration.

Consider also taking a plug, painting it solid white and adding glitter flake and black ribs to the surface. This "rib and glitter" effect can often convert an old beat-up bait into a dynamite new lure.

On the other hand, add a simple long lateral line to your big crankbaits using a red marker. This changes a big deep-diver into a planted rainbow trout—a popular morsel for trophy Florida bass.

Hooks

Most of us naturally accept manufacturer's stock treble hooks as the appropriate match for a particular plug. This may not always be correct. Many pros prefer to remove chrome or cadmium hooks and replace them with duller, less "flashy" bronze trebles. The bronze models may also retain a sharper point.

In some situations, the factory stock treble hooks on crankbaits are simply too small. The manufacturers may have been technically remiss in not switching to larger hooks when it comes to serious bassin'. You have to be careful not to alter the delicate balance of the lure by changing over to larger trebles. Always test the new bait with the larger hooks by making a few trial casts before employing it in a tournament situation.

When fishing bass in a shallow river with expensive minnow-shaped plugs, we will often replace the factory trebles with long-shank single Siwash hooks. This modification permits us to run these lures over the rockiest bottoms without hanging up.

More Tricks

There are a few other tips worth passing along that you may want to use in doctoring your crankplugs. First, the particular action of the crankbait can often be made to track differently by sanding or shaving down the sides of the lure's diving bill. Usually this modification will make the plug track with a "tighter" side-to-side wobble. You can also carefully shave the diving bill somewhat to correct for proper tracking.

Next, drill a small hole into the hollow cavity of a crankplug or top-water lure that doesn't come stocked with a sound chamber. Add a few tiny BB shots and seal the hole with epoxy. This will convert the lure into a "rattler."

A variation on this is passed along by one of the most innovative serious bassers out West, Dave Nollar. This big fish expert sometimes drills a hole in a hollow plastic crankbait and fills the cavity with various liquids, then reseals the hole with epoxy.

Some fluids like mineral or cooking oil provide a nearly neutral buoyancy effect with the lure. As you pause in the retrieve, the plug may now remain at that depth without sinking. Other heavier liquids such as water may actually add weight to the crankplug, allowing it to go deeper but without altering the action that sometimes occurs when a spot of lead is added to the surface.

Finally, scale-like prism paper is a real boon for making quick modifications to plugs while in the field. Often a small subtle patch of this self-adhesive paper applied to a crankbait or a surface lure will be all it takes to generate renewed interest in the plug. This prism paper is sold in a multitude of brilliant scale-like finishes including some fluorescent shades.

Above all, be experimental! These are only a few suggestions for "doctoring" your plugs.

Spoons for All Reasons

Spoons are, without a doubt, the most underrated lures in the recreational bass fisherman's tackle box. For most anglers, these simple baits are usually earmarked for the sporadic wintertime bite. Many of us have come to believe that "spoonin'" is something you do in the colder months when the fish are sluggish and nothing else seems to work. Similarly, we were taught the basic "lift-and-drop" technique as the primary way to properly use spoons for bass. This is "hardware" bassin' at its more boring.

The fact of the matter is that these lures have year-round effectiveness. Spoons can be employed in many different presentations apart from the vertical, deep-water approach. Thus, if anglers can avoid stereotyping these baits, they will find that there is a wide range of interesting applications for this kind of serious "hardware." Let's review the finer points of using spoons working from shallow to deep water.

Pitchin' Spoons

During the late spring through the fall, spoons can be pitched tight into shoreline cover. The bright reflective surface of a metal spoon can often trigger strikes from shallow water bass when more traditional strategies fail. The erratic "flash" from the lure's polished surface simulates an errant baitfish venturing too close to the bank.

The trick with pitchin' spoons in shallow terrain like this is to match the weight of the lure proportionally to the density of the cover. For example, if you were pitchin' along a lake shore tightly lined with trees or thick brush, a heavier spoon like the Hopkins 075 or Cordell-CC would be a good choice. These models weigh roughly 3/

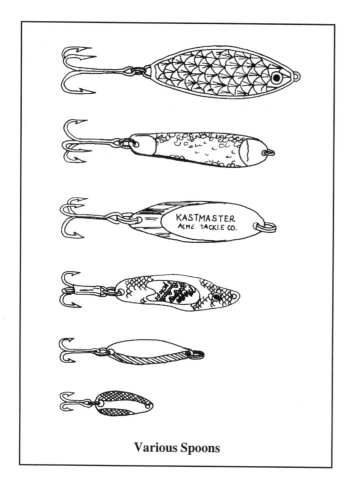

Various Spoons

4 ounce. They are normally used for deep-water bassin'. However, with dense brush or limbs it will take a modicum of weight for the lure to pierce the cover to get to the fish.

As this heavier spoon sinks through the submerged structure it will seductively deflect off the branches or limbs, imitating a wounded minnow. A lighter spoon may not be able to penetrate the brush or deflect the structure. However, often a more subtle model like the small Hopkins or Acme Kastmaster in 1/4 to 3/8 ounces will be more suitable for pitchin' around riprap, limited vegetation, docks, piers, or shallow vertical walls. In this situation, penetration may not be that critical. Also, the bass may actually be suspended a few feet off the bottom. Hence, a lighter weight spoon with a slow, fluttering action may generate more strikes than a heavier model.

Using spoons in this manner is similar to pitchin' a jig. Make short, quick underhand or sidearm casts to the target. Try to gently "parachute" the spoon into the strike zone with a splashless entry. Be prepared for a majority of

your strikes to occur on the fall. Any interruption in the sinking action of the spoon such as a "tick" or slackening in the line may signal a bass has inhaled the lure. Swing and set!

If you are not bit on the sink, give the rod 2 to 3 short "pumps" to make the spoon rise and fall once more through the cover. If you fail to get a strike, quickly reel up and pitch the spoon to the next viable target.

Surprisingly, spoons with stock treble hooks can often be shaken loose from brush or rock if snagged during a shallow pitch. Slack up on the line a little and sort of jiggle the lure free with short twitches with the rod tip. If the spoon persists in getting hung up, replace the treble with a single short-shank live bait hook.

Flippin' Spoons

Taking the shallow water approach one step further, consider flippin' spoons. This can be an intriguing option, particularly in the warmer months when the bass are more active. During this time, it is not uncommon to find a lot of baitfish schooled tight near the bank, especially inside tules and reeds. A metal spoon carefully flipped into this vegetation can be highly potent.

Again, the secret is to flip the lure with minimal commotion and a fairly slow sinking action. One way to facilitate this is to add a trailer to the spoon to ease the splash and retard the fall.

The old standbys, Johnson Weedless Silver Minnow and its modern counterpart made by Rapala, are also excellent options. Although this type of spoon has enjoyed its greatest popularity in the South and Midwest, it can be an excellent flip bait wherever weeds are found. Recently, many bass fishermen have discovered this lure as the perfect flippin' spoon for big Florida bass rooted in tight to the tules. Many of the pros like to add either a solid white #11 Uncle Josh Pork Frog or #U-2 Split Tail Eel for extra bulk. The white pork combined with a silver spoon also resembles the silhouette, action, and coloration of larger, summer shad minnows.

Sub-Surface Spoons

Spoons can also be utilized like a spinnerbait or crankplug working extensive shorelines or expanses of open water. There are times when the bass have been thoroughly hammered by the repetitive hum of spinners and plugs. This is commonly the case on a crowded tournament weekend. This is the time to switch to the subtle action of a spoon. Work the same water you would with a spinnerbait or crankplug, however using a relatively slower retrieve with the spoon.

Many of the silver, gold, copper, and brass-colored spoons relegated to your trout tackle box will be equally effective as bassin' lures. Smaller models in the 1/8 to 3/8 ounce range can be particularly deadly retrieved slowly under the surface when the bass seem super finicky. Spoons fished in this manner can be allowed to sink, counting down to a certain depth, then retrieved through that strike zone.

One key strategy is to use what is termed the "stop-and-go." During the retrieve, simply intermittently stop winding the spoon while letting it sink. Quite frequently, the bass will attack the bait as it starts to fall, presumably representing a dying baitfish.

There is a tendency for some anglers to want to add a snap-swivel to these tiny spoons to minimize line twist. Avoid the temptation! You may find that the snap-swivel combination serves to deaden the subtle side-to-side wobble of these little baits. Instead, scale down to 6 to 8 pound test monofilament.

Tie your line to either a solitary snap or a split ring. This will insure proper action from the lure.

Sub-surface spoons can be a real "sleeper" lure, especially in ultraclear water. With lightweight tackle, these baits can be cast a long distance with a fairly quiet entry. The slow, seductive wobble of these lures often produce strikes when conventional bass lures can't seem to interest the fish.

Surface Spoons

At certain times of the year, bass will often crash on the surface chasing schools of baitfish. Spoons can be an intriguing alternative to the common top-water baits.

In clear water conditions, although the surface feeding activity can be intense, the fish may still be quite skittish and hesitant to attack a plug or buzzbait. Tie on a small 1/8 to 3/8 ounce wobbling spoon using light 4 to 8 pound test line and a spinning outfit. The fine diameter monofilament allows you to make a long cast, preferably over the surface boils where the fish were seen.

Slowly retrieve the spoon using rhythmic twitches with the rod tip. The trick is to actually make the lure dance and dart on top of the water. The light line and tiny bait create minimal resistance as you pull the spoon to the surface. Another ploy is to quickly stop the retrieve as the lure is worked into the area of the commotion. Let the spoon slowly sink. Be prepared for a vicious strike within the first few seconds following the pause.

In Western bassin' circles, this phenomenon of a surface feeding frenzy is quite common at big fish reservoirs such as San Diego's Lake Hodges, Sutherland, and Lower Otay. Local bass anglers have designed a specialized spoon to be used for this kind of top-water action called the Schurmy Shad. This is a hollow-bodied aluminum spoon with brilliant scale-like, prismlite finishes. The aluminum body allows this lure to sink slowly compared to spoons made from brass or heavier metals. While making long casts with light line, twitch the Schurmy Shad across the surface when the big Floridas start herding schools of shad.

Hoppin' Spoons

Moving further off the bank, spoons can be used in place of jigs or plastic worms for exploring deeper underwater terrain. "Spoon hoppin'" can be effective for maintaining good bottom contact and covering considerable territory in a short amount of time.

The most viable places to hop a spoon are along gentle inclines, stair-step ledges, the sides of underwater river channels and down the face of a dam. As a rule, select a heavier spoon in the 1/2 to 3/4 ounce range. Casting out either uphill or downhill, work the lure back to the boat, using short "pumps" with the rod.

This should not be confused with the more commonly practiced lift-and-drop strategy used with deep-water spoonin'. The object of hoppin' the spoon is to make solid contact with the lure so that it kind of flip-flops along the bottom. This is similar to the pitchin' method only staying further off the bank with extensive retrieves. At times, a spoon will work better than a jig in the summer because the bass are more aggressive. The fish chase schools of shad into the bank, then the bait flutters erratically as they are wounded. A well-placed spoon is highly effective here. If you can fish it fast, the spoon will bounce off the bank mimicking a shad that is under attack.

For this hoppin' approach, we recommend a 1/2 to 3/4 ounce Crippled Herring, Kastmaster, or Hopkins model. Fish these spoons with 10 to 12 pound test line and work it almost as fast as a crankbait.

Vertical Spoonin'

As was mentioned, this is the basic presentation usually associated with spoonin'. Even with this method there are certain details that novice spoon fishermen often overlook.

First, it's important not to overexaggerate this lift-and-drop motion. Too often, anglers can be seen making pronounced five or six foot rod lifts, practically jerking the spoon through the water.

Sometimes, if the bass are suspended a few feet off the bottom, this strategy can be quite effective. However, if the fish are in a slow-down state, especially in colder weather, they won't move too far or too fast to attack a bait. Hence, a short series of rod twitches creating the "flip-flop" effect may be more productive.

The bass slow way down when the weather turns cold. Under these conditions, the short twitch works best moving the rod tip only about a foot. The fish orient close to structure so the long rod sweep isn't necessary. Keep the spoon in the strike zone more by using a short "pop" with the rod tip.

Secondly, with the vertical approach, it pays to be selective with regard to the size of the spoon you use. Bass situated in this deep environment are typically wary and relatively hook shy. Try to match the size of the spoon to the size of the indigenous baitfish the bass are foraging on. The same 3/4 ounce spoon you used for summer hoppin' may be too large to replicate the immature shad found in the early spring. A smaller 1/4 to 3/8 ounce model may be more effective.

Mix It Up!

Try to be somewhat creative with regard to color, design and presentation, whether you use a spoon shallow or deep. Don't make the mistake of using only the ubiquitous nickel-plated pattern. Other colors can be even more effective at times. For instance, if the bass are keying on shiners or even small rainbow trout, try spoons in gold, brass, or prismlite finishes. Similarly, if the water is murky or the sky is overcast, bronze, or black-colored spoons may prove to be the best choices.

If the bass fail to respond to one type of spoon, switch to another. Some models have flatter surfaces with great reflective qualities. Other spoons are more concave, refracting light erratically, but with excellent fluttering motion. At times, the bass will clearly prefer one design and action over the other.

Finally, mix up your presentations. Nothing is etched in stone when it comes to spoon fishing. Shift gears and use a faster retrieve if the slow wind doesn't produce. Switch to the other, more dramatic, lift-and-drop tactic if the "flip-flop" strategy doesn't generate any strikes from bass on the bottom.

Wherever and whenever you fish bass—don't forget spoons. They are indeed "serious hardware"!

Precise Spinnerbait Selection

Upon first glance the spinnerbait appears to be a rather uncomplicated lure. However, the professional angler or guide puts a considerable amount of forethought into the proper selection of these baits when it comes to this serious form of fishing.

Here is a brief summary of the three most important dimensions the pros use to decide which spinnerbait to toss in competition.

Single or Tandem?

As a rough rule of thumb, a single-bladed spinner is more suitable as a "stall" bait when you want the lure to moderately fall on the sink. If you are fishing stick-ups, for example, and wish to have the spinnerbait "helicopter" down into the base of the structure, the single-blade models are the best choice.

Tandem-bladed spinnerbaits on the other hand are excellent for running through grass or sub-surface structure. The addition of the extra blade serves to hold the lure up longer so it won't sink as fast.

Even with this basic distinction, there are situations where you can improvise with either blade configuration. For instance, in the winter and spring we usually prefer to use a 3/8 to 1/2 ounce single-blade model so we can get it down quicker to bass holding deeper. However, if you want to switch to a tandem-blade version to fish deep, all you have to do is add a little weight to the head and throw a 1/2 to 5/8 ounce tandem-blade spinnerbait.

Blade Design

Another major variable in spinnerbait selection is which blade to use. Here again we can simplify the decision with the following basic guidelines:

1. Use the round Colorado blade if you want the greatest "thumping" action that serves to "call in" the fish. This blade turns the widest circle and will generate greatest torque. It's an excellent choice for fishing off-colored water. The Colorado blade also excels in deep water as the excessive vibrations permit you to feel the lure bumping along the bottom more easily.

2. The narrow willowleaf turns with the tightest rotation. It is superior for working the spinnerbait through grass and similar vegetation with minimal fouling of the blade.

3. The Indiana design falls between the Colorado and the willowleaf in terms of water displacement and torque. It is most commonly used in tandem as the lead blade with either the Colorado or the willowleaf models.

Coloration

With regard to color, start with the blades. Silver or nickel-colored blades seem to perform best in clear water and bright skies. Darker-colored blades such as copper,

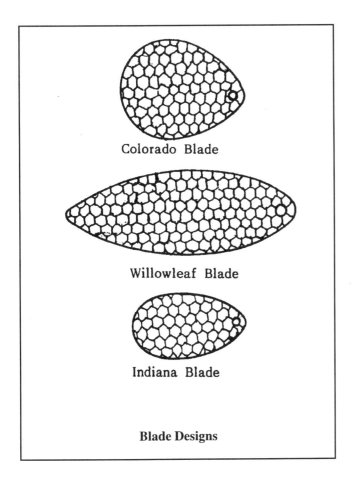

Colorado Blade

Willowleaf Blade

Indiana Blade

Blade Designs

Serious Spinnerbait Secrets

Adjusting the Spinnerbait

Carefully examine every spinnerbait you purchase over the counter or through the mail. Serious bassin' requires serious scrutiny of your personal baits.

The first thing to do with a stock spinnerbait is to intentionally bend open the hook with pliers approximately 5 degrees more. Do this in order to expose the hook slightly so it is not exactly parallel to the shank. You will find that you will actually stick more bass with this minor adjustment than by using the lure as is. The spinnerbait still remains quite weedless with the more exposed hook.

Next, while holding your spinnerbait upside down, carefully give the rear blade a flick with your finger to check for proper rotation. If the blade does not turn freely, replace the factory swivel with a ball bearing version made by Sampo where the blade attaches to the wire arm. Even with the addition of the ball bearing swivel you may still reject up to 50 percent of the spinnerbaits purchased. You need that blade to spin so freely that the weight of the lure itself will be enough to make the blade turn when the bait slowly falls.

Consider adding 5 to 10 strands of fine mylar strips to the stock live rubber skirts of the lure. Make certain that the mylar strands extend slightly out beyond the existing skirt material. You will find that the mylar creates some spectacular erratic flashes when added to the skirt. Now the spinnerbait looks more like a frenzied shad minnow. The mylar sometimes works better than any other trailers, especially in dirty water.

Another secret tactic is to add a soft plastic shad-tail bait as a trailer combined with the live rubber skirt. Use a shad-tail with that eerie pearlescent color to give the spinner a more natural shad-like appearance under water. The tiny shad-tail pulsates behind the spinnerbait often generating strikes under tough conditions and in clear water.

Selecting the Right Blades

Many recreational bassers rarely take the time to contemplate which specific blade design will work best with the changing seasonal patterns. Many trophy hunters who specialize with blades feel that of all the things you can do to receive strikes from a spinnerbait, none is more critical than selecting the proper blade.

In the early winter all the way up through early spring during the pre-spawn period, fish will be slowly moving

brass, gold, bronze, or painted finishes work best in stained or muddy water or with an overcast sky.

Spinnerbait skirt materials should be light-colored to match both prevailing water and weather conditions along with indigenous forage bait. For instance, white, silver, or gray skirts have always been effective for replicating threadfin shad, while brown/orange skirts are used to mimic crawdads.

The chartreuse spinnerbait skirt has been the longtime standard for fishing in stained or muddy water usually in some combination with a copper or brass blade.

Always remember bass fishing is not an exact "science." These are the three major considerations for spinnerbait selection. Always allow yourself enough latitude to be somewhat experimental and to deviate from these generalizations when traditional methods fail to produce.

toward the bank. The water will be typically colder and often off-colored. Use a fairly large #5 to #7 Colorado-style blade with your spinnerbaits during these times. Retrieve it S-L-O-W-L-Y. The big Colorado blade generates greater vibration than any other blade type. The intense vibrations given off by the lure will excite the bass as sound is received along their lateral lines.

You must use a fairly heavy spinnerbait in the 3/8 to 1 ounce range to power the large Colorado blade. It will take a lot of "pull" or resistance to keep a blade this size rotating.

Switch to the more subtle and seldom-used Indiana blade during the spawning period. This blade shape requires less pull than the Colorado and also gives off fewer vibrations. Try retrieving a spinnerbait with the smaller Indiana blade or willowleaf near the bank and through limited weed growth to trigger strikes from bass near the shallow spawning beds.

By summertime, the vegetation on many lakes across the country is in full bloom. This is the time to select the narrow shape of the willowleaf blade design. This style of spinnerbait will pull through the grass, moss, hydrilla, and other weeds better than those with Colorado or Indiana blades. The ultratight rotational pattern of the willowleaf also serves to generate strikes from more aggressive warm weather bass through any heavy cover in all seasons.

More on Innovative Retrieves

Perhaps the biggest mistake made by novice anglers is to fish spinnerbaits too shallow. Forget the notion that a spinnerbait works best near the surface where you can see it. Instead practice fishing it out of sight. Retrieve it deep enough so it cannot be seen from above the water, somewhat like a crankbait. You'll find that you will draw strikes from fish swimming 8 and 10 feet below the surface with this type of slow-down presentation.

Most recreational anglers are simply not inventive enough when it comes to adding more erratic action to their spinnerbaits. For example, learn to intentionally hesitate during the retrieve. Then give the lure a *hard pull* with the rod to increase its speed. This "hard pull" and the hesitation that follows is precisely what simulates a fleeing baitfish.

Be Creative!

As a final note, perhaps the most important secret of all when using a spinnerbait is to *be creative!* Try to expand upon the basic spinnerbait design and the routine cast-and-retrieve presentation. Be aware that most strikes occur by bumping into an object that might be either visible or out of sight underwater. These are terrific year-round lures. As with any popular bass bait, the serious basser will always try to give the fish something different to look at.

14 lb. 3 oz. Spinnerbait Fish

Serious Flippin'

Serious Flippin'

Of all the different techniques we outline in this book, none is probably as demanding as shallow water flippin'. This is serious bassin' at its maximum. A good flip fisherman might make literally thousands of quick, tight "flip" casts in a single day! The serious flipper must thus have stamina, perseverance, and a strong commitment to this specialized approach. Let's look at some of the more serious dimensions of the flippin' approach.

You're Always in the Strike Zone!

In the past few years, flippin' has emerged as one of the most viable strategies for shallow water bassin'. Accomplished flippers can catch fish regularly on an all-year basis. They point out that the strength of the flippin' technique is the ability of the angler to keep the bait in the strike zone 90 percent of the time. How is this possible?

To begin with, water near the bank is typically where tules, brush, rocks, and similar prime ambush points can be found. Simply put, when serious bassers flip their lures into this shoreline structure, they are working the areas where fish live. Because the flipped bait is presented in such a confined pocket, the extraneous water between the bank and the boat is not usually fished. A lot of "dead" water can be eliminated by a competent flipper or flip-caster. Thus, lures that are flipped into this shoreline territory remain in the major strike zone for the optimal amount of time.

Bass anglers usually talk about flippin' in terms of stout, 7 to 7 1/2 foot rods and baitcasting reels loaded with 20 to 30 pound test monofilament. Heavy-duty gear like this is characteristically necessary to pry bass out of these shallow haunts laden with riprap, heavy brush, trees, and tules. Flippin' occurs primarily in off-colored, stained water. It is important to note that flip-casting by contrast is more viable when the angler must work shallow but remain further off the bank so as not to spook the fish. Most bassers have also come to rely upon a narrow range of baits to use while flippin'. These include the basic pig'n jig, plastic worms, and occasionally lizards.

However, sometimes bass can become wary and tough to catch in shallow water. For instance, on many impoundments, the water near the bank is sometimes fairly clear with sparse shoreline cover. In this situation, a standard flippin' approach won't always work as the fish become somewhat spooky. Bassers have to revise their methodology at times in their attempts to flip bass from this kind of water. By using lighter line and more exotic baits, bassers will find that new avenues of success are possible with the flippin' game.

Flip All Year Long[1]

Recreational bass fishermen often view flippin' as a shallow water tactic practiced primarily in the spring. The fact of the matter is that Mike and Ron employ this technique any time of the year when the bass are situated tight to the bank.

Many serious bassers believe that at least a portion of the fish in a given body of water will inevitably be found in the shallows some part of the day. This is regardless of the prevailing climate, water temperature, or whether you fish in a river or a lake.

However, it is important to note that although it is indeed possible to flip bass throughout the year, the actual selection of lures, line, and overall presentation may vary significantly as the seasons change.

Spring

As the water temperature warms in the early spring, the different bass species begin to stage a major migration

[1] Portions of this section previously appeared in *Bassmaster Magazine*

from deeper water, moving into the shallow zones. As mentioned, it is during this pre-spawn ritual that flippin' excels, particularly for larger trophy fish.

Most shallow water enthusiasts would recommend flippin' a pig'n jig combo if they had to select one bait for this early season approach. One theory often cited to explain the popularity of this lure in the spring focuses on the bass' need to replenish both calcium and protein stock expended during the migration and nest-building period. Crawdads are a natural source of these compounds for the fish needing to re-energize themselves.

The widely used Uncle Josh #11 "frog" thus has practically become the generic offering for pork rind tipped jigs. Combined with either a live rubber or nylon-skirted lead head, the #11 Pork Frog closely replicates the size, texture, and silhouette of a spring crayfish.

However, this is also the time of the year when lunker class fish may key in on an extraordinarily large bait.

Many serious bassers will switch from the basic #11 frog to either the much more prominent Uncle Josh #1 Jumbo Frog or the giant Big Daddy pork chunk. Interestingly, veteran flippin' specialists believe that bigger fish become aggravated in the spring when confronted by a large black-on-black pig'n jig.

Similarly, if the angler subscribes to the adage: "BIG BAITS = BIG BASS," then other large lures may be effective when flipped in the spring shallows. A live rubber jig, for example, with a big pork rind trailer such as Uncle Josh's #2 or #1 Big Daddy Pork Frog is an excellent alternative to the more popular #11 Pork Frog. Soft plastic lizard imitations are sometimes even more potent than their pork rind counterparts in the spring. Lures in this genre closely resemble an errant lizard as it tumbles down the bank.

Many pros and guides believe that the soft plastic lizards are particularly effective in the spring due to the

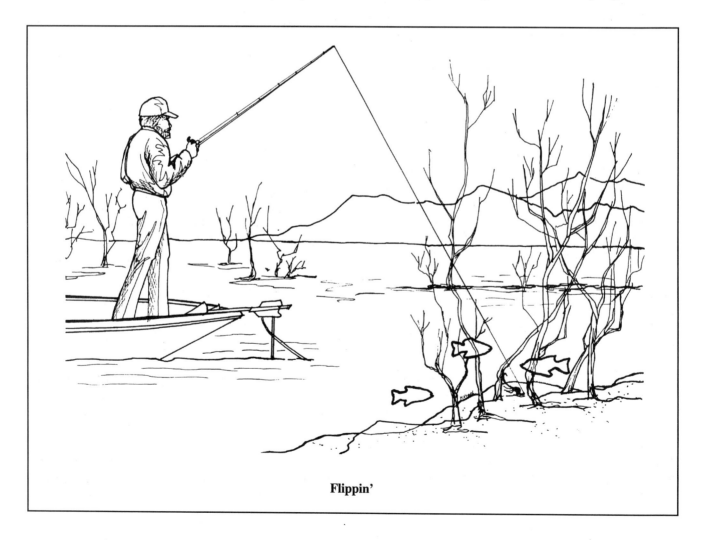

Flippin'

tiny legs that protrude from most of these baits. Presumably, with an abundance of natural food near the shoreline, spring bass can still become quite finicky. However, in contrast to a slow-moving worm, the plastic lizard creates more excitement as its little legs start to move on the retrieve. The lizard's 6 to 8 inch body size and the curl-tail legs drive springtime bass crazy. Big bass may sense that they have to strike fast at this particular bait or it may rapidly scurry away. Another theory suggests that the bass realizes lizards and other similarly shaped salamanders might attack the female's nest and eat the eggs, and thus they strike these imitations with a vengeance.

What about plastic worms? These lures are a mainstay in the flip fisherman's spring arsenal apart from the pork frog and the lizard replicas. Instead of flippin' the basic 4 to 6 inch length worms, consider switching to longer 8 to 12 inch models.

Here again, the larger "kicker" fish may be keying in on a magnum-size bait, especially if they are being barraged by a parade of smaller, more compact offerings. These longer worms perhaps create the illusion of a small snake that is swimming near the bank.

One thing we have learned, however, is that you must be patient and let the fish really eat the bait. Instead of swinging instantly as many anglers do after feeling a strike when flippin', allow the bass to mouth the jumbo worm a little longer, setting up as the fish begins to actually move off with the lure.

Tackle for spring flippin' tends to lean on the heavy side across the country. This is when you have a chance at a wallhanger, which may be rooted into thick dense cover. Mike and Ron opt for 20 to 30 pound test line, and prefer the supertough Berkley Big Game monofilament. The drag on the baitcasting reel is usually hammered down tight.

Summer

As water temperatures increase, bass along the shoreline may become more active in their feeding behavior. That's the good news. On the downside, it may require somewhat more finesse and forethought in lure selection to get the summer fish to attack a flip bait. This is the time of the year that the bank on a given lake receives the greatest amount of recreational traffic. The bass may thus be somewhat skittish from this sort of pressure.

Also, bass suspend more during the summer when shoreline food sources—for example, shad—move off the bank. Flippin' is still effective in rivers in the summer but generally poor in lakes when the quantity of shallow

fish is low. However this time of the year you may find limited success using smaller baits, lighter line, and lighter action rods to flip a modest amount of bass during the warmer months.

Therefore, be prepared to use lighter 12 to 15 pound line and smaller baits if necessary. Granted, you may lose some fish with the lighter tackle, but you may also get bit when the bass shy away from the heavier tackle and larger lures.

In the summer, you may have to switch from the pig and jig combos to plastic jigs with swimming tails. Baits like the Garland Spider Jig, Yamamoto's Hula Grub, or the Haddock Kreepy Krawler may excite the bass into striking as they seductively flutter down on the fall if there are signs of shad minnows in the shallows.

Plastic worms with pronounced sickle-shaped tails will produce a similar effect. These large whip-tailed worms in shades of silver, gray, or smoke will displace a lot of water and generate an erratic "flash" as they are flipped matched with light 1/8 to 3/16 ounce bullet sinkers.

Along this same line, hollow-bodied tube baits like the Berkley Power Tube or Bobby Garland's Fat Gitzit, particularly in light color schemes, will often trigger strikes from summer bass gorged on shad when other larger lures fail to get bit.

Larger plastic grubs such as Mr. Twister or Berkley's Power Grub similarly can generate spectacular results flipped Texas-rigged with the light bullet sinker. Patterns like salt'n pepper, smoke/sparkle, or black/laminated gray will imitate a dying shad minnow as they are gently flipped near the bank, in brush, or in trees away from the shore where shad might be suspended.

Another seldom-used entry in the summer flippin' sweepstakes is the classic shad-profile baits such as those made by A.A. Worms and Mr. Twister. This type of soft plastic bait has a popular following in saltwater circles. It has a distinctive, large knobby tail that pulsates back and forth on a slow retrieve.

Some anglers have discovered that the Mr. Twister Sassy Shad and the A.A. Shad make great flippin' baits when the shad are ranging from 2 to 4 inches in length. As you flip one of these lures on a light jig head with a weed guard, it creates a pronounced silhouette fluttering on its wide sides mimicking a large frantic shad minnow.

If there is an indication that the summer fish are still feeding shallow, then by all means continue throwing pork. However, if weed growth is extensive, you may be better off flippin' an Uncle Josh U-2 or 3 Split-Tail Eel. This is a much slimmer piece of pork than the #11 frog. It will slither better through the narrow openings found in moss beds and similar vegetation.

Plastic worms in basic black, brown, or purple patterns will also flip quite well through summer weeds and closely match the crawdad forage. Consider switching to a slightly more compact worm in the 4 inch length as an alternative to give these more pressured fish something different to look at.

A compromise between pork and plastic would be to flip craw-worms during this time of the year. These are distinguished by a head portion molded to look like a crayfish with pinchers and a torso that is basically the thicker portion of a 4 inch plastic worm. These flip well on either a Texas rig or a jig head. Or flip other soft plastic crawdad replicas like the Billy's C-Dad, Guido Bug, Hales' Craw Worm, Haddock Kreepy Krawdad, or Berkley Power Craw. All of these baits can be flipped on a jig head or rigged Texas style.

Finally, if you encounter bass "herding" schools of bait up into the shallows, it might pay to flip a spoon. The Johnson Silver Minnow, Rapala Spoon, and Cordell-CC models in bright polished chrome finish actually can be flipped if you are careful to make a quiet splashless entry. Strikes can be vicious with these lures, though few anglers ever think of flippin' them.

Fall

If we had to summarize an approach to flippin' bass in the autumn, it would be a return to basics. There will still be some residual action on fish that are finding shad to feed on near the bank. Many of those lures that imitate these minnows used in the summer may continue to produce in early fall.

Look for the fish to key in once again on crawdads. Switch back to the standard #11 Pork Frog and gear back up with 20 to 30 pound test line. This combination is hard to beat.

Medium-size, 6 inch plastic worms in a range of "earth tone" patterns will also provide an alternative to the pig'n jig flipped in the fall. Select your worms in mottled shades combining black, brown, green, and orange.

Large 5 inch long plastic grubs will also be effective in the fall, especially as the weather turns colder. The fluttering tail on these baits will still trigger strikes when the blander worms or jigs stop getting bit.

The trick with the grubs is to move away from primarily shad-like color schemes and instead flip darker patterns that look more like a crawdad. Pumpkin/pepper, tomato/pepper, bubble gum/pepper along with solid purple or brown would be my choice in colors for flippin' a grub in the fall.

With autumn weather often being unpredictable be prepared for the shallow water bite to vary from hot to cold. Some days the bass will readily attack a flipped bait as they do in the prime spring and summer period. Other days, a slow, methodical presentation will be in order with the fish start to make the transition into a wintertime feeding mode.

Flippin' a 7" Power Worm

Winter

It is amazing that the dedicated flipper often will find bass in less than a foot of water during the dead of winter. When most anglers are probing the outside, deep structure during these colder months, a small legion of hard-core shallow water experts continue to find fish along the bank.

Most wintertime flippers overwhelmingly prefer to use the pig'n jig in cold water. One explanation is that the fish want to expend as little energy as possible looking for a substantial morsel of food. After capturing their prey, they can then return to the prolonged slow-down state characteristic of cold water bass.

Crawdads provide this type of bulkier winter forage. Hence, the pig'n jig combo is again a wise choice, even when water surface temperatures drop below 45 degrees.

The Uncle Josh Spring Lizard and #1 Jumbo Frog pork rind trailers discussed for spring will also meet the criteria for a winter bait with a prominent silhouette. These may be used in place of the standard #11 size frog.

If you can find pockets of warmer water during the winter months, then by all means try to flip plastic worms, grubs, crawdads, or lizards instead of pork as an alternative. Look for matted, decaying tules, or the backs or coves where the wind may have blown chunks of wood and similar flotsam as potential shallow warm water spots for winter flippin'.

Above all, if the weather and water are extremely cold do not expect the bass to move too far or too fast to ambush a flipped lure. It is imperative that you make a delicate presentation, occasionally pausing to leave the bait in the strike zone longer than you would during the warmer months.

Winter bass may be holding extremely tight to shoreline cover such as tree trunks, dock pilings, or the center of brush piles. You might also have to make repeated flips into one of these winter targets to interest the fish into striking. Heavier 20 to 30 pound monofilament line using stronger forged jig or worm hooks is recommended for penetrating this sort of cover.

Above all, be prepared to flip very S-L-O-W-L-Y if you expect to catch bass during this part of the year. Patience will be a major component of the winter flip fisherman's overall strategy.

Flip All Year!

So, as you can see, the serious basser who prefers to work the shallows stalking his fish flippin' or flip casting, can utilize this technique through the four seasons. In contrast to other anglers who may have to settle for exploring vast expanses of deeper water, flippin' allows the serious basser to keep his baits in the potential strike zone 90 percent of the time. This fact, combined with the propensity of flippin' to consistently put solid "keeper" fish in the live well, is why this method remains a serious weapon in the tournament pro's and veteran guide's bag of tricks—all year long!

Serious Jiggin'

Serious Jiggin'

We are both veteran jig fishermen. Unfortunately, many recreational anglers have a tendency to shy away from this lure. Some feel that it gets hung up too often; others say they can't really tell when they are bit with a jig.

If you are to become a serious bass fisherman, there is no way around it—you are going to have to master the art of jig fishing, both shallow and deep! Here are some pointers that may help you to perfect your techniques when throwing these remarkably simple lures.

The Most Versatile Lure Ever?

Regardless of what you hear from the various lure manufacturers, there is no such thing as a "miracle" bait. However, some pros and guides feel that if they had to pick just one single lure to depend on day after day, the simple jig would be their choice. This bait is very versatile. It can be fished all through the year, allows the angler to explore the bottom, and can be worked fairly quickly. Under tournament and guiding conditions, you can cover a lot of different terrain with a jig.

Don't underestimate what seems to be the oversimplicity of this lure. Closer scrutiny reveals that the serious basser puts a lot of forethought into selecting the proper jig for specific situations. Every part of this bait including lead head shape, skirt type, brush guard, and trailer material contributes to its overall effectiveness.

If we break this lure down into its basic parts, it becomes apparent why one kind of jig works better than another depending on prevailing conditions. We'll start this "anatomy lesson" by examining the trailer and build the lure up from there.

Pork and Plastic

For years, bass fishermen have been debating among themselves as to which jig trailer is best, plastic or pork. In reality, both materials have great effectiveness when fished in the right context.

Pork rind trailers have been around for decades. It is only with the rise of the "pig'n jig" as a major tournament bait that these trailers skyrocketed in popularity. "Pork" can imitate numerous creatures that plod along the bottom, such as newts, eels, salamanders, or worms. Interestingly, the popular pork "frog" is to some degree a misnomer. In most parts of the country this style of pork rind is selected to replicate a crawdad and not a frog. These little crustaceans comprise an integral portion of the major forage found in most impoundments. This certainly attributes much to the effectiveness of this kind of jig trailer.

Many pros also feel that the natural texture of the pork rind itself is another critical feature. Although research is not conclusive, some lure makers are adamant that bass will hold on to a soft bait longer if it is impregnated with salt. This is evident in recent marketing blitzes offering plastic worms, grubs, and lizards with salt mixed in.

As a rule, pork rind tipped jigs are made to be fished along the bottom. Many bassers err in believing that the pig'n jig is primarily a cold water bait. Far too often anglers have a tendency to put away the pork with the onset of summer only to take it out again in the cooler autumn weather. The truth of the matter is that pork will work all year long.

Serious bassers must become proficient as both deep water specialists and masters of the shallow water game.

The one common ingredient that motivates them to toss pork is whether or not there are crawdads in the lake. More than likely, fishermen will throw pork if they sense that the bass are feeding on 'dads.

Many anglers stop using pork in the summer because of increases in algae growth and a rise in the metabolism of the bass.

Some bassers opt for a plastic worm over pork when fishing weedy, mossy areas. They reckon the thinner plastic baits will slither through the vegetation better than a bulkier pork frog. Similarly with more active feeding occurring in the warmer months, some fishermen prefer a faster moving bait. They may select a crankplug, spinnerbait, or even a plastic swimming jig.

Again, these are oversights on both counts. Pork is available in a variety of styles not just the widely used "frog." Pork "chunks" such as these are a little bulky for fishing thick, slimy weed growth. Simply switch to a slimmer piece of pork such as an Uncle Josh #U-2 or #U-3 Split-Tail Eel. This thin pork strip will slide through the vegetation in a manner similar to a plastic worm.

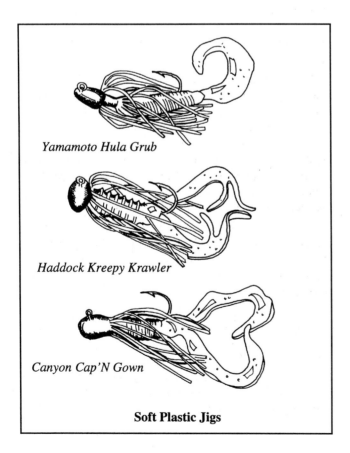

Yamamoto Hula Grub

Haddock Kreepy Krawler

Canyon Cap'N Gown

Soft Plastic Jigs

The pig'n jig doesn't have to be fished slowly all the time. Accomplished jig fishermen will flip, pitch, or even swim a pork frog quickly along a potentially good shoreline or riverbank any time of the year looking for aggressive fish.

By comparison, plastic jigs can have even more versatility than their pork counterparts, but they lack that soft, natural composition. However, the array of possibilities that are available with plastic trailers is endless. The double-tail, swimming type is the most popular. Manufacturers such as Yamamoto and Mr. Twister have been producing this fork-tail design for years. This configuration will generate the most fluttering action while displacing a lot of water.

Other possibilities include large single-tail versions that yield a very tight vibration. The Mr. Twister and Yamamoto grubs for example exemplify this prominent whip-tail trailer. There are also flat-tail grubs such as Haddock's Split Tail, lifelike crawdads and lizards, assorted plastic worms, and even tube baits like the Fatzee that can be used as jig trailers.

Still another bait that has been drawing a lot of attention along the tournament trail is the craw worm. This unique lure combines the best features of both a crayfish and a worm. It can be used as a sensational trailer and can be super potent when the bass are foraging on crawdads.

Skirting Materials

The live rubber skirt featuring multiple thin, rubber band-like tentacles is probably the most popular combination teamed with pork rind baits. The pros feel that this type of skirt fishes fairly well throughout the year, and especially in warmer water. The rubber seems to respond very well in water over 55 degrees with the skirt pulsating as the jig is moved along. Plastic trailers such as worms, imitation crayfish, and lizards also combine well with the live rubber skirt.

As live rubber-skirted jigs have proliferated, vinyl-skirted jigs have become less popular. However, some old-time tournament bassers are still absolutely convinced that vinyl-skirted jigs are the best for cold-water conditions. Fished in conjunction with either a pork rind or plastic trailer, the vinyl resembles a crawdad slowly raising its claws in its last line of defense.

Bucktail jigs seem to be even rarer than vinyl skirted models. Some tournament anglers with a lot of savvy persist in throwing the bucktail versions when they want a slick-looking bait. Fished with either a pork rind or a plastic worm trailer, the bucktail jig can be outstanding when a sensuous, slow presentation is in order. Deer hair breathes well at all temperatures. Most color combinations used with bucktail jigs cater to the crawdad tones: browns, blacks, and purples. A real "sleeper" is a white bucktail jig with corresponding white worm trailer. It can be a "killer" when the bass are keying in on threadfin shad, and the bass want a lure with a very soft vibration.

Plastic skirts including Yamamoto's have been quietly producing some remarkable results in tournament circles across the country. The most popular combination is to use a plastic skirt with a double-tail grub trailer. Yamamoto's baits best exemplify this type of jig. It is estimated that more tournaments have been won in the West on Spyder Jigs than all other lures combined!

Haddock Lures of Torrance, California has taken the plastic skirt-trailer design one step further. Using injection-molding technology, they have come up with a plastic jig body that has the skirt and thorax section of the critter formed into a single unit. This lure, called the Kreepy Krawler, has enjoyed considerable popularity in Southwestern tournament circles. You can pitch, flip, or swim this lure. The Kreepy Krawler has been a terror on such lakes as Roosevelt in Arizona or New Mexico's Elephant Butte Reservoir.

Plastic jig skirts can also be matched with worm trailers when less dynamic swimming action is desired. A "hot" secret bait for Alabama spotted bass, for example, is to use a black and chartreuse spider skirt with a "mean green" Super Float Worm. Similarly, plastic skirts can be used with pork rind for some sensational flippin' action. Because of the huge array of unique colors available in these skirts, shallow water fishermen have been able to customize a whole new generation of "pig'n jig" baits. It is important at times to be a little experimental, particularly with this flippin' approach. Too often even the most seasoned bassers get stuck into a rut, flippin' the basic black, brown, and purple patterns to shallow water targets.

Jig Head Design

Interestingly, the shape of the lead head itself can be essential to jig performance. For example, the popular banana head is made to be fished in scattered rock, brush, or riprap or when you are flippin' or pitchin'. The narrow profile permits this jig to be slid or shaken through the underwater obstructions.

In contrast, some jig heads are designed to be sort of bulldozed along the bottom. The unique barrel or football style is very suitable for maintaining maximum contact when fishing deep on more rocky bottoms and ledges especially those found in western desert lakes.

Other lead heads are designed as compromises for both bottom-bouncing and hopping through the brush. The spade head is very versatile as it stands up at on angle at rest. This also has the effect of making the jig trailer protrude up off the bottom, tantalizingly waving back and forth in the underwater current.

Brush Guards

An overlooked component of the jig is the type of brush guard selected. These devices serve to limit the lure from getting snagged. To begin with, understand that the best hook penetration will be with a jig fished with an open hook without a brush guard. Over water with minimal rock and brush and a fairly smooth bottom, you're better off working the jig with an exposed hook. However, if the jig seems to be getting hung up too frequently, then there are a variety of options to consider. Remember that the more protection provided by the brush guard, the more difficult it will be to set the hook.

Nylon bristle guards are widely sold with many commercially made jigs. The trick in using this type of guard is to compress the bristles down a few times, passing them through the hook, before using the jig. Sometimes the bristles are too stiff, with a residue of glue. This little tip makes the nylon more pliable, while maximizing hook penetration.

Polypropylene guards look like a small piece of rope extending over the hook eye of the jig. This material is much softer and more malleable in contrast to the nylon bristles. The secret here is to "fan out" the polypropylene. The more the polypropylene is spread out, the greater the potential for a hook set but, at the same time, the weedless capability of the jig correspondingly decreases. Also, by fanning out the polypropylene, you can make the jig displace more water and, hence, drop slower.

The Y-guard is composed of a moderately stiff, Y-shaped piece of nylon. This type of brush guard offers modest protection, while providing fairly good hook-setting potential. It is excellent for fishing in broken rock or scattered brush.

Two other more unusual brush guards are also occasionally used by accomplished jig fishermen. The wire guard is constructed from a fine strand of wire bent into a diamond shape. This guard is fairly flexible and works best in light cover. A mono guard consists of a thick piece of 20 pound (+) monofilament molded into the jig head then looped back into the plastic body of the trailer. It is

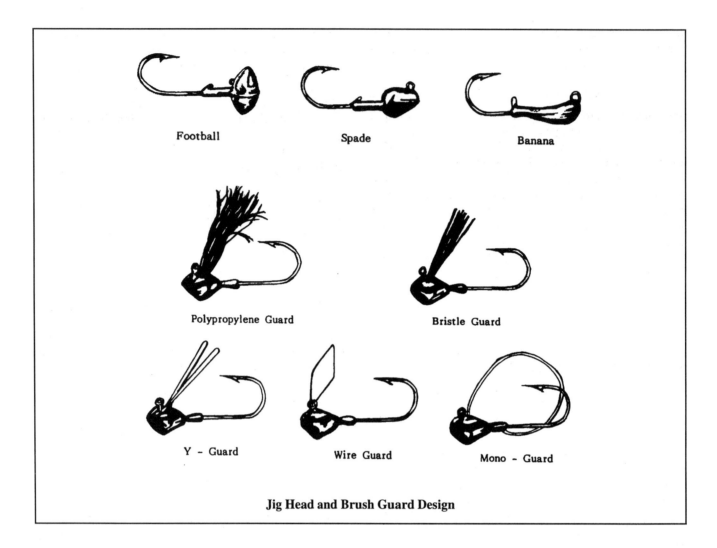

Football   Spade   Banana

Polypropylene Guard   Bristle Guard

Y - Guard   Wire Guard   Mono - Guard

Jig Head and Brush Guard Design

also very flexible and provides for excellent hook penetration with light, plastic jigs.

Finally, a recent innovation has been marketed by Gary Garland of Canyon Lures. Garland has designed a special brush guard made from super soft plastic tubing. His "stick guard," as he terms it, fits over the jig eye on one end. Then the hook is carefully embedded into the hollow portion of the other end of the guard. Upon the hook set, the point quickly drives through the soft plastic for excellent penetration. The stick guard is particularly effective with light line or jigs fished over deep structure when a fast hook set is imperative.

What About Hooks?

The lead head portion of the jig is cast around either a wire or a forged hook. This subtle difference can also be a significant factor in selecting the right jig for specific conditions.

For example, wire hooks can be honed to needle-point sharpness. Ease of penetration is increased with this type of hook, particularly when combined with lighter 8 to 12 pound monofilament. On the other hand, if you are flippin' in dense wooded cover, for example, a forged hook is better. This style is considerably stronger than the wire hook and will not stress or bend with heavier 15 to 30 pound line. In contrast, a forged hook is a little more difficult to sharpen and to drive home into the fish, especially if you use light monofilament.

So, when it comes to choosing a jig, those with wire hooks are better for open water and light lines. Forged hooks are more suitable for fishing thick cover, stalking large fish, and when using heavier lines.

Also, the open gap portion of the hook is important to examine when picking the right jig. This is the space formed between the point and the shark of the hook. Most pros try to fish with as large a gap that they can get away and still keep the jig fairly weedless. The wider the gap, the better "bite" you get when you drive the hook home into the bass' hard mouth.

Be Creative with Jigs!

As you can see, there can be a lot of calculated reasoning that goes into proper jig selection. These lures are incredibly versatile and not too complicated to master. However, it is important to be a little imaginative and creative at times when fishing jigs. Bass fishing is not an exact science. Too often recreational bassers—and to a certain extent, serious bassers too—can become too conservative, sticking with historically proven lure choices. There is an extensive range of combinations that can be considered in using these simple lures. Trailers, skirting material, different head designs, and brush guards are available in so many different options. The possibilities are virtually unlimited when selecting a jig for your specific needs.

Deep Structure Jigging

This style of bassin' requires stiffer baitcasting rods in medium-heavy to heavy actions. It will take some backbone in the rod to get a solid hook set at depths over 20 feet. A high-speed casting reel is also a boon to this vertical approach. Bass will tend to sometimes skyrocket up from the depths once the hook is set. A reel with a fast gear ratio will pick up slack line quickly.

Let's focus then on some of the ways to utilize these lures to pattern bass holding on deep structure.

Plastic vs. Pork

It is important to decide between a pork rind and plastic trailer in putting together a jig for the vertical game. There are pros and cons to each material.

Most bassers prefer the plastic jig due to the great diversity of skirts and tails that are available. Popular models include Yamamoto Hula Grub, Spyder, Canyon Lure's Cap'N Gown, and the Haddock Kreepy Krawler. All of these baits are sold in a variety of shades. Stay with the lighter colors such as smoke/sparkle, clear, or firecracker if you want the jig to imitate a threadfin shad minnow. Shift to darker patterns like brown, black, purple, or pumpkin/pepper to replicate a crawdad.

Plastic jigs in this genre also are excellent to load up with Berkley Strike fish attractant. The bass at these depths can be highly lethargic and finicky feeders. With a jig worked slowly, strikes may be induced more readily with the application of scent. The Berkley Strike can be squeezed onto the plastic skirts at the head portion of the bait. In the case of the Haddock Kreepy Krawler, apply the scent along the ribbed thorax.

This style of jig also has tremendous fluttering action. The movement of the twin-tail section generates considerable water displacement and vibration. Bass will frequently home in on a plastic jig to investigate all the commotion from the plastic tail-swimming action, especially when they are feeding on shad minnows.

Pork, on the other hand, does not have any of the built-in action exemplified by plastic jigs. It does, however, have a more natural texture. This factor may also help hook-shy bass hold onto the jig longer than they would with a plastic model.

Most anglers fish the standard #11 Uncle Josh or Strike King Bo-Hawg "frog." For deep-water vertical jigging, consider some other options. For example, a worm-like silhouette such as Uncle Josh's U-3 Split-tail Eel can be very sensuous when worked in a vertical presentation. These baits can be "shaken" in the same manner you would when doodling a worm.

Jig Heads, Hooks, and Skirts

In working a jig over vertical structure, practically any head design will work. Try a football, barrel, spade, or banana-head shape—whatever you have the most confidence in. However, be somewhat more selective when it comes to hooks.

For the vertical format, you will be typically fishing deep. This translates into a lot of potential line stretch, "pressure" bites, and invariably, lost fish. These problems are inherent in this style of structure fishing.

Choose jigs with fine wire hooks. These hooks are lighter than the forged version used when flippin'. Granted, the fine wire is not as strong as a forged hook, but it will take a sharper point. In a vertical presentation, the jig will be dragged less through obstructions and dense cover such as occurs in a shallow water program. Thus, it is not too important that the hook be super strong. It is more critical that you get a good hook set at depths over 20 feet. Use a carefully sharpened wire hook when it comes to vertical structure jigs.

Skirting material is again a matter of personal preference. Most pros overwhelmingly prefer live rubber or plastic skirts. An even smaller minority throws bucktail models, though this can be a real "sleeper" at times. The deer hair sort of gently "sashays" in the water with the slightest rod action. This can be quite seductive in a vertical presentation.

Deep-Water Tactics

There are four basic strategies you can employ when working jigs over deep structure: crawlin', shakin', yo-yoing or bangin'.

Crawlin'. This technique involves throwing the jig out from deep-water towards a shallow incline. (This could be the bank or a ledge.) The trick is to slowly inch the bait all the way back to the boat. We emphasize S-L-O-W-L-Y.

Crawlin' entails absolutely no erratic motion imparted to the bait. Instead, you must make the jig slowly nudge through every piece of underwater cover on its way back to the boat. Don't be surprised if you get bit as you begin to reel the bait in as it moves directly under the boat. Bass will sometimes "snap" at the jig as it begins to leave the bottom, sensing that the errant critter is about to get away.

Shakin'. This is a more vertical tactic than crawlin'. The jig can be fished almost completely straight up and down. It is similar to the doodlin' method. The angler simply employs a series of rhythmic twitches with the rod tip to make the jig erratically dance and dart through and around the structure.

With this strategy be prepared for pressure bites. The bass will often become aggravated with the jumping jig and literally inhale it. At greater depths, this may take the form of dull resistance on the end of the line. There will be minimal obstructions to contend with in a vertical pattern. So if you feel any sense of "pressure," swing and set—it's probably a fish!

Yo-yoing. In this situation, the fisherman can utilize the jig similar to a spoon. The object is to use a modest lift-and-drop action with the rod to make the jig rise and flutter vertically over structure. Yamamoto's Double-Tail jig is one of our favorites. We rarely use pork rinds for yo-yoing.

Expect most of your strikes to occur on the "fall" as the bait swims back down to the bottom. Be aware that the "strike" may be signaled by only a little "tick" in the line as the fish eats the jig with slack mono on the drop.

As with spoonin', it is not uncommon for the bass to intercept the bait as it glides to the bottom following the initial drop with the reel in free spool. Here too, the strike may be quite subtle—sometimes evidenced by sudden slack in the line.

Bangin'. This method was pioneered by Western pros who wanted to fish jigs ultra deep on large impoundments like Mead, Mojave, Elephant Butte, and Roosevelt. The secret to bangin' involves using extraordinarily heavy jigs. Like those used in saltwater, the lead head sometimes weighs up to 1 ounce.

The heavier lead head gets the jig down quickly and helps to maintain constant contact with the bottom. It also serves another important purpose. Working vertical structure, the pros have found that if they give the heavy jig some sharp twitches with the rod tip, it will "bang" into the submerged rocks and brush. The extra weight in the jig head generates considerable noise as the bait "bangs" into the structure. Lethargic bass holding deep are thus attracted to the commotion and often strike. The bangin' technique has proven successful, remarkably to depths approaching 90 feet!

Patience and Perseverance

Deep structure jigging is an art. It is not a simple strategy to master. It will take considerable practice with good equipment, premium line, and sharp hooks. It will also require confidence in the program and a good knowledge of using electronics in locating structure. Bass holding on structure at these greater depths are not commonly aggressive feeders. They can be enticed to bite. You must employ a meticulous well-thought-out presentation to generate strikes. Above all, considerable patience and perseverance is required to refine jigging over vertical structure. The number one item in deep jig fishing is boat control over the structure. If you are off 5 feet your odds for success go way down. It takes many years of practice to become a successful deep-water bass fisherman.

Swim the Jig[1]

Most recreational bass fishermen perceive jigs as slow, bottom-plodding lures. Without a doubt, when the fish are in a more lethargic slow-down state, a jig methodically inched along the bottom can be a potent bait.

These simple lures should not be overlooked when the bass appear to be in a more active feeding mode. Shrewd serious bassers often see this as an opportunity to literally "swim" the jig.

Let's take a closer look at some of the more specific techniques the pros use when swimming these baits to approach more aggressive fish.

Types of Swimming Jigs

Technically speaking, almost any kind of jig can be utilized in a swimming capacity. The most popular is the pig'n jig and double-tail model. This skirted lead head with a pork rind trailer was indeed designed as a slow bottom-grabbing bait. However, there are times, particularly in the late spring, when a faster moving jig in this genre can be deadly.

[1] Portions of this section previously appeared in *Bassmaster Magazine*

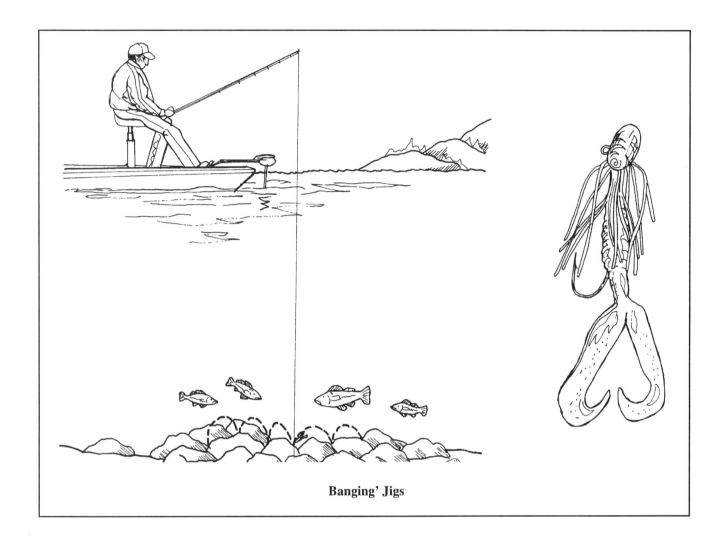

Banging' Jigs

To convert the basic #11 Uncle Josh Pork Frog into a swimming lure, take scissors or knife and carefully make a cut from the intersection of the two "legs" all the way up into the pork pad. Now the legs will have more of a paddling action, replicating a fast fleeing crawdad.

To increase the swimming action further, make another lateral incision across the pad, being careful not to cut all the way through the "frog." This creates a hinged effect that allows it to flutter faster behind the lead head. Run you knife across the pork pad from the side, actually trimming the pad down to half its original thickness. This will make the pig'n jig even lighter, allowing it to move with less restriction.

Other straight-tail jigs such as bucktails and lead heads with plastic tube bait trailers should also be considered for a faster moving presentation. Sometimes the bass will prefer either the overall silhouette or more subtle action of one of these baits as it glides through the water when used as a "swimmer."

Similarly, jigs constructed from plastic worm trailers also excel as swimming baits. The long-time favorite out West is made by adding half of a Superfloater worm behind a lead head with either a plastic or vinyl skirt. The trick, however, is to slice the worm portion almost in two, making a cut from the tail, stopping at the base of the jig hook. By doing this, the tail of the bait will again have a swimming scissors-like motion as the lure is "pumped" through the water.

The most obvious swimming jigs are those featuring either a single curl-tail or double fork-tail plastic trailer. The more aerodynamic design of plastic jigs such as Yamamoto's Hula Grub or Mr. Twister and Haddock's Kreepy Krawler generate terrific fluttering action underwater.

On some occasions, the bass will key in on the greater vibration and water displacement from swimming a lead head with a prominent curl-tail grub behind it. At other times, the more subtle fluttering action of a double fork-tail jig swimming over underwater structure triggers the most strikes.

With regard to selecting the proper swimming jig, the choices are varied. You can use dark-colored pork rind and bucktail, along with similar shades in plastic trailers to simulate crawdads. Shift to lighter patterns such as salt and pepper, smoke/sparkle, or clear "firecracker" to rep- licate shad minnows. A sometimes forgotten, but still potent option, is to use a white bucktail. With a quick twitch of the rod tip, you can make this jig sashay through the water, mimicking a wounded threadfin shad.

Regardless of which jig material you elect to try, you may have to scale down the size of the lead head you are using if you want it to "swim." For instance, a customized pork frog will appear more lifelike when it is being retrieved if you stay with a 1/4 to 1/2 ounce jig. The heavier head on a small compact trailer will likewise drag the bait down too quickly and thus eliminate a more subtle swimming action particularly on the fall.

Along this same vein, consider using lighter monofila- ment when swimming a jig. Heavier 12 to 20 pound test line is fine for pitching to thick shoreline cover or flippin', but it may impede the delicate swimming action of the bait. Lighter 8 to 10 pound mono will let the jig swim with minimal drag or resistance. Again this can be especially helpful in generating strikes as the lure sinks.

Ways to Swim the Jig

If the bass appear to be in a more active state, there is a good chance they will attack a swimming jig. Here are some of the key methods the pros have devised to fish the bait in this manner.

On Suspended Bass. This is an excellent situation in which to swim the jig. Frequently, the fish may be sus- pended in say, 15 to 40 feet of water. It is often difficult to maintain a steady depth with a deep-diving crankbait. In addition, the large silhouette of these magnum-size plugs may spook schools of hook-shy suspended bass. The jig, on the other hand, presents a far less imposing morsel to these fish.

As with crankplugs, you can manipulate the jig so that it swims through a multitude of strike zones. By simply counting down the bait as it sinks, then retrieving it through various depths, you will be able to key in on the different strata the fish are holding at without changing lures.

You can swim the jig through suspended bass in a variety of ways. One favorite is the simple stop-and-go retrieve. After you count the jig down to the desired depth, start reeling at a steady pace back to the boat. Every so often, stop winding completely. Let the jig sink a few seconds, then start the retrieve again. Invariably, the bass will hit the bait as it begins to slowly flutter down right after you stop.

Another ploy is to sort of "pump" the jig back to the boat. To do this, lift the rod up to about the 11 o'clock

14 Pounder on a Hair Jig

position and drop it back parallel to the water and follow the bait with a tight line. Wind until the line is taunt. Touch bottom, then lift the rod up again. This "pumping" action makes the jig swim in a rising-and-falling motion, simulating an erratic wounded minnow. Be sure and let the jig hit bottom between pumps. The key to this method is to keep in mind that most bites occur on the descent.

Over Ledges. Deep structure experts rely heavily on swimming jigs working underwater ledges. Serious bassers always look for "shade breaks" as prime territory for swimming a jig. Cast your jig out towards a light-colored ledge that has dark water on its edges. Then let the jig hit the bottom, and crank fast, with maybe 5 to 6 turns of the reel handle to make it speed up off the bottom. Come to a dead stop and follow your line as the jig glides back down towards the bottom. This really triggers the strikes! We estimate that 75 percent of the strikes are on the fall. The bass sees the jig moving fast, picks up the vibration, then runs right into it as the retrieve stops and the bait starts to sink. This method also works well on suspended bass and along long underwater flat points.

We recommend a similar ploy when prospecting down an ultra-steep staircase bank. In this situation, we prefer a heavier 1/2 to 1 ounce lead head. Try to swim the jig off this kind of bank at a 45 degree angle then rip it up real quick. We like to do this on a deep bank over an outside point. If we don't get bit, we quickly move onto the next ledge. The key is not to pick up the slack at all. You need the slack to let the jig descend to the next level. The fish will be either on top, mid-range, or on the bottom. You will soon be able to isolate the zone where the bass are with the swimming jig—this works great in winter and summer!

Steep Walls and Banks. We have also noticed that there are times when it pays to fish vertical rocky walls by swimming a jig. In this situation, we prefer a double-tail plastic trailer, but a well-trimmed pork frog will also be effective.

While moving down the bank quickly pitch the jig up against the face of the wall. It is important to let the bait slowly sink, but the trick is to maintain a relatively taunt line. Many strikes will occur on the fall as the jig swims down the face of the wall. If the line is too loose, you will be late in detecting the strike—or miss it completely.

After the jig swims down approximately half way to the bottom, reel it quickly back up to the surface. Large expansive rocky walls can be easily covered with this vertical swimming tactic. Some rocky walls feather this staircase terrain. Be prepared to "walk" the jig down this staircase ledge formation, resting at each level for a moment.

The Yo-Yo. On occasion an even more dramatic vertical presentation will produce when working a swimming jig over deep structure. In this context, the Bassmaster can utilize the jig in a manner similar to a spoon. By raising and lowering the rod tip, the lure will "jump" off the bottom and flutter down, representing a wounded baitfish or frantic crawdad. Always be prepared for strikes on the fall when practicing this lift-and-drop strategy with a jig.

7 Pounder on a Rubber Jig

Yo-yoing in this fashion can be highly effective when you are able to pinpoint clusters of bass holding on a deep outside ledge or submerged pinnacle, tree, or brush pile.

Over Limbs and Brush. Working a swimming jig, preferably a banana-head shape design with brush guard, through submerged tree limbs and brush requires somewhat more expertise than using these baits over deep structure. The crucial aspect of swimming a jig through this kind of cover is to watch for deflections. Without letting the bait touch the bottom, retrieve it steadily through the maze of brush or limbs. The instant it makes contact with the structure, let it gently fall off to the edge.

Usually this act of deflection stimulates the bass into eating the jig. Presumably, the bait appears to be wounded and hence vulnerable to attack when it starts to fall following impact with structure. We should point out that you should not necessarily expect a spectacular strike when the fish hits the swimming jig in this scenario. Instead, be prepared for a quick subtle "tick" or just pressure in the line signaling the strike.

Working Current. One of the most often overlooked places to use a swimming jig is in a river, canal, or culvert where there is flowing water. As a rule, the bass will typically be facing upstream, waiting for the current to push bait to them. Thus, it is usually best to work a downstream drift.

Cast the jig upstream, ahead of the fish and let it drift down with the current. It is imperative to give the bait enough slack line to drift naturally in the flow. However, if the line is too loose, the jig may sink to the bottom and hang up. You must maintain the bare amount of tension on the line to keep the lure from snagging as well as being able to discern the strike.

Depending upon the current, use a 1/4 to 3/8 ounce lead head for the "gliding" jig and a 1/2 to 3/4 ounce for the bottom-bouncing variety. The weight of the jig is clearly more important in establishing a pattern when fishing current then is the type of trailer utilized. Both pork and soft plastic jigs perform equally well in the current.

Swim Those Jigs!

Whenever you sense that the bass are in an active feeding phase, consider swimming a jig instead of tossing a crankplug or spinnerbait. These lures have tremendous versatility. What you choose to "swim" is mostly an issue of what you have confidence in rather than what the fish prefer. You can pick from pork rind, bucktail, soft plastic single and curl-tail grubs, or modified worm-trailers. Try to match these in terms of size and color with indigenous forage baits. Customize the trailers as needed to generate more tail action from these baits. When the bass are on the move, serious bassers realize that it is time to "swim the jig"!

Tune Your Jigs

As we have noted, a jig can be divided into three basic components: 1) the lead head, 2) the skirting material, and 3) the trailer body. Each of these parts can be "fine tuned," so to speak, to dramatically improve the overall effectiveness of the lure.

Here then, are some of the things you can do to perfect each of the three basic parts of a jig.

Lead Heads

Mike and Ron feel that the lead jig head is actually the most integral part of the bait. The shape, weight, weed guard, and hook that comprise the lead head may significantly effect the performance of the lure.

To begin with, the seasoned basser will carefully sharpen the hooks on these baits to needle-point perfection. Penetration is enhanced dramatically if the jig hook is pre-sharpened whether you are shallow water flippin', or draggin' a jig over deep structure.

Next, if some sort of weed guard is built into the lead head, it should be examined closely before you fish the jig. Sometimes, for instance, the polypropylene brush guard is matted down too much near the shank of the hook. It will thus have to be lifted slightly so the bait is able to brush by obstructions.

If you feel the bass will prefer a jig that falls slowly through the water, it might be best to spread open the polypropylene weed guard creating a fan-like effect. This will add more resistance to the jig as it moves through the water, resulting in a slow-sinking bait. When the weed guard is fanned out, a certain amount of weedlessness is lost.

Similarly, the nylon strands of a bristle guard frequently may be stuck together because excessive glue or enamel may have been used in assembling the jig. In this case, the bristles must be carefully spread open and out somewhat to increase the weedlessness of the bait.

Sometimes weed guards extend back past the hook. The jig is now almost too weedless so that penetration is difficult with more subtle bites. The bass may strike the bait, but the long weed guard doesn't compress down far

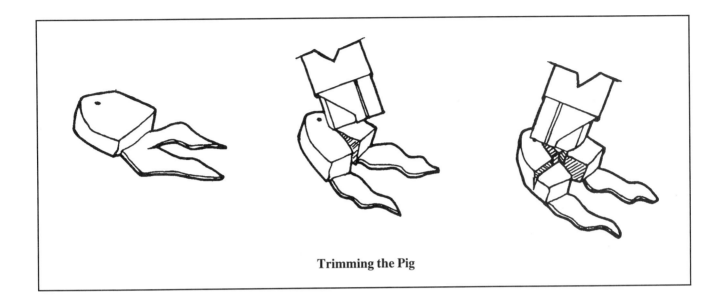

Trimming the Pig

enough to allow the hook to dig in. In this situation, the accomplished jig fisherman may actually cut a portion of the weed guard off to enhance the potential for a quick effective hook set.

You can also carefully "shave" the lead head, removing small amounts of lead with a pocket knife. Perhaps you carry only 3/8 and 1/2 ounce jig heads in your tackle box, but discover the fish prefer a bait that is closer to 7/16 ounces. You can easily shave that amount of lead off one of your 1/2 ounce jig heads.

Occasionally you may want to create a narrower, more sleek-looking lead head than the one currently in your tackle box. Here again, you can simply shave some of the lead off the stock jig heads to create your own custom slim design. This little ploy often works perfectly when you need a narrower lead head that will penetrate through grass or brush more easily than a bulkier more traditional shape.

Skirting Material

The bucktail, vinyl, plastic, or live rubber that is used to form the skirt of the jig gives the lure its silhouette. The most frequent thing the veteran bass pro does to these skirts is to inspect their overall length. This is done by turning the lead head upside down and examining how the skirt hangs around the heads. This will give you an idea of how the skirt looks to the bass as it flares out underwater.

Next, take scissors and trim the skirt back so it barely reaches the point of the hook. If the skirt is too long as it often is with many commercially sold jigs, the fish will have a tendency to short-strike the bait, often missing the hook entirely.

It is also important to make sure all the strands of soft plastic, vinyl, or live rubber are not sticking together. The strands should be carefully separated so that at rest they flare out to generate that lifelike "breathing" effect.

You might also consider adding a find strand of reflective mylar to the skirt by either wrapping it on with thread or gluing it to the lead head. The mylar material is sold at fly-tying shops. It will give a subtle "flash" to otherwise dull vinyl, live rubber, or bucktail jig skirts, providing you with a seldom-seen customized lure.

Mike and Ron break off a small piece of plastic worm and thread it onto the shaft of the jig hook. This gives the lure more body instead of having only the bare wire shaft surrounded by the skirting material. A colorful chunk of plastic on the hook shaft also adds some contrast to otherwise bland-looking brown, purple, or black lead heads and skirts. This ploy works especially well with a pig'n jig combination. The small piece of plastic helps the pork rind trailer to lie flat in the water instead of bunching up on the shaft of the hook.

Trailer Bodies

Plastic jig trailers are overwhelmingly the easiest component to work with. They can be mixed or matched with either vinyl, bucktail, soft plastic, or live rubber skirts.

The main concern in using plastic trailers is that they are laced onto the lead head so that precise symmetry is maintained. In my own guiding experiences, for example, we have watched novice clients quickly thread a fork-tail plastic trailer onto the jig head. They frequently disregard details like making certain the trailer is not bunched up on the hook. They may not take the time to insure that the hook is threaded directly onto the center of the trailer body so that the jig swims perfectly straight on the retrieve.

Some soft plastic trailers are too large for a particular lead head and skirt combo. The remedy is to cut off a portion of the trailer body. This will also shorten up the overall length of the lure. Otherwise, you may encounter many short-strikes as the bass nips at a trailer situated too far from the hook.

As was mentioned with skirting material, you can also adjust the fall of the jig by increasing or decreasing the size of the trailer. This holds true for both soft plastic and pork rind jig trailers. A larger trailer will reduce the speed of the jig as it sinks. A more compact trailer will increase the speed of the fall.

In contrast to pork rind trailers, the soft plastic versions will often have a tendency to slide down the shaft of the hook. A simple trick is to Super Glue the plastic trailer to the lead head.

These are only a few of the possible ways Mike and Ron prepare jigs for serious bassin'. These are terrific all-season lures. They are relatively inexpensive and simple to master. The trick is to keep your jigs "tuned." Many of the biggest bass tallied each year are caught on these popular baits!

Tenderize Pork

Serious bassers who routinely use pork rind jig trailers commonly prefer to customize their baits. Certainly, the pork rind packed in the factory jars will catch its share of fish. Still, many pros feel that by altering the factory stock baits they will gain an edge over other fishermen throwing pork.

We have been using another more "scientific" approach to generate a similar effect. We will take pork rind directly from the jar and place it on a rock tumbler. This device is used by rock hounds to smooth and polish semi-precious stones. The tumbler thoroughly "tenderizes" the pork, making it exceptionally malleable.

As an added bonus, when pork rind has been "customized" with either cuts or through tumbling, it also becomes more porous. This is important when fish attractants are added to this bait. The liquid scents will seep into the grooves or into the softer texture. These attractants will stay in the customized pork longer than in the harder factory stock rinds.

Coloring the Pig

Along with the concern for proper texture and flexibility, Mike and Ron prefer to custom color their pork. There are numerous little tricks you can try.

We firmly believe that pork rind baits straight out of the jar are typically too saturated with color dye. An "insider's" favorite color is a purplish-blue tint that is not available from any of the manufacturers. Take white pork with green dots—frog color—out of the jar. Rinse it off with water, then take equal numbers of purple and blue pork and do the same thing with them. Put them all in a jar with just water in it—just enough to cover the pork. Set it out in the sun for a couple of days. The color comes out of the purple and blue and goes into the frog-colored baits making an off-blue with spots on it. This is a terrific color in the spring.

Another simple coloration trick is worth mentioning here. Take solid white pork trailers. Leave them in the saline solution. Add varying amounts of Rit Dye to different jars to create a panorama of unique shades. Write down how much dye went into each jar. When you find a particular batch that seems to work especially well, you can then duplicate the blend by referring to your notes. Or heat a pot of water—don't boil it. Add the Rit Dye and let the pork rind soak until you reach the desired shade. Remove the pork and rinse in cold water to set dye in the bait.

Rig It Right

Most recreational anglers remove the pork from the jar and simply impale it on a hook. The pros on the other hand will spend a little more time scrutinizing the bait, making sure it is hooked correctly.

When it comes to frog-shaped baits, there is an ongoing debate whether to hook the pork with the pad up or pad down. The best jig fishermen believe the pad should ride down. In this way the pork rind "legs" or tails wave up higher off the bottom and their movement is less restricted.

Be Pig Creative!

Pork rind trailers have enjoyed phenomenal success under a full gamut of conditions. As frequently happens with any "hot" bait, the bass can become conditioned to the same basic offerings.

The manufacturers are continually introducing new, innovative designs and colors in pork rind trailers. Be experimental and try some of these other shapes, shades and textures as an alternative to the basic frog, lizard, or eel. Keep an assortment of pork handy at all times, adding trailers to spinnerbaits and spoons as well as to various jigs.

Pork rind is an extraordinary offering—one of the few baits that come remarkably close to natural prey. Use it often—all year long!

Serious Soft Plastics

Serious Soft Plastics

Across the country it is safe to say that upwards of 90 percent of the bass caught are tallied on some sort of soft plastic bait. The basic worm still leads the parade among this collection of lures because of its wide range of seasonal applications and overall versatility.

In recent years, tournament pros, guides, and other serious bass fishermen have had to devise more innovative strategies when using these worms and their various cousins in the soft plastic category, especially under tough conditions. Here then, is a concise survey of some of the more interesting ways these anglers have found to use soft plastics to consistently put fish in the live wells.

Suspending Worms

Many of the plastic worms sold today have a certain amount of natural buoyancy. Some are enhanced with hundreds of tiny air bubbles injected into the plastic. When bass suspend off the bottom, however, almost any plastic worm can be rigged to reach these fish, irrespective of its built-in buoyancy. The trick is to lace it onto the styrofoam jig head, as we previously discussed, and fish it Carolina-style, trailing behind a 3/16 to 5/8 ounce bullet sinker. (The same simplified crimping technique we mentioned for the Do-Nothing rig will also work with the floating jig head.)

The styrofoam jig head will float most worms off the bottom into the suspended fish. Interestingly, the bass will frequently strike this open-hook bait while it remains practically motionless following a pause in the retrieve. The open-hook feature of the jig head diminishes the worm's weedless quality to some degree. It also encourages better hook sets on light line in deep water.

Swimming Worms

Mike and Ron like to employ darter head technology in the tournament ranks. These ultralight, 1/16 to 1/4 ounce tiny lead heads are teamed with small 2 to 4 inch long plastic worms, fished on 4 to 8 pound line. These so-called "sissy baits" have been highly effective when shaken, twitched, or made to "swim" through offshore structure.

Tadpoles and Sculpins

West Coast worm manufacturers who specialize in the custom hand-poured process have begun to miniaturize their baits, scaling down even further from the popular 4 inch models. The object has been to create lures that may closely replicate other indigenous prey in these waters apart from either shad or crawdads.

The "Slinkee" mentioned in the chapter "Split-Shottin': The Next Generation" has indeed been an excellent alternative to the basic straight-tail worm. It excels when split-shotted, shakin' on a 1/8 to 1/4 ounce darter head over deep structure, or slowly crawled Texas-style behind a small 1/8 ounce bullet sinker with light line. It is a perfect replica of an immature tadpole.

When fishing Lake Castaic, a popular trophy bass reservoir near Los Angeles, lure inventor Brian Delashmutt stumbled upon another form of indigenous forage in the presence of sculpin that he was able duplicate with his custom hand-poured process.

Delashmutt then designed a series of 3 to 3 1/2 inch long baits that would replicate the sculpin population. His "Beaver-tails" and "Sculpin Tadpole" lures again utilize the head portion of a plastic worm with flat and tapered tail sections to appear more like a sculpin minnow. These two soft plastic lures have generated excellent results with the split-shot method.

Snakes

Now let's look at plastic worms at the other end of the spectrum. For years, some Southern bass fishermen have been fishing magnum-size 8 to 20 inch baits that are almost snake-like in appearance. Even with the heavy emphasis on "finesse" lures in the West, more and more serious bassers are throwing these big worms, looking for lunker-class fish.

On many occasions, we have watched highly successful lake locals, for instance, avoid the temptation to catch smaller tournament-size fish and instead concentrate on that one strike of the day that might produce a double-digit weight wallhanger.

While other anglers are catching "keepers" split-shottin' minuscule 2 to 4 inch hand-poured "weenie" style worms, they might prefer to S-L-O-W-L-Y crawl an 8 to 10 inch "snake" along the bottom looking for that double-digit Florida.

The secret is to inch the big worm slowly covering every little piece of structure on the bottom. Keep in mind that it may take a number of minutes to complete a single cast using these larger worms.

Tandem-Hook Worms

As we noted earlier, plastic worms featuring a rear "stinger" hook have been sold for a long time. For many years, most serious bassers scoffed at such lures as gimmickry or a "crutch" for anglers who couldn't catch fish on the basic Texas rig.

In the past few years, however, tournament pros and veteran guides across the country have "rediscovered" these worms as a highly effective lure for deep structure fishing.

Arizona pro Danny Westphal popularized this style of tandem-hook bait with his Westy Worms. Similarly, Dave Nollar of Redlands, California began experimenting by placing "stinger hooks" into simple Super Floaters threaded onto a 1/8 to 1/4 ounce lead head.

Westphal's lures soon became a staple for bass anglers fishing deep desert lakes while Nollar's innovation received considerable attention for its success at fooling

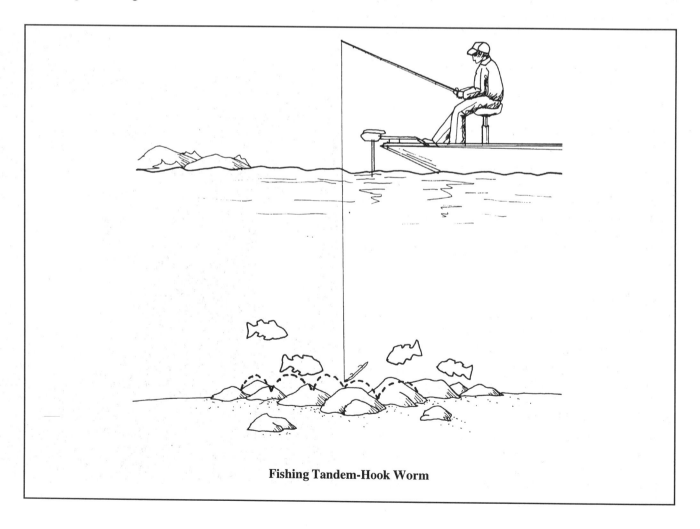

Fishing Tandem-Hook Worm

otherwise very temperamental world-class Alabama spotted bass at Lake Perris.

We feel it is necessary to mention this unique bait once more. In deep water the tandem-hook worm takes away the hook-setting problem and having to detect the strike. You can reel into the fish and set the hook with minimal effort when using this kind of worm. At the shallower depths, this worm allows you to feel even the lightest pick-up as many bass will often just strike the tail. So, especially with spotted bass, you may be able to nail fish that you otherwise wouldn't get without that rear hook. On the negative side, tandem-hook worms obviously won't work very well deep or shallow where there is a lot of cover.

Secret Lighting

For nighttime bassin', we have experimented with a rather unusual approach. Using a thicker-bodied 4 to 6 inch long plastic worm in either clear, smoke, or salt'n pepper shade, we carefully insert a small cylume light stick termed a Lunker Light into the thickest portion of a large plastic worm.

These tiny chemical light sticks are made for fishing and are similar to what is used in larger versions as emergency highway flares. As you gently break the stick, a chemical reaction begins which produces an eerie soft fluorescent light. Inside a plastic worm, this has the effect of making the bait practically "glow."

This little ploy can be particularly effective using plastic worms at night with either a Carolina rig or split-shot setup. You can also fish the "glowing" worm behind a styrofoam jig head for even greater buoyancy. Be prepared for strikes to occur as the worm suspends motionless off the bottom, "glowing" as you pause in the retrieve.

Noisy Worms

Bass anglers have experimented for years trying to make plastic worms more enticing to the fish by adding some sort of noise-making device to the bait.

The Clatter Weight made by Culprit takes this idea one step further. This sinker has a specially designed core to produce a subtle clattering sound, presumably imitating the noise generated by natural bait.

Similarly, Woodies Rattlers and Venom Glass Worm Rattles are miniature sound chambers designed to be conveniently inserted into a plastic worm. Shaking the bait with the rod tip will produce noise from the tiny pellets encapsulated in the plastic or glass chamber.

Most recently, some touring pros and guides began using brass rather than lead bullet weights with a faceted glass bead that comprises a doodlin' setup. Brass weights seem to be somewhat noisier underwater than lead weights when they are used with glass beads.

Pork Worms

As a final option, serious bassers who prefer to fish plastic worms might consider trying a pork rind version of these popular lures. The Uncle Josh Pork Worms are an unusual but intriguing bait. Not as popular as the common pork

4" Power Worm

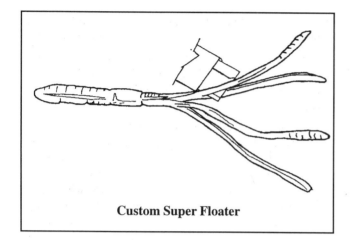

Custom Super Floater

frog series of jig trailers, the Pork Worm would appear to be an afterthought for most serious worm aficionados.

The fact remains that all bass species will attack a pork rind tipped lure. The natural taste and texture of this substance often trigger strikes when both hard and soft plastic offerings fail to get bit. The same holds true for natural pork rind baits shaped like a worm.

In colder water, in particular, Pork Worms will often get bit as the bass reluctantly "mouth" or "taste" the bait. They are an excellent alternative for S-L-O-W crawling with a Texas rig or used when flippin' on lethargic finicky fish.

Expand Your Wormin' Horizons

More anglers learn how to fish bass with plastic worms than any other lures. These baits are the foundation of the sport. However, don't get into a rut by staying with that same initial array of worms and strategies that you mastered at an early stage in your fishing career.

These are incredibly versatile, all-season lures. The designs and methods used to fish worms change more frequently than any other style of bait. The shrewd Bassmaster will expand his tackle repertoire to include these newer innovations to go beyond simple worms!

The Super Floater: A Special Case Study

One of the best-kept secrets in tournament circles has been the Super Floater. This plastic worm, manufactured by the Johnson Tackle Company, has had a remarkable life cycle of sorts.

There have been periods where consumer interest of this rather unspectacular worm has dwindled and manu-facturing has declined. The bait has actually been taken out of production three times in the past. Then, suddenly, word leaked out that some pro tallied a big limit with the Super Floater and consequently anglers started to hoard the remaining stock of these lures. Retailers in turn responded by requesting a new production run of the worm.

The Super Floater itself is a rather bland-looking, injection-molded bait. The basic worm is 4 or 6 inches long, made from fairly stiff plastic and designed with a straight, round tail. With all the interest in hand-poured, salt-impregnated, ultrasoft plastic worms, it's amazing that the simple Super Floater still catches fish and continues to have a following among hard-core bassers.

The secret to this worm is the air that is trapped in the plastic to give the bait extraordinary flotation. This feature, combined with some special customizing the pros do to the lure, accounts for the Super Floater's success.

Let's examine some of the inside tricks the Western pros employ to more effectively fish the "'Float."

The Straight Worm

The Super Floater crawled with the basic Texas rig can be fairly potent at times. With all the air in the plastic, the tail of the worm will stick up high off the bottom. This presumably provides the fish with the illusion of a crawdad rooting in the mud, rocks, or similar structure.

However, you can make the stock worm even more potent by slicing the tail portion up the middle. Take a sharp knife, razor blade, or scissors, and carefully slice the worm in half, starting from the tail to the base of the prominent sex collar.

Now, when you inch the 'Float along the bottom, the two half portions of the tail create a scissors-like effect. This resembles the claws of a crawdad raised in a stance of self-defense as the bass approaches.

This type of customization can be taken one step further. Carefully cut each of the two tail sections in half again, running your blade from the tip of the tail to the base of the sex band.

This creates four superthin tentacles. When the worm sits still, the four strands of plastic wave sensuously under water. This can be a deadly attractant when traditional plastic worm styles fail to produce.

Split-Shot the 'Float

The Super Floater is a terrific split-shot bait. Because of its exceptional buoyancy, the split-shot or Carolina setup allows the serious basser to effectively suspend the worm some distance above obstructions.

There is a subtle technique you can use for hooking that will improve your strike-catch ratio when split-shottin' the 'Float with light line. This worm is thick and tough. Hook penetration can be particularly difficult if you embed the point of the hook into the center of the bait. You will simply have too much stretch with light 4 to 8 pound test mono to drive the hook through the body of the lure.

Instead, gently "skin-hook" the Super Floater. Run the point of your worm hook off to the edge of the bait, barely under the outside layer of plastic. Use one of the new generation of fine needle-sharp worm hooks. Then, when you go to set with the light line, the hook will quickly pull through the thick plastic.

Super Floater Jigs

A long-time favorite with Mike and Ron is a jig constructed using a 4 inch Super Floater. Tournament veterans have been quietly using this jig for years when other anglers have opted for the more popular pork rind or plastic fork-tail models.

This lure is easy to construct. Take a four-inch 'Float and cut it across the bait to form two equal halves. Next, slice the almost the full length of each section, taking care to leave about 3/8 to 1/2 inch of the plastic in tact. (It

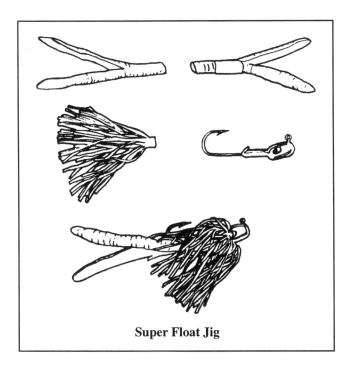

Super Float Jig

doesn't matter whether you start your cut from the thick or thin portion of each half. It works well either way.)

What you now have is two separate split-tail trailers made from a single 4 inch worm. Lace these short split-tails behind a lead head jig with either a soft plastic or vinyl skirt.

This custom-made jig is an excellent cold water bait, especially on lethargic fish. Largemouths, bronzebacks, and Alabama spotted bass have been caught on this lure. The trick is to fish it S-L-O-W. As you gently hop it on the bottom, the Super Floater tails rise up and twitch in a scissors-like fashion, mimicking a crawdad clacking its pinchers. Many early season trophies have been tallied with this jig on Western reservoirs by the pros who fish these instead of commercially sold baits.

A Year-Round Worm

The Super Floater is one of the most utilitarian lures you can add to your tackle repertoire. As a worm, it can be crawled, split-shotted, or flipped. Fish it shallow or deep with the special tandem-hook ploy. Cut it up to form seductive "tentacles" or use it as a jig trailer.

Experiment with this simple yet useful bait. Don't be totally enamored by the new wave of fancy hand-poured worms. Smart bassers always leave space in their tackle boxes for the 'Float.

The Remarkable Reaper

They say that "great things come in small packages." Well, this certainly seems to be the case with the minuscule soft plastic bait called the "reaper." Like the Super Floater, this simple little lure has been accounting for a lot of bass limits across the country.

This feather or leech-like lure measures 2 to 3 inches in length. It, too, is quite unspectacular looking and actually had its origins back over 25 years ago with the Mar-Lynn Tackle Company.

Then, in the last few years, local hand-pour manufacturers in California began to experiment with this Southern-bred bait and found that it produced remarkable results on typically deep, clear Western impoundments.

Now, with that word of its success out, the reaper (also sometimes known as a "reefer") is sold throughout the country by both hand-pour and injection-molded lure companies. So, why is this tiny bait so effective?

To begin with, the length and silhouette of the reaper closely matches the size of a threadfin shad minnow and small panfish found on many lakes. Secondly, the unhurried fluttering action that results when the reaper is worked S-L-O-W-L-Y, mimics the action of a dying baitfish.

Finally, because most serious bassers fish the reaper with extraordinarily light, 4 to 6 pound test monofilament, the potency of the lure is increased as even the most hook-shy bass become tempted by the little bait.

Let's take a look then at some popular ways to fish the reaper as well as some of the more obscure methods.

Split-Shottin'

The split-shot strategy Mike and Ron recommend is overwhelmingly the most common method for using the reaper. Serious 'shotters prefer a long 6 to 7 foot medium to light-medium action spinning rod and a spinning reel spooled with 4 to 10 pound, premium-grade Berkley Trilene XL or Select mono.

The simplest way to split-shot the reaper is to crimp a small lead shot about 18 to 36 inches above a #1 to #2 plastic worm hook. Worm aficionados will quickly note the rather small size hooks recommended for this soft plastic lure. Remember, the reaper is only 2 to 3 inches long.

Care must be taken when hooking the reaper. The worm hooks should be needle sharp and preferably made from light gauge wire. Most reapers have a certain amount of buoyancy that will be restricted if you thread it onto a heavy-duty worm hook. The ability of the bait to momentarily suspend dramatically enhances its effectiveness.

You will find that when you fish the gossamer monofilament there is a lot of line stretch. A softer rod tip helps to some degree to prevent inadvertently snapping the mono on the hook set as might happen with a more traditional stiffer wormin' rod. Also, try "skin-hooking" the reaper to improve instant hook penetration.

To do this, after beginning to Texas-rig the lure, gently re-embed the point of the hook into the side portion of the reaper instead of down the center. The point of the small worm hook should barely under the outer edge or "skin" of the bait. Now, when you go to set up on the bass, an easy sweep with the rod tip will generate enough force to drive the point through the soft plastic "skin" of the reaper, insuring a solid hook set.

We cannot emphasize enough how important it is to retrieve this lure in the S-L-O-W-E-S-T manner. Interestingly, many bass actually strike the reaper as it rests practically motionless following a pause in the retrieve. If you retrieve this bait too rapidly, it will spin and twist the line.

The so-called "strike" that commonly occurs while split-shottin' the reaper is usually nothing more than that dull mushy pressure we've mentioned before. However, there are times, especially when the lure is allowed to remain motionless, semi-suspended, that all of a sudden you may receive a startling jolt from a big bass that has literally inhaled the little bait.

A variation on the split-shot technique is to use a larger sinker butted to a swivel with an 18 to 36 inch length of leader attached. Instead of using a Texas rigging, switch to a floating styrofoam jig head with an exposed hook.

This is a basic Carolina setup and is used for fishing the reaper in deep water all the way down to 90 feet. The styrofoam jig head keeps the feather-like bait suspended well above the bottom. At greater depths underwater obstructions are minimized so the exposed hooking rarely snags, enhancing quick positive penetration.

Darters and P-heads with Reapers

Many bass anglers rely upon these miniature lead heads when conditions get tough. We have found that these heads also have tremendous application with the reapers. The darter heads in 1/16 to 1/4 ounce sizes are perfect teamed with a 2 to 3 inch long reaper and 4 to 10 pound test monofilament. Use this same setup for the p-head jig with the more rounded shape.

When rigged with a darter jig head, the reaper will dart from side to side on the fall. With the p-head, the bait will sink in more of a straight line. The broad tail design of the little bait flutters seductively as the jig and reaper combo falls. Always be prepared for strikes to occur as the reaper sinks.

You can either stop the tiny lead head midway to probe for suspended bass or let it hit the bottom. Throw the reel into gear as you gently and rhythmically twitch or shake the rod tip to make the lure dart and dance, replicating a frantic baitfish.

This type of vertical finesse bassin' requires a lot of patience and a high level of alertness. Frequently the fish will hit the reaper as it is being made to jump back and forth. The light mono may all of a sudden go slack then seem to slowly swim off to one side. Gather up the slack and quickly swing and set! This bait is so small and subtle, that combined with the minimal resistance of light line and soft tip rod, the bass may not even know it is hooked as it lazily swims off with the reaper.

As for colors, the most popular combination for reaper fishing is salt and pepper since it replicates shad minnows.

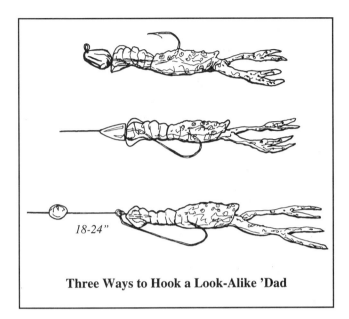

18-24"

Three Ways to Hook a Look-Alike 'Dad

Even with this pattern, there are distinct differences in the size, quantity, and color of glitter added to the clear-bodied bait. Some reapers, for example, will be clear, with chunky black flakes. Others are sold with red or silver flakes added. Day in and day out, some variation of this salt and pepper color combination will undoubtedly get bit in your favorite lake. Other colors to try are panfish colors or earth tone browns, pumpkin, and greens.

More Reaper Secrets

Reaper fishing is an art. Frequently many strikes are missed due to the way in which the bass often seem to "mouth" the bait. One way to improve your odds is to switch to a small #8 long-shank baitholder hook when split-shottin'.

This style of hook is used for live bait fishing with two small barbs on the shank. Carefully thread a reaper on the baitholder leaving the point totally exposed. The hook is so small it rarely gets hung up. When the bass mouths the bait, it practically sticks itself on the little baitholder hook.

Also try splitting the tail section of this minuscule lure. Create two, three, or four separate tails using a small pen knife or razor blade. As the reaper is motionless on the stop of a "stop-and-go" retrieve, the small tentacles will sashay about creating a most tantalizing morsel.

Finally, Mike and Ron feel that the effectiveness of the reaper is enhanced even more with the addition of Berkley Strike fish attractant. This finesse bait is commonly used when bassin' is toughest. Every few casts, coat the reaper with an ample amount of scent. The bass will hold onto this tiny lure for some time with this trick so that pressure bites are more easily detected.

Look-Alike 'Dads

No matter where you stalk bass, you will invariably find that the fish feed on crawdads. There are different species of this small crustacean across the country and all kinds of bass thrive on this key forage bait. Largemouth, small-mouth, and Alabama spotted bass rely upon crayfish as a major component of their natural diets.

In recent years there has been a rash of new and innovative imitation crawdads introduced into the bassin' market. These soft plastic replicas come in a variety of designs. Some, like Hale's Craw Worm and Berkley's Power Craw, are actually half worm, half crayfish. The front portion of these lures is tubular shaped, similar to a plastic worm. The rear section has pronounced claws. These pinchers tend to stand up when the lure is at rest. They give the illusion of a creature that is staging a line of last defense.

Other artificial 'dads such as Haddock's Kreepy Krawdad, Advanced Angler Technology's Billy's C-Dad, and Renosky's Superclaw are remarkably lifelike. They are carefully molded to look like the real McCoy.

Bass will attack a crayfish all year long. For this simple reason, these plastic replicas can prove to be a valuable addition to any basser's lure arsenal. There are, moreover, some distinctive methods that are highly effective in using look-alike 'dads.

Jiggin' 'Dads

Almost all of the crawdad-shaped lures can be utilized laced behind a lead head. Many veteran bass fishermen feel that a plastic jig will frequently outperform the more traditional pork rind trailer used in the popular pig'n jig combo. They claim this is particularly true in the summer months. Some anglers often mistakenly assume that bass stop feeding on crayfish following the spring spawn. However this is not true; bass feed on crawdads year-round.

The trick is to use a jig with more swimming action during hotter weather. Imitation 'dads perform well under these conditions. The soft plastic is pliable and moves seductively in the warm water. Furthermore, in contrast to pork rind bait, the plastic crawdads won't dry out in the summer heat.

The easiest way to jig these lures is to thread them onto a 1/4 to 5/8 ounce lead head and bounce them along the bottom. You can add either a vinyl, plastic, or live rubber skirt to the jig for greater bulk if the bass want a more prominent bait. The skirting material also pulsates underwater giving the imitation 'dad a more lifelike appearance.

Sometimes it is better to use a tiny 1/16 to 1/8 ounce lead head with these lures. If the water is clear and the bass are skittish, try fishing the plastic 'dad on light 6 to 8 pound test line and the little jig head. The small lead head allows the crawdads to slowly glide down the bank. This strategy is particularly effective when the bass are holding tight to submerged cover like salt cedar trees. Always be alert for strikes to occur on the fall with this method.

Crawl the 'Dad

Another technique is to rig a plastic crayfish with a weedless hook and a slide sinker, Texas style. The Craw Worm and Berkley's Power Craw are best suited for this kind of presentation. The bullet weight rests against the tubular front portion of the lure as it would with a conventional plastic worm.

It is important to observe that this type of bait has a somewhat thicker body than a standard plastic worm. Thus it is often necessary to gently run the worm hook off to the side of the bait, barely penetrating the plastic. By "skin-hooking" the 'dad in this manner, the hook will quickly pull through the plastic upon the set.

Look-alike 'dads can be slowly inched along the bottom with the Texas rigging. The slide sinker allows you to present the bait in the thickest cover. This slow-down approach is especially effective in the winter. Simply crawl the plastic crawdad along outside points and ledges, working both uphill and downhill with the lure.

Flippin' and Pitchin'

Almost all of these fake crawdads can be flipped on a jig head. The Kreepy Krawdad, the Flip'n Craw, Billy's C-Dad, and the Super Claw can also be rigged Texas style and pitched in the shoreline brush. Simply crimp the bullet weight against the head of the 'dad, or use one of the screw-on bullet weights made by Gambler. These will not slide up the line and are perfect for flippin' or pitchin' where you might get hung up more with a moveable sinker.

Split-Shotting 'Dads

Soft plastic, look-alike crawdads are compatible baits to use with this finesse method. The bass will usually attack a look-alike 'dad on the lure on the fall, so it is important to pay attention to your line following the cast. The split-shottin' technique is equally applicable along shallow moss beds. Cast the 'dad to the edge of the weeds and again be alert for strikes as it slowly sinks. You can also fish the fake crayfish totally weightless with only a worm hook. Drag the lure on top of the moss beds until you come to an opening in the weeds. Let the plastic 'dad slowly fall down into the hole in the moss. Be prepared for a vicious strike as the bass skyrockets up through the opening to attack the lifelike imitation.

Don't hesitate to fish plastic crawdads at extreme depths. In this situation, the Carolina setup is recommended instead of the lighter split-shot rig. Slowly drag the look-alike 'dad along the bottom. It is possible to actually fish this setup well below 40 feet. Every so often, give the rod tip a quick "twitch." This will make the lure "jump," simulating the action of a live crayfish. Then, let the plastic 'dad rest motionless on the bottom for a few seconds. Occasionally the bass will eat the "dead bait" as it lays still.

An All-Season Lure

As you can see, these lifelike, fake crawdads have year-round potential when fished for any species of bass. They are made in a multitude of sizes and colors. On this note, here's a tip that will help to make these lures even more potent: try to visit local bait shops and observe length and coloration of the live crayfish they are currently selling. Most bait vendors capture crawdads from local waters. Thus, it's a safe bet that the live 'dads they are selling are the same size and shade of those in the nearby lakes. Try then to match both the length and the color tones of the natural crawfish with those available in the soft plastic imitations. Bass love 'dads—fool them with one of these plastic replicas!

New Grub Secrets

For many years, the soft plastic grub had little appeal among the bass fishing community. Most of these lures were initially designed as short pieces of fat, stubby plastic with simple flat tails. Many anglers considered grubs an afterthought—something to try when the plastic worm failed to produce.

Times have changed. Plastic grubs have now assumed a new status in the serious basser's bag of tricks. Many tournaments are being won and stellar catches are being made from coast to coast with these lures. What has triggered this dramatic rise in popularity?

Two answers come to mind: innovative changes in design and materials; and new techniques for fishing these baits.

The most important revolution involved a new shape and action with the formation of prominent, sickle-like curly tails. Those flat-tail grubs from yesteryear simply did not have much pizzazz as far as movement was concerned. Anglers could make the old-style grub "jump" with a twitch of the rod tip (which still often proves effective, especially in cold water) but not much more.

Once manufacturers redesigned their grubs with large, pronounced swimming tails, a whole new era opened. Bass seem to key in on the sensuous moving tail action and attack the grubs with a vengeance.

Similarly, the addition of salt crystals impregnated into these lures, combined with using softer plastics, has apparently made today's grubs quite palatable to the fish. Some bassers feel that the issue of salt is overrated or perhaps mythical. Other pros adamantly feel that bass simply eat the softer grubs with salt concentrations best. They seem to hold onto these baits longer.

Let's review for a moment. The traditional method for fishing grubs—both the older flat-tail models and the latest curl-tails—has been with a scaled-down jig head. Practically any small 1/16 to 1/4 ounce lead head is compatible with 3 to 5 inch grubs. You can add a weed guard for areas with a lot of brush and rocks or fish the grub with an open-hook jig head if there are few obstructions. Cast out, let the grub sink to the bottom, and "jig" it back in with short hops, or swim the grub back to the boat or the bank in a steady even motion, working the bait through a particular strike zone.

That's the most rudimentary way to fish this lure. Now let's take a look at some of the more subtle tactics the pros have come up with for using these lures.

Grubs, Texas Style

Many anglers are remiss in not working these baits with a conventional Texas setup. In contrast to a plastic worm, the grub is seemingly too thick to lend itself to a slide sinker and a Texas rig. However, with a little ingenuity, this lure can be fished weedless, Texas style.

To begin with, use a needle-sharp worm hook with a wide gap. The offset round bend Gamakatsu hook in size #2/0 to #3/0 is excellent with a larger grub such as the 4 inch models made by Mr. Twister or Yamamoto's 5 inch grub. The Gamakatsu offset round bend worm hooks in sizes #1 to #1/0 match perfectly with smaller 3 inch grubs like Yamamoto's popular models. The wide gap provides for better penetration and improved setting power as the hook pulls loose from the thick plastic.

Here is another trick used by the pros. Even with wide gapped, super sharp hooks, a certain amount of strikes will be missed. This is especially true if the hook is implanted directly into the center of the bait. This "meaty" section of the grub is fine for hiding the hook, but it is tough to pull the point through. Switch to the skin-hooking strategy.

Split-Shottin' Grubs

Mike and Ron have had great success split-shottin' plastic worms. Pinch a medium-size lead split-shot, anywhere from 12 to 18 inches above the hook. Fine diameter 4 to 10 pound line is preferred, along with miniature plastic baits. Curl-tail grubs are perfectly suited for the split-shot approach. Both smaller 3 inch models on up to the larger 5 inch versions are deadly baits to use with this method.

Generally in the summer when the bass are suspended off the bottom and feeding on baitfish, it's time to fish the grub. With the split-shot or Carolina rig, the grub glides down after the sinker hits the bottom. This really triggers the strikes on deep-water bass.

Even with skin-hooking the grub, strikes may often be missed fishing the light line. In our experience we have encountered this situation numerous times with Alabama spotted bass. Unlike their largemouth cousins, the 'spots school over deep structure. They will definitely eat a grub on the split-shot rig, but the "strike" is typically nothing more than subtle pressure.

Rather than hooking the grubs Texas style, we switch to a standard Mustad or Eagle Claw baitholder hook in #4 to 1/0 sizes and thread it through the bait. We leave the hook totally open or exposed. On some lakes there may not be too many obstructions in the deep water for the open-hook setup to get snagged on. When the spots hit the grub, penetration and a solid hook set occur instantly. This little ploy will work for largemouths and small-mouths as well if the bottom terrain is fairly snag-free.

Flippin' Grubs

Most recreational bassers conceptualize flippin' as a shallow water attack using primarily jigs and worms. Many of the pros have been quietly flippin' grubs instead of these more traditional baits.

There are two ways to effectively flip grubs. You can lace a larger curl-tail model on a 1/4 to 5/8 ounce jig head, preferably with a brush guard, and flip the grub into the thickest shoreline cover.

Use the lighter lead head when a slower fall is desired or add a plastic skirt to the jig head to create more bulk and to make the grub drop into the pockets even more slowly. A heavier 5/8 ounce jig head can be used to penetrate through dense brush or timber.

Sometimes, however, the bass want a more subtle bait, especially in clear, shallow water. Here is where a grub flipped on 12 to 15 pound mono rigged with a sliding sinker, Texas style, excels. Peg the bullet weight with a toothpick to keep it from moving up the line or use the Gambler screw-on sinker we previously mentioned. Once again, skin-hook the grub off to its side for quick hook sets. Schools of threadfin shad often move up into the tules. Try flippin' a clear shaded grub in this situation. Swing and set with the slightest "tick" in the line or anything that feels different or the slightest movement in the monofilament.

Grub Trailers

Curl-tail grubs also make sensational trailers with assorted spinnerbaits. They can be used separately, with a safety pin-style spinner or with a twin-spin. If a slower fall is the key, simply thread the grub onto an existing spinnerbait behind the skirt. You will find that the prominent flagellating tail portion of the grub adds tremendous action to the rear portion of the versatile spinnerbait and creates a bigger silhouette.

Top-water enthusiasts can similarly dress up bland-looking buzzbaits by using grub trailers. The longer 4 to 5 inch models create a lot of vibration when combined with the whirling prop-like blades, and fished as a buzzer trailer in shallow water. For nighttime bassin', a grub combined with a buzzbait creates an imposing silhouette, especially under a moonlit sky. Black is the best color.

More Grub Secrets

These thick curl-tail baits are a valuable addition to the recreational basser's tackle box. Grubs perform under the most diverse conditions. They are effective on aggressive bass in the warmer months and lethargic feeders during the winter.

Because of the proportionate size of these lures, they also soak up a lot of fish attractant. Many of the pro bassers are adamant that by adding Berkley Strike to these baits their potency is doubled.

Grubs also replicate a wide range of dominant forage baits. Manufacturers such as Yamamoto, Mr. Twister, Haddock, and A.A.T. color their grubs to imitate the major natural food sources. Use salt'n pepper shades to mimic shad. Tomato, brown, or purple appears very much like a crawdad under water. The latest pumpkin tones with traces of blue and green are the "hot" secret for replicating small bluegill—a favorite food for lunker bass.

Be experimental with these curl-tail baits. Try grubs in place of plastic worms, and don't hesitate to work them all year long. They can be rigged Texas-style, slow-crawled, doodled, doodle-stitched, or shaked. You can also use a worm-gutter, a small boring tool, to create a pocket cavity in the grub so you can insert a rattle, scent, or styrofoam to make it float. A number of top bass pros have been collecting some hefty paychecks thanks to these little baits!

More Serious Secrets

More Serious Secrets

Mini Lead Heads[1]

We have told you that many bass fishermen subscribe to the theory that states "big baits catch big fish." There are times certainly such as in the spring, when larger lures definitely seem to catch lunker bass.

On deep, clear, man-made lakes, you might have to rely upon an arsenal of scaled-down, so-called "finesse baits" to bring bass to the scales. One of the most effective lures in this repertoire of finesse baits is the mini lead head.

Mini lead heads can be divided into many different designs, each requiring a distinctive presentation. The basic categories are as follows: 1) p-heads, 2) darters, 3) sliders, 4) pony heads and 5) marabous.

Let's examine each of these mini lead head baits separately and the specific ways to fish them.

Mini P-heads

One of the simplest lures found in pro tackle boxes is composed of nothing more than a tiny rounded lead head, about the size of a garden pea. The pea-shaped head on these minuscule baits sinks relatively fast and straight when fished on light 4-8 pound monofilament. The most popular size p-head is a 1/8 ounce, though models range from a minute 1/16 ounce up to larger 1/4 ounce p-heads for ultradeep bassin'.

The most common way serious bassers fish the p-head is to thread on a small 2-4 inch long soft plastic trailer. Almost any curl, paddle or straight-tail Anglers' Choice worm will convert easily to a p-head bait. The curl-tail combo seems to perform best when the bass want a more active lure. A simple cast-sink-retrieve sequence will work with the p-head using the curl-tail worm trailer.

In a post-spawn period or during the winter months when fish are more lethargic, subtle paddle-tail and straight-tail trailers work best teamed with the p-head. With this type of soft plastic trailer, the tiny p-head can be gently "hopped" along the bottom, pausing occasionally in the retrieve to allow the bait to rest motionless on the bottom.

Darters

These distinctively shaped arrowhead or sharp-nose lead heads have also become a staple among finesse fishermen. In contrast to the rounded p-head baits, darters actually "dart" from side to side on the fall following the cast.

Most darter jigs consist of a light 1/6 to 1/4 ounce lead head, with a small soft plastic trailer. Curl-tail grubs, reapers, Power Worms, and Slinkees are common darter-head trailers. The key to fishing these little lures is to monitor for strikes on the sink. As the bait darts from side to side, invariably the bass will practically inhale the lure creating nothing more than a sudden slackening on the light line. You must quickly reel up the slack and set.

Softer-tipped, medium or medium-light action spinning rods are perfect for fishing both p-heads and darters. The hooks must be honed to needle-sharp perfection, since there isn't much gap between the shank and the point as there is in, say, a conventional lead head.

Sliders

One of the most intriguing and certainly underfished lures in the mini lead head parade is the strange-looking slider jig. The wafer-thin thicknesses of these 1/16 to 3/16 ounce lead heads create almost an aerodynamic effect with the lure.

[1] Portions of this section previously appeared in *Bassmaster Magazine*

Tiny soft-plastic worms, grubs or feather-like reapers used as trailers behind a slider head can be fished both shallow and deep, as the ultimate slow-down, fall bait.

You can fish the slider in deep clear water as you would with any other finesse-style lure, using 4-8 pound test mono. More than ever, be patient in allowing this lead head to literally glide to the bottom. Strikes almost always occur on the sink, either following the cast or while pausing on the retrieve.

Another rather strange-looking innovation, is to carefully insert the slider head up inside a hollow-tube bait. Then push the hook eyelet up through the soft plastic body. The wafer-like head remains encased by the soft plastic. You will find that the slider-tube combination falls somewhat differently then traditional tube baits, with more of that slow gliding effect as it sinks to the bottom.

Sliders also make excellent pitching lures while working around shallow brush, riprap and similar shoreline structure. Using heavier 8-12 pound test monofilament, fire off casts with the slider into this type of cover. The slider hook can actually be rigged Texas-style into the soft plastic worm or trailer.

Frequently the bass will be suspended among the rocks or branches. A maximum slow-down fall on the presentation can be deadly to get these fish to dart out of the structure to attack the subtle bait. A slider pitched in this manner allows the Bassmaster to basically use a finesse bait in dense cover, while minimizing the chances of getting hung up due to the small size and shape of this type of mini lead head.

Pony Heads

The unique thing about lures in this class is the distinctive horse-shaped or "pony" head design that forms the lead head, combined with the tiniest of spinners affixed to spin *under* the head.

Lures like the Blakemore Roadrunner are dynamite in the hands of a skilled finesse fisherman. Once again, the trick will be to throw the pony heads on light action spinning gear using 4-6 pound test line.

We have found the tiny pony heads to be quite deadly on marauding Florida-strain bass. On some lakes, for example, it is not uncommon to see "meatballs" of big Floridas intermittently crashing near the surface on schools of small threadfin shad.

One highly effective tactic is to stalk these marauding Floridas with your electric trolling motor. Make long casts, with light mono, tossing the little pony head baits

Pony Head

some distance *beyond* where the bass boil occurred. Allow the tiny lure to sink for a moment, then start an uninterrupted retrieve.

The subtle appearance of these mini lead heads, combined with the tight flash and whirring noise from the small spinner blade, often generates strikes when conventional top-water tactics fail.

Marabous and Deer Hair

One of the oldest lures to be found in bassin' war chests is the marabou feather or deer hair. Although somewhat relegated to a panfish or trout bait, marabou feathers or deer hair should be tried more often when a subtle presentation is needed, and the baitfish are small.

White, chartreuse, or yellow marabou feathers or deer hair are frequently effective tied on to a 1/16 to 1/4 ounce lead head. The feathers and hair breathe well at rest and can be fished at a reduced slow-down pace in cold water or tough conditions.

The marabou, like the pony head jig, can also be a real sleeper when it comes to throwing on bass chasing shad and crashing on the surface. After the marabou lands behind the boil, give it a few long pulls with the rod tip to make the little lead head dart rapidly—then stop—as it swims through the bass boil. Hold on for a jolting shake!

Mini Frogs

The standard #11 size Uncle Josh Pork Frog has become a hallmark bait for bass fishermen throughout the country, pinned behind a 3/16 to 1 ounce jig. This popular pig'n jig combination produces limit catches from shallow to deep all season long. Although not a mini lead head, per se, the frog trailers team well with small jig heads.

Again, when conditions are tough, as is common in the West, it pays to switch to a more subtle offering. As with other classes of baits, the so-called "frog" can also be scaled-down for the finesse approach.

The Uncle Josh #101 Spin Frog is basically the standard #11 bait dramatically reduced to miniature proportions. Similarly, hand-pour operations in the West, such as Sweetwater, Ambusher, Advanced Angler Technology and A.A. Worms, have brought out their own line of scaled-down "frog" trailers in soft plastic versions.

These tiny 1-2 inch long trailers must be matched with smaller 1/8-1/4 ounce lead heads. It is critical that the lead heads themselves feature fine wire hooks. The fine wire style hook creates a mini lead head that is lighter so the tiny jig will sink slowly for the tough bite. The fine wire hook will not tear up the soft plastic trailers as the lure is dragged through thicker structure.

Again, a light to medium action spinning combo is highly suitable for throwing these mini frogs. Many of the new ultralight baitcasting reels are now able to be spooled with gossamer 4-8 pound monofilament, which is perfect for casting these mini lead heads.

Versatile Finesse Baits

Although so much has been written about finesse techniques, the fact remains that the subtle baits have great application wherever bass become reluctant feeders.

Spinning gear, light premium grade monofilament, sharp hooks, patience, and great sense of timing are integral when using this variety of mini lead heads. These lures consistently catch not only the basic keeper class fish, but trophy bass as well. Always be prepared for the most subtle of strikes, particularly as you allow this kind of light lure to sink.

Mini lead heads are inexpensive to assemble, yet remain highly versatile and deadly baits when bassin' turns tough.

Ultralight Bassin'[2]

As urban density increases, there may be an awesome amount of pressure exerted on our local bass lakes. Serious bass fishermen are perpetually on the lookout for new ways to put fish in the boat. On this note, there is an emergent dimension to the serious bassin' tournament scene that has been drawing attention—ultralight bass angling. Instead of chuckin' and windin' with the traditional baitcasting outfits and 12 to 17 pound test line, this approach depends on spider web-thin mono, hi-tech ultralight reels, and light action rods.

Ultralight bassin' matches perfectly with the current trend toward using smaller and smaller artificial lures. We agree that to some extent, the adage that "Big Baits = Big Fish" has validity. The problem is that there are not that many bass in some lakes to begin with, let alone lunkers. Hence, most weekend anglers are more content with catching a few legal fish than trying to nail a wallhanger.

As we discussed earlier, studies have indicated that the average size of forage bait found in the stomach contents of dissected bass measures a mere 3 inches in length. This finding holds true for both threadfin shad and crawdads, the two major food sources for the bass species. The latest parade of miniature crankbaits, hand-poured worms, reapers, and small curl-tail grubs attest to the fish's preference for these more lifelike replicas. Ultralight tackle can be teamed perfectly with the diminutive bass lures.

Basic Gear

A compact, ultralight spinning reel is the pivotal piece of equipment for this kind of fishing. The most important feature of this reel is a precision drag mechanism. The stern drag design has been the most popular for spinning reels in this genre. The angler is able to make quick adjustments by turning the drag knob at the rear portion of the reel.

The stern drag however is usually not as smooth as most front-loaded systems. This is due to the size of the drag washers used in the reel. Manufacturers are able to place larger drag washers on top of the spool where more room is available. The larger drag washers have more surface area to dissipate heat and friction build-up. This results in a smoother drag when having to play bass on light line. Expect to spend anywhere from $35 to $100 for a quality ultralight reel.

You will have considerable latitude when it comes to selecting a companion rod. Stay with a blank in the 6 to 6 1/2 foot range. It should have a fast taper. A single piece model is also recommended. Remember, this fishing requires using fine diameter mono. It will have a moderate amount of stretch. The rod — even an ultralight model— has to have some backbone to it to get a solid hook set.

As for line, invest in premium grade monofilament. Don't shortchange yourself here. Top quality 4 to 10 pound test mono has high abrasion resistance, consistency, and superior knot strength. These are important features for any form of serious bassin'.

---

[2] Portions of this section previously appeared in *Bassmaster Magazine*

Tiny Hardbaits

There is a wealth of ultralight lures from which to choose. Some, such as in-line spinners like the Roostertail, Shyster, or Mepps, are primarily used for trout. Others are nothing more than reduced versions of bona fide bass plugs. The new ultralight Cordell Spot, Rapala Mini-Fat Rap, and CD 5-minnow, Rebel Pop-R, and Heddon Sonic exemplify this recent wave of tiny hardbaits.

Small spoons can also be presented quite effectively with this type of tackle. Models such as the 1/8 ounce Kastmaster, Krocadile, or Mepps Syclops can be thrown a long way on light monofilament. When the bass are feeding on shad near the surface in super clear water, these little spoons can be dynamite. The angler can fire off long casts without coming too close to spook the fish. The trick then is to rhythmically twitch the rod tip as you retrieve the spoon back in. This has the effect of making the lure dart and dance along the surface, mimicking a frantic minnow.

Another type of lure that is highly suitable for ultralight bassin' is the Mini-Scrounger. This is basically a curl-tail grub with a unique oscillating plastic lip. It is another crappie lure perfectly suited for the ultralight game. This simple panfish lure provides a silhouette to the bass that closely resembles a small, immature shad. The fine diameter monofilament allows the angler to impart considerable swimming action to these otherwise rather uncomplicated lures.

More Soft Plastics for Ultralight Bassin'

In recent years there have been many innovative tactics using soft plastic baits. One of these—the split-shot technique—has probably revolutionized bass fishing on heavily pressured waters more than any method to come along in years.

Even with the split-shot approach using primarily 6 to 10 pound test line, the bass found in heavily pressured impoundments can become quite finicky at times. More weekend tournament anglers are now resorting to ultralight tackle and 4 pound mono to bring bass to the scales. Small plastic worms, 2 inch feather-like reapers, and little curl-tail grubs swim perfectly when split-shotted with superthin line. The fish can also be fooled more easily with this nearly invisible monofilament.

This form of finesse bassin' requires considerable skill. However, there are some specific tricks Mike and Ron use to maximize their chances of nailing fish with the ultralight split-shot approach.

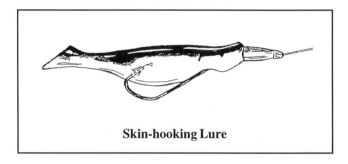

Skin-hooking Lure

To begin with, split-shotters most always rig their plastic baits Texas-style with the hook buried into the lure. With the ultralight outfit, the hooks used will have to be exceptionally sharp since the rod tips are softer and the fine mono will stretch. It may still be difficult to tear the hook away from the soft plastic bait with ultralight gear. A simple way around this problem is to "skin-hook" the lure.

A final option is to use a small #4 to #8 long-shank baitholder hook in place of the more prominent plastic worm hook. Thread the soft plastic lure onto the baitholder hook leaving the point exposed. Split-shotting with an open hook in this manner requires hardly any setting power at all. However, there is a trade-off: you lose a lot of the weedless quality of the setup characteristic of the Texas-rigged bait.

Best Times

The ultralight approach can be utilized any time anglers want to add considerable challenge to their sport. Apart from the sheer excitement of fighting bass on superlight line, this presentation can be a potent strategy under intense tournament conditions. The smaller lures closely replicate natural forage baits. These artificials swim and perform better on extremely light line. Highly pressured largemouth, bronzeback, and spotted bass are also less suspicious of 2 to 4 pound test mono. They are thus prone to attack tiny artificials. Give ultralight bassin' a try!

Applying Scents[3]

In recent years, one of the most important breakthroughs in serious bassin' technology has been the advent of chemical fish attractants. Some anglers swear by them; others feel they are nothing more than "confidence builders." The fact of the matter is that more and more pros are taking a serious look at these smelly concoctions and

---

[3] Portions of this section previously appeared in *B.A.S.S. Times*

using them to enhance their baits under high stakes tournament conditions.

With the liquid products, simply squeeze a few drops on the head of the lure. This is the major portion of the bait where strikes occur. As an added effect, rub the drops down along the worm or grub by sliding the lure through your fingers.

Attractants that are in pump bottles are often wasted as the angler tries to "hit the target" with the bait dangling on the line. Here's a simple tip used by the pros. Squirt a few drops of the scent in a small plastic bag. Then roll the lure in the bag, fully coating it with the attractant prior to the cast.

Other soft baits such as pork rind trailers can also be customized so they will retain the attractants. Several lateral cuts across the thick pad of a pork frog, for instance, will allow the scent to seep deep into the bait.

The recent wave of hollow-bodied tube baits also lend themselves to scent technology. A trick we have used for years is to squirt liquid attractants into the hollow cavity of a tube bait. As the tiny tube sashays through the water, a vapor cloud or "chum slick" of scent is emitted calling in lethargic bass to investigate.

Anglers may also want to consider adding either liquid or aerosol attractant to their baits. Some pros squirt a few drops of liquid scent into jars of pork rind weeks before using the trailers. The compound will to some degree impregnate into the pork.

In sum, there are many different fish attractants on the market today. It pays to be experimental, trying them with a variety of lures under diverse conditions. The manufacturers often have difficulty educating bass anglers as to the merits of these concoctions. The serious basser has to give the scents a fair chance. Too frequently, the angler has unrealistic expectations for these compounds. They are not "miracle" chemicals, but they will frequently improve the bite. The trick is to stay with them long enough, re-applying the scent intermittently to give the attractants a chance to work.

Live Critters for Bass[4]

The true mark of a tournament angler is his prowess at catching bass on artificial lures. Still, many recreational bass fishermen rely upon natural baits to maximize their chances. The fact remains that bass are a temperamental species, frequently reluctant to attack anything unless it is alive.

Veteran guides often have to resort to using "critters" under tough conditions to generate at least minimal action. This is particularly true when guiding novices or weekenders are fishing smaller, heavily pressured waters.

Fishing with live bait, however, does not automatically guarantee success. Even with natural offerings, there are definite methodologies in terms of selection, rigging, and presentation. Here then are some of the basic techniques serious bassers can utilize to catch fish on live baits.

16 lb. 3 oz. Bass Caught on a 9" Worm Soaked in Berkley Strike

---

[4] Portions of this section previously appeared in *Bassmaster Magazine*

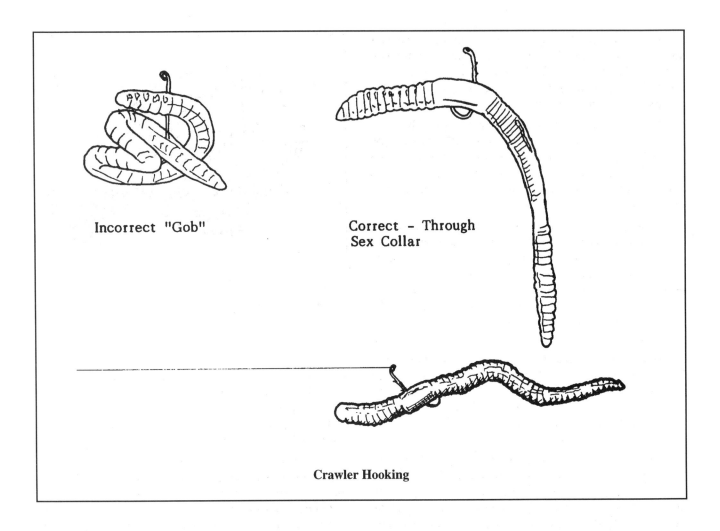

Incorrect "Gob"

Correct – Through
Sex Collar

Crawler Hooking

Nightcrawlers

These magnum-size worms remain one of the most popular entrées on the live bait menu. Most 'crawlers are sold by commercial bait vendors. It is important to be rather selective when purchasing a container of these worms.

'Crawlers are often packaged in terms of size. Some bait dealers may actually sort their containers in this manner—designating small, medium and large nightcrawlers. As a rule, the bigger the better when it comes to fishing 'crawlers for bass.

However, in our own guiding experiences, we have encountered situations where the bass actually preferred only the small to medium length worms, perhaps intimidated by the longer "snakes."

It is in your best interest to empty the container at the bait shop before you buy the 'crawlers. It is possible that an unethical wholesaler or dealer might intentionally "salt" a container with, say, a few larger worms nestled on top of much smaller baits. This most often occurs during periods of high bait usage—for example, during a holiday weekend—when all the wholesalers have left are primarily short, immature 'crawlers. Don't hesitate to ask to see the bait before you leave the store.

The best method we have found for fishing nightcrawlers is to rig them weedless using a #6 to #8 long-shank bronze baitholder hook. These hooks are small as compared to the specialized hooks used for rigging plastic worms.

Tie this hook onto 6 to 10 pound monofilament. The lighter line will let the 'crawler move with minimal restriction. Next, carefully hook the worm through the prominent sex band located at the upper third of the body behind the head portion of the bait. Then—and here's the trick—re-embed the point of the hook back into the thick collar to make the bait practically weedless. This also allows the worm to seductively slither and twist as it does in its natural state.

Avoid hooking the nightcrawler more than once as is sometimes done by the novice bait dunker. Bass will clearly strike a 'crawler delicately rigged with the small hook in the sex band more often than a "gob" of bait that results from multiple hookings.

In many situations such as fishing heavy brush, rocky riprap, thick moss beds, or particularly clear water, you can make a gentle lob-cast using the 'crawler without any sinker. The bait will slowly sink to the bottom. Expect to get bit many times on the fall as the bass literally inhales the worm.

If you are working a nightcrawler in deeper water or in windy conditions, it may be necessary to add some weight. A small BB-size lead shot crimped about 12 to 18 inches above the hook works fine. Before you tie on the baitholder hook, run your line through a little 1/16 to 1/8 ounce sliding bullet sinker. Then carefully crimp the nose of the weight so it is permanently affixed 12 to 18 inches above the worm.

Nightcrawlers can also be fished under a small plastic float to keep them suspended off the bottom. A tiny snap-on bobber will work fine with the bait suspended anywhere from 1 to 8 feet under the float. This strategy works especially well for fishing a 'crawler on the outside edge of a tule bank or moss bed.

Regardless of how you present the nightcrawler, always try to keep it moving to some degree. By "inching" the worm along with a slow intermittent retrieve, you will not only cover more territory, but will also insure that the bait isn't lodged behind a rock or has become invisible because it is stuck inside a weed bed.

Unlike plastic worms, the live version should be fished with a modest amount of slack line. When a bass strikes the crawler, gather up the slack. While maintaining slight tension, let the fish swim off with the worm following it with the rod tip. This will insure that the bass will feel only minimal resistance while eating the bait. After the fish has moved one to two feet of line, swing and set!

Crawdads

Some of the largest bass tallied each season from coast to coast are caught on live 'dads. Crayfish comprise a major source of forage on most inland waters. All the bass species will readily attack these small crustaceans. In some areas, adept anglers may catch their own 'dads using baited traps or nets. Crayfish are usually sold in specialized bait shops.

As with nightcrawlers, it pays to be selective when purchasing a bucket of crawdads. It helps if you know the

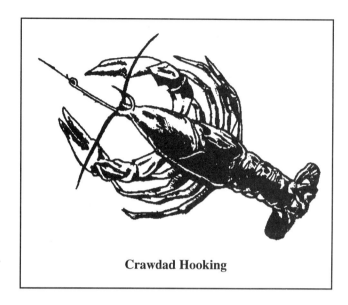

Crawdad Hooking

shell color of the 'dads in the lake you are fishing. For example, on one of my home lakes in the West, the crawfish population has a mottled greenish brown shell all year long. Thus, we look for 'dads with this coloration instead of, say, buying baits with bright red shells.

Similarly, the size of the crawdad can be important when picking your stock from a bait store. For instance, on that same lake, the indigenous crayfish population usually averages less than 3 inches in length. When we fish this water, we try to purchase only those crawdads that are mottled greenish-brown, and under 3 inches long. Larger, off-colored 'dads seldom get bit on this particular reservoir.

The most effective way to hook a crawdad is using a long-shank Eagle Claw #181 bronze baitholder hook. A larger #2 to #8 hook is more suitable for fishing 'dads depending on the size of the bait. You can also scale up in line diameter working crayfish on anywhere from 6 to 12 pound test mono. Run the baitholder through the gristly, bony structure between the crawdad's eyes. This permits the 'dad free tail movement to enhance swimming and crawling.

These baits perform best using minimal, if any, added weight. Use a sinker only if necessary and then a #4 to #7 split-shot. As was noted when working a 'crawler, it is best to slowly retrieve the 'dad—pausing and starting up again. The best way to work the crayfish is to slowly "stitch" the bait in pulling your line a few feet by hand, then gathering up the slack.

When you stitch crayfish on the bottom, watch for telltale signs that a bass is contemplating attacking the bait. Fish the 'dad on a small amount of slack line. If the bait gets excited when a hungry bass is in the vicinity, it may frantically swim, signaled by quick twitches in the line. Stay alert!

When the bass decides to eat the crawdad, usually you will feel a more prominent "thump" on the line or the line moves off as the fish starts to crush the bait. Then, the bass will turn with the 'dad, starting its run. Pick up the slack, follow the fish for a few seconds with the rod tip, then use a steady gentle sweep of the rod to set the hook.

Shiners

Bass fishermen in the South and West will attest to the effectiveness of shiner minnows as an all around big fish bait. In less populated areas, anglers often catch their own shiners using small gold trout hooks baited with everything from bread dough to meal worms. Some retail bait vendors will also stock these minnows that require special aerated tanks to keep them alive.

Shiners may also be sorted into small, medium, and large sizes. The adage BIG BAITS = BIG BASS definitely holds true for shiner fishing. Dedicated trophy hunters looking for big Florida-strain bass usually try to buy the biggest shiners available.

If the bass are holding on deeper structure, you can split-shot the smaller shiners. Crimp on a 1/8 to 1/4 ounce lead shot about 18 to 24 inches above the bait. The minnow will usually swim above the bottom trailing behind the weight.

The most common way to fish these minnows is to suspend them underneath a bobber. The float will serve to keep the shiner from swimming too far back into the tules or weeds near the bank.

Another strategy is to simply "fly-line" the bait, totally weightless, without a sinker. The minnow will feel hardly any drag or resistance as it swims freely.

One of the simplest ways to rig a shiner is to run a long-shank baitholder hook through the minnow's upper and lower lips. By sealing the minnow's lips in this manner, you can minimize the chances of accidentally drowning the baitfish by forcing too much water through its gills. Hook size may vary from a #4 to #2/0 depending on the size of the shiner.

If you cast shiners in heavy cover or over rocky terrain, consider switching to a short-shank live bait hook in sizes #4 to #4/0. This style hook is normally used in saltwater circles. Although you won't generate as much leverage with the short-shank model compared to the longer baitholder, this small ocean hook will get hung up less.

As was noted for nightcrawlers and crawdads, it is also important to give the bass plenty of time to eat the shiner. Quite frequently, the fish will make an initial pass at the minnow but without really taking the bait. In this situation, try reeling the shiner in a few feet. Often the bass senses that its prey is scurrying away so it quickly moves in to make a final "kill." A sustained run with the shiner will follow the second attack.

Shiners should also be kept in either your boat's live well or in a separate aerated bait box. An aquarium dip net is useful for selecting the smaller minnows from the bait tank.

Shad Minnows

Along with crayfish, shad minnows comprise the other major forage in many impoundments. Although somewhat fragile, shad are also a potent option for the serious bait soaker.

Shad minnows can be caught using throw nets, casted into schools of the baitfish as they concentrate in the shallows. Shad can also be caught or snagged by dropping shiny spoons after deep schools of baitfish have been metered.

Like shiners, shad must be kept in an aerated environment and handled gingerly. They should be hooked either through both lips, or once across the back, behind the dorsal fin. A thin wire Sealy hook in #1 to #6 size will work best with the smaller baits, doing minimal damage to the minnow. Switch to stronger forged live bait hooks with palm-size shad, or when using these minnows in thick cover.

Shad can be fished shallow or deep. At times, they are a red hot secret bait fly-lined weightless into shallow brush lines where finicky bass may be rooted in tight.

For the deep-water approach, crimp on a small lead shot and fish shad all the way down to 60 feet. Allow the bass to run off 1 to 2 feet of line before setting up on the fish. You can scale down with 6 to 10 pound mono split-shottin' shad deep, since hooks will usually pull out easily from this bait.

Mudsuckers

Fishermen on the West Coast will find that some bait shops stock mudsuckers as a prime deep-water offering. 'Suckers are actually small 2 to 6 inch saltwater tidal fish and are members of the gobi family.

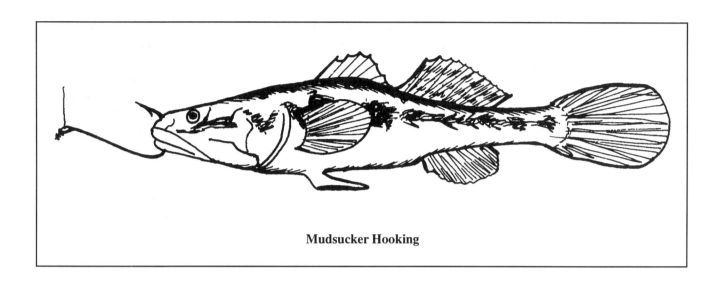

Mudsucker Hooking

It is often necessary on deep clear Western lakes to cover as much ground as possible over large expanses of water. It is also difficult to make repeated rapid-fire casts with nightcrawlers, shiners, or 'dads. In both situations mudsuckers excel.

Pin the 'sucker on a #4 to #1/0 long-shank baitholder or a fine diameter wire Sealy hook tied to 8 to 15 pound line. Run the hook through both the lower and upper lips of the baitfish. Crimp a fairly large lead shot about 18 to 24 inches above the bait.

Although the natural environment of the mudsucker is shallow tidal flats, it swims remarkably well at depths beyond 30 feet. Largemouths and spotted bass in particular will eagerly pounce on a 'sucker split-shotted at these depths.

This is also an excellent bait to slow-drift on submerged ledges, along river channels, and over hard, muddy bottoms. The instant you feel either a pronounced strike or perhaps only subtle pressure, maintain tension on the line. Again, follow the fish with your rod tip, letting the bass run 12 to 18 inches before setting the hook.

Mudsuckers are also excellent for covering long stretches of shoreline as you would with a crankplug or spinnerbait. You can make repeated casts fly-lining the bait without a sinker or add a small split-shot and swim the 'sucker at the 10 to 20 foot mid-range depths.

Waterdogs

These are actually amphibians and not baitfish per se. With their four little legs, waterdogs are the larval stage of the tiger salamander. 'Dogs are not quite as hearty as mudsuckers. They can be fished shallow or deep however, but in a slow-down fashion. This slow movement of the bait matches well when bass are situated on deep structure and especially in cold water conditions.

In wintertime trips, we have often salvaged the day by fishing waterdogs all the way down to 60 feet in sub-50 degree water. Usually the "bite" will be mushy pressure on the end of the line. In this situation it is not necessary to give the bass much more additional time to swallow the bait. Quickly swing and set, reeling fast to offset excessive line stretch.

Hook waterdogs in the same manner as mudsuckers. They can be fly-lined in shallow water or split-shotted at greater depths. Also, be selective when purchasing 'dogs at the local bait store. These amphibians are frequently marketed in a mix of different sizes. Occasionally you will find some giant waterdogs approaching 13 inches in length. Bait this size may be a potential meal for only the largest bass in the lake.

Insects

An assortment of insects can sometimes prove to be remarkably effective bass baits when larger offerings won't produce. Crickets and grasshoppers are two primary forms of insect forage that often interest hungry smallmouth and spotted bass.

Crickets are frequently sold in local bait stores, packaged in miniature wire cages. Grasshoppers usually have to be caught by anglers canvassing their nearby fields with insect nets.

The best way to hook insects in this genre is to carefully run a #12 to #16 long-shank baitholder hook under and through the collar section of the bait behind the head. To enhance casting, add either a small split-shot 12 to 18 inches above the insect or snap on a little bobber and let the 'hopper or cricket drift under the float.

Expect to catch a lot of smaller bass with live insects. This makes for great sport on ultralight gear! However, sometimes in farm ponds, on streams, and smaller, more pressured lakes, "bugs" can become a potent menu due to a lack of other indigenous forage.

Fishing Critters Weedless

Frequently one of the problems the live bait fisherman faces when using an open hook point with his offerings is getting snagged on brush, rock, and similar obstructions. You can quickly remedy this by making your live bait hooks weedless.

After threading a shiner, crawdad, mudsucker, or waterdog on the hook, take a tiny piece of plastic worm and embed it on the point of the hook. Be sure to cover up the barb. Try to match the chunk of soft plastic with the color of the natural bait for maximum camouflage.

The soft plastic cap will now make the live bait hook remarkably weedless, without impeding the movement of the critter. When you decide to set up on the bass, the hook point will easily pass through the soft plastic cap making penetration quick and solid.

Catch and Release!

The catch and release ethic has become the central tenet of the Bass Anglers Sportsman Society and similar tournament organizations. There is no reason why this practice cannot be maintained by fishermen desiring to use live bait instead of artificial lures.

To enhance the chances for release when baitfishing, try to keep your hooks on the small side so if the bass swallows the bait minimal damage will result.

Next, try to get your timing down, so to speak, as to when to set the hook while using live bait. Granted, you have to let the fish run with the natural offering a little

longer than you would with, say, a plastic worm. Still, you don't want to deep-hook bass on live bait as a result of letting the fish run too long following the initial strike.

Finally carry a surgical hemostat in your tackle box to remove hooks with the least amount of injury to the bass. If the hook is too deep, cut the line without hesitation and release the fish. The bass' natural digestive enzymes will soon dissolve the small live bait hook.

Bassin' with live critters is another dimension of this sport that adds both fun and excitement as well as the potential for catching a lunker-class fish. Always check your state regulations with regard to using live bait. Keep it legal—and practice catch and release.

Spotted Bass Myths[5]

One of the most intriguing bass species is the Alabama spot. Volumes of literature are available on large and smallmouths. For most anglers, the "spot" remains somewhat of a mystery fish. This species was originally indigenous to the South. In recent years they have been stocked in a handful of Western reservoirs in order to diversify the bass fishing in this part of the country. Lake Perris, in Southern California, has received the most publicity from this transplant program. Perris was initially established by the California Department of Fish and Game as a trophy spotted bass reservoir. The plan was that no other bass species would be introduced into this 2000 acre impoundment.

In the last decade, numerous line class and all tackle marks for "spots" have been set at Perris, including the world record 9:4 pound fish. Local guides claim to have seen "spots" in the water that eclipse 11 pounds. Keep in mind that the behavioral characteristics we found to hold true at Lake Perris are also evident wherever spots are found across the country.

"Spots" Are Bottom Feeders???

The belief has been that these bass rely heavily upon crayfish as their major forage food. Much of the time, "spots" do indeed root on the bottom for these crustaceans. However, large groups of spotted bass become "marauders," cruising at a variety of depths following schools of threadfin shad, minnows, or sometimes small planted rainbow trout. It is not uncommon to see spectacular "boils" of "spots" crashing the surface chasing bait. It would appear then, based on the guides' logs at Perris, that these fish will adapt to whatever food source is most readily available.

---

[5] Portions of this section previously appeared in *B.A.S.S. Times*

"Spots" Are Seldom Found Below 35 Feet???

At one time, many so-called spotted bass experts firmly believed that "spots" would rarely be found below 35 foot depths. There is evidence from the Perris logs that spots will migrate to deep water, particularly following massive schools of bait.

At Perris, many fish are routinely taken in the 35 to 45 foot range, working deep structure in the form of outside ledges, tire reefs, and isolated rock piles. During the winter months in particular when water temperatures drop below 55 degrees, Perris' "spots" will be found as deep as 90 feet. Serious bassers who monitor their electronics over these depths will find huge schools of shad clustered in tight "meatballs."

These ultradeep fish have been taken on spoons, Carolina rigs, and floating minnows fished on a dropper sinker. It is amazing how hard these bass will strike an artificial lure at such extreme depths.

"Spots" Need Rocky Terrain???

The theory was that when the Alabama spotted bass were originally planted in a reservoir, they would be more akin to smallmouths in their behavioral patterns. Perris is a stark lake, with minimal structure.

Speculation was that the fish would take up residence in the limited rocky areas in the deeper water. In reality, we have found these bass to be once again, highly migratory in their movements. The key seems to be the location of the dominant forage baits.

If there is an ample supply of crawdads or shad up near the bank, the "spots" will be close by. If the shad are situated in deeper water, as noted, the spotted bass will follow. Furthermore, there appears to be no set pattern of shallow versus deep based on the time of the year. It is not uncommon, for instance, to find "spots" at Perris well below the 35 foot level in the middle of summer and on the bank in the dead of winter.

"Spots" Feed by Pressure???

One of the more frustrating elements of fishing spotted bass is the manner in which they often attack the bait. The "strike" is that "mushy" pressure bite we've mentioned. Anglers accustomed to the prominent "tap tap" of a largemouth inhaling a plastic worm are frequently caught off guard by the "pressure bite" of spotted bass.

Here again, this may be only one of many feeding modes these fish can demonstrate in a single day. For example, it is not atypical for one angler slow-crawling a split-shotted grub to experience the pressure bite from a wary spot, while his partner gets bushwhacked hard by another spotted bass attacking a crankplug or spinnerbait.

Presumably, it would seem that "spots" key in on the lure and strike it depending upon the speed it is being retrieved. Those who split-shot or crawl soft plastics over the bottom frequently talk about the "pressure bite." Other anglers who prefer to throw faster-moving reaction baits, mention the incredible, viciousness of the strike when a spotted bass decided to eat the lure.

"Spots" School Alone???

On some lakes, spotted bass seem to travel in small schools of 3 to 6 fish. It is not uncommon to nail 2 or 3 fish in successive casts from a small area on a particular reservoir.

However, we have also found that "spots" too often mix with their largemouth cousins. Interestingly, the largest fish taken out of a school of fish may invariably be an Alabama spotted bass and not a largemouth. This would seem to suggest that many of the "spots" in a specific lake may become larger, solitary "rouge" fish that are schooling less with their own kind.

"Spots" Only Eat Small Baits???

It was widely believed that these fish, due to their smaller mouth structure, would be less likely to eat a prominent size lure. When we first encountered "spots" we avoided throwing such offerings as pig'n jigs, larger crankplugs, longer plastic worms, or magnum willowleaf spinners, fearing these bigger lures would intimidate this sensitive species.

Over the course of time, however, this was yet another theory that had to be discounted. It is now clear that, although these fish seem to prefer a more compact bait such as a reaper, grub, or Westy Worm, they will at times hit larger lures with reckless abandon.

Some of the biggest "spots" have been taken on such man-size offerings as jigs with a #1 Uncle Josh Jumbo Pork Frog, longer 8 to 10 inch plastic snakes, large alphabet-style crankplugs, and giant spinnerbaits. The adage "big baits catch big fish" would seem to be highly applicable for Alabama spotted bass at lakes across the United States.

"Spots" Won't Eat Top-Water Lures???

A similar misconception was that spotted bass, because of their presumed bottom orientation, will not eat a surface plug. Nothing could be further from the truth based on the Perris data.

These fish will clearly attack floating minnows, poppers, chuggers, and large cigar-shaped stickbaits if they are feeding on shad near the surface. What is even more remarkable is that "spots" on many lakes are prone to ambush a top-water lure all season long if the baitfish are near the surface.

Throw Out the Book!

It is thus apparent that many of the original notions we had about spotted bass no longer hold up at Lake Perris. This complicated species is highly adaptable. They can be found shallow or deep, foraging on different prey. Spotted bass can be taken on a variety of methods ranging from slow-crawling worms to big top-water baits. The fact remains that the general way this unique species behaves at Perris is reflective of spotted bass patterns across the United States.

Getting Serious—The Lives and Times of Guides and Pros

Getting Serious—The Lives and Times of Guides and Pros

Getting Serious—Buying a Bass Boat

Selecting the right boat for serious freshwater bass fishing is not always an easy decision. There are a variety of things that have to be considered before the angler makes this kind of significant investment. As both veteran guide and tournament fishermen, we want to give the prospective bass boater a brief shopping list of the major factors that should be weighed before he purchases this kind of craft.

Hull Shape

Perhaps the most rudimentary variable to consider is the hull design. Novice bassers sometimes fail to recognize that hull shape can play a prominent role in the overall performance of the boat they select.

For example, if you are interested in primarily fishing while traveling slowly or at anchor, a flat bottom or "duck boat" design might be best. This type of hull is particularly stable when the boat is moving slowly or if you want to fish from a stationary position. This basic design is typified by today's modern aluminum and fiberglass bass boats. The fisherman can stand on top of sturdy casting platforms and quietly maneuver the flat-bottom boats in and out of shoreline cover with an electric trolling motor.

You should also closely scrutinize the casting platforms. For example, if you like to practice the art of shallow water flippin', you will be standing up all the time. With this technique the angler must make repeated tight casts to shoreline cover. It pays to have a boat with ample platform space to move around in the bow while flippin'. Also, if you want to fish bass tournaments, you will need a wide casting platform to permit your partner to share the prime flippin' water while fishing next to you in the bow.

The more traditional deep-V is found in some fiberglass crafts, such as the Ranger models, but is modified somewhat in aluminum bass boats. This hull construction is clearly safer and smoother riding in rough water. Recreational anglers who frequent big, windy lakes might be better served with a V-shaped hull. You will simply get pounded less while riding through wave and wind chop with the V-hull cutting through the water. Keep in mind that the bow casting platform may be considerably limited with this hull design.

Hull materials also play an important role in the overall performance of the craft. Aluminum bass boats are the least expensive. They are easy to maintain and withstand most cosmetic damage since the hull is a uniform dull finish. On the other hand, high-speed fiberglass rigs are snazzy, with their brilliant metal flake hulls. Washing, polishing, and careful handling are routine for maintaining these more expensive bass boats.

Fiberglass bass boats also provide the angler with a more comfortable ride and evidence stronger hull construction and overall safety features. The Ranger models, for example, won't sink due to special flotation features even when the boat is sampled. Here then, the issue of one's recreational budget and time commitment to boat upkeep should be evaluated in picking between a fiberglass and an aluminum bass boat.

Boat Size

As a rule, the longer the boat, the more stable it tends to be. Smaller, 12 to 14 foot aluminum skiffs are highly practical for car-top hauling or trailing with compact vehicles. However, remember that you will be limited somewhat not only in terms of available deck space, but also with regard to weather. Smaller craft up to about 16 feet will not provide the modicum of safety needed to handle rough water. A 14 foot outboard can be a dangerous vessel on expansive waterways like Mead, Mojave, or Havasu when the wind begins to whip up some formidable swells.

If you prefer to fish bass on the big inland waters, definitely consider boats that are 17 to 18 feet minimum length. The added length will obviously provide more space for the family or for fishing buddies. More importantly, a bigger boat will be safer in the long run should water conditions take a turn for the worse. These are the typical Ranger tournament-style boats popularized by pros and guides like Mike and Ron.

Power Choices

There are two ways to go in selecting a serious bass boat when it comes to engines, inboard or outboard. On this note, there are no split decisions. The choice is clear. Both veteran anglers and dealers emphatically recommend an outboard system for fishing bass.

There are tremendous advantages to owning one of today's modern outboards in contrast to an inboard engine. To begin with, outboards typically have better horsepower-to-weight ratios than inboards. Put simply, these are lighter motors with comparable power. This has the added bonus of having less towing weight with an outboard than an inboard bass boat of similar length and hull design. This means greater fuel economy and less wear and tear on your towing vehicle.

It is also important to note that outboards have fewer moving parts than high-speed inboard engines. This translates into fewer repairs, fewer replacement parts, and greater maintenance value for the freshwater bass fisherman.

Finally, in recent years more and more outboard motors have switched to an oil injection system such as the new popular Yamahas. This means no more messy inconvenience of having to add oil to the gasoline by hand to come up with the correct oil-to-gas ratio. Many manufacturers now have stock oil injection features on outboards 35 horsepower or greater with similar options available on smaller models.

Fuel Capacity

This is an often overlooked dimension when it comes to deciding which kind of bass rig to buy. Before purchasing a particular model, you must contemplate how much range you need from your boat. For example, if most of your angling is done on small local lakes, you will probably be traveling short distances at reduced speeds and, hence, be using a modest amount of fuel. It is hard to burn up a lot of gas on a 600 acre impoundment that has a 10 mph speed limit.

Let's say you want to fish a lake with over 1,000 miles of shoreline for some serious bassin'. It is conceivable that you may launch from one marina but have to motor 10 to 30 miles to find the best concentration of largemouth bass. This round trip distance, compounded with an unlimited high speed run, obviously requires greater fuel capacity than casually fishing at a local lake. So, it might be best to visualize a "worse case" scenario in terms of the maximum range you need from a boat and under what conditions.

Most smaller aluminum boats are stocked with standard 6 gallon gas tanks. Additional tanks can be added as an option. Fiberglass models used for tournament fishing have anywhere from 12 to 24 gallon tanks. However, larger tanks up to 50 gallons are available for bigger boats or for long, sustained runs.

Before you select a bass boat, discuss the craft's approximate range under ideal conditions with your dealer. He will take into consideration 1) the length and weight of the boat, 2) the size of the outboard, 3) fuel capacity with the existing gas tanks, and 4) how fast the angler is traveling, in order to ascertain the approximate range of the rig.

An example of this assessment can be made for a 16 foot aluminum flat bottom boat with a 40 horsepower outboard. We can calculate that cruising at 30 mph, with the factory stocked 6 gallon tank, the fisherman will have an approximate range of 50 to 60 miles. Thus, if you wanted to use this boat on a big lake where you might have to make a 40 mile run one way, you have to either add another tank or plan to refuel at another marina to safely complete the return trip.

Trolling Motors

The electric trolling motor is a marvelous invention. It affixes to either the bow or the stern and permits the angler to quietly move along without scaring the fish. This is an absolutely essential piece of boat equipment for serious bass fishing. It is important to note that these powerful little electric engines are not made strictly for trolling as their name implies. Freshwater bass anglers who must stalk their prey near the bank use these motors to quietly sneak up on the fish.

Trolling motors are available in either hand or foot-operated versions. Most anglers on the West Coast seem to prefer the foot control models while Southern bassers like the hand-held style. With the foot-control model, you are able to keep both hands free while running the troll motor by pressing down on a mounted foot pedal. This is very similar to a sewing machine rheostat. The pedal unit directs the motor through cables connected to the steering arm.

The hand-operated trolling motors are easiest to use and you will never have to worry about a cable breaking. These units are mounted in either the bow or the stern, depending upon the position from which the angler prefers to fish. Most tournament-style bass boats use a bow-mounted trolling motor.

These electric dynamos are scaled in terms of the pounds of thrust generated. A smaller 12 foot aluminum car-topper requires not much more than an electric trolling motor with 18 pounds of thrust. A 14 to 16 foot aluminum model needs roughly 24 to 28 pounds to propel it along. However, heavier fiberglass hulls require approximately 34 pounds or more of thrust. Some manufacturers such as MinnKota now have magnum-sized electric motors that put out a whopping 48 pounds of thrust. These would be suitable for 18 to 20 foot fiberglass rigs that are used in the roughest conditions. These particular motors are also one of the quietest ever designed with a Maximizer system that has minimal draw down on your batteries.

Batteries

As far as batteries are concerned, there are a number of options available. Many dealers, for instance, recommend 6 volt batteries; others prefer 12 volt models. Each boat and its electronic package is different. Discuss these options with your rigging specialist. Be prepared to purchase one battery for cranking up the engine and at least one other to power your electronics, if you are running a big outboard over 75 horsepower. We prefer the Delco Voyager series.

Consoles

Many aluminum and fiberglass bass boats have built-in consoles. These house the in-dash instruments and provide some protection from wind and spray. The single console model is the most popular. It is located on the right side of the boat and is designed for the operator to sit or stand behind.

Another option to explore is the sporty-looking double-console plan. This is typically what you will find in so-called "fish-and-ski" models. There is a console on both the driver and passenger side, usually connected by one long bench seat. On chilly mornings, your passenger may be highly grateful for this option as it provides protection from the winds for both of you.

Seats

Most boats in this size range have either bench seats or pedestal seats. Tournament level bass fishermen prefer the pedestal seat. This high-back chair is both comfortable and functional. The angler is situated well above the water for optimal vision. You will also be able to swivel 360 degrees to either cast or play the fish with this seat design.

Straight bench seats are more comfortable for cruising but less practical for fishing. Some boaters settle on a compromise. A pedestal seat may be placed only on the bow, or on the bow and stern as is done with tournament-style bass boats. Bench or jump seats are also included and are used while the boat is running or simply for relaxing.

Storage Space

Before deciding upon a particular bass boat, contemplate how much gear you might take with you on a typical trip. Too often the buyer may settle on a less expensive model to minimize the initial monetary outlay. Then he discovers that the boat does not have ample storage compartments for his equipment.

Make a list of what you think you will stow away on your craft. Bring it to the dealer and review it with the salesperson to make sure your space requirements are met. You might also inquire as to which compartments, if any, are 100 percent dry storage. These will have special locks and seals so that no water can penetrate into the compartment. These will be the areas where you will want to store cameras, tackle boxes, and other valuables.

What about a rod locker? Frequently, would-be buyers fail to ask about this essential feature for a bass rig. This may be one option worth considering. It is convenient and safe to have rods tucked away while under power in rough water.

Live Wells

If you want to fish tournaments, the bass must be released alive after weigh in. Therefore, your boat will have to have a live well system. Some rigs, like the Rangers, have a live well in the bow for the frontseater and one in the rear for the backseat partner. Other Rangers are set up with two large live wells behind the back seat or one compartment with a divider to separate each competitor's catch.

More Electronics

The final critical item to consider in consolidating your boat purchase is the electronics package. The most popular units are the new liquid crystal recorders. These are easier to read than a flasher and are more compact. Either unit can be mounted near the steering console for easy monitoring.

A more sophisticated setup is to have an LCR affixed to a bow-mounted troll motor and a second unit placed near the console. The transducer attached to the trolling motor will give the angler an immediate reading of the bottom directly under the bow. The unit mounted on the console allows the boater to view the bottom while the rig is under power.

The transducers for these console units perform best if the dealer mounts them through the hull on fiberglass boats. This gives the least distorted reading. The fiberglass is almost the same density as water. The electronic signal will thus shoot through the fiberglass hull at roughly the same speed as through water.

However, for aluminum rigs, the transducer has to be mounted on the transom. This is because aluminum hulls won't absorb vibration. If you put the transducer through the aluminum hull, the whole bottom would become a distorted, vibrating transducer.

Outline Your Needs

In sum then, there is a wealth of things to carefully weigh before plunging in and buying a freshwater bass boat. Prior to visiting the dealer, it might be helpful to construct an outline of the various things you will need from your new rig. Examine length, power, comfort, safely, accessories and, of course, affordable cost as well as long-term investment. Don't feel intimidated to ask questions. It's in the dealer's best interest to make certain you are happy with a choice that meets your own personal needs.

Bass Guaranteed—
Becoming a Professional Guide

So, you're a good fisherman and you think you might want to become a bass guide. This work is often depicted as an exciting adventure. Some anglers see the guide in an enviable light. Here's the fisherman who has the best of both worlds. He can be on the water to his heart's content while being paid for it. But romantic images aside, finding "fish for pay" can be a high pressure job. It requires a certain profile to become an accomplished bass guide.

This type of professional angler stands apart from other fishing guides. The major difference is the quarry he seeks. Bass are a highly temperamental species. They are difficult to fool, particularly with artificial lures. Unlike say trout, you usually won't find them schooled tight in great numbers. So the bass guide has to "scratch" for a fish here and a fish there.

The bass guide is also relegated to locating one specific gamefish. By comparison, saltwater guides have more options open for their clients. If the sea trout don't bite along the Gulf Coast, for example, the marine guide can switch to redfish or snook. If, on the other hand, the largemouth develop a case of lockjaw, the bass guide has his back to the wall. This results in some considerable built-in pressure for the bass guide, since he must perform with only one species available.

Different regions of the country also provide inherent pressure. For instance bass guides in the South have considerably more water to fish. Their lakes are larger with less angling pressure. In contrast, Western guides work under somewhat more difficult conditions. Much of their territory consists of smaller 1000 acre impoundments that are commonly deep and clear. Weekend traffic on these waters is also intense. This can put additional pressure on Western guides who must often take clients out on weekends.

Young aggressive bass fishermen routinely ask what it is like to guide for money. This feature — the money — is probably one of the most significant aspects of guiding a professional must contend with. Even good tournament anglers sometimes fail to understand this. Fishing in high-stakes contests with your own money on the line is one thing; having clients pay you to put them on fish is another.

Guiding for bass can be like fishing with a loaded gun against your head. Without a doubt, the pressure can intensify once you and your party leave the dock. To a large degree, the success of their angling day is now in your hands. However, on the up side, if the outing proves to be successful in terms of shared camaraderie, instruction, and maybe even catching some fish, then the pressure may be worth it.

Becoming a Guide

To become a bass guide, the angler will have to develop a mental attitude that can handle the pressure of "fishing for pay.— This is true whether he does it as a part-time or full-time profession. In addition, the angler must demonstrate a high level of patience in working with people. Clients can come from all walks of life, with a wide range of expertise and bassin' savvy.

The would-be guide also has to be more than a mechanically sound angler himself. *He must know his water.* For some eager bassers, this may require that they spend an additional season or two on their home lakes before setting up a guide business. The guide must fully understand the seasonal patterns and idiosyncrasies of each different lake on which he may wish to guide. Paying customers expect him to know what are the best chances for locating bass on a particular impoundment. There is simply no shortcut for garnering experience and knowledge by spending time on the water *before* you become a bona fide guide.

When you feel you have both the technical skills and experience to lead clients to fish, it's time to assume professional status. This procedure varies from state to state. Most Departments of Fish and Game have some sort of licensing procedure you will have to go through in order to be a certified professional bass guide.

Don't' underestimate the value of being registered as a "professional." Many customers will not part with their money unless their guide is clearly identified as legitimate. The fishing and hunting guide business has been plagued with both rank amateurs and charlatans who prey upon unsuspecting clients. Your customers will value your credentials as a professional angler.

Working with Clients

The financial arrangements between the guide and his clients must be discussed in precise detail. The guide should not presume what the customers expect from the fees they pay. The length of the trip and the incidentals provided need to be explained before the charter is finalized.

Once the clients have contracted with the guide, he should try to size up their specific needs. Making this assessment is important. To begin with, what is it that the charter party expects from the outing? For example, are they business people out for a relaxing day on the water

President Bush with Mike Folkestad (right) Holding a 10 Pounder

with minimal interest in nailing fish? Are they there primarily for instructional purposes, to master a certain technique, or to learn the "hot spots" on a given lake, or are they trophy hunters with one single goal in mind—a double-digit weight wallhanger?

The guide also has to assess the client's level of expertise. Ascertain whether you are dealing with new beginners or veteran bassers. Determine the appropriate equipment they will need to bring or that you will supply (i.e., spinning tackle for neophytes, baitcasters for the more seasoned clients).

Once on the water, it is absolutely essential to re-evaluate your customers' prowess. You may find that in contrast to what was claimed dockside, your client is relatively "green." It may be important then for you to slow down the pace considerably and perhaps spend some time working on fundamentals and presentation. It also helps to change methods and baits frequently until your customers get bit. Rotate tactics until they stick a bass to instill confidence in novice anglers.

On the other hand, your passenger may turn out to be a fast learner. This allows you to pick up the pace, covering greater terrain and increasing the potential for landing more fish.

In sum, the conscientious bass guide will be sensitive to the ways in which his clients "flow" into the day. Don't try to impose either your pace or your bassin' personality onto your customers. Many people charter guides for a one-time experience. Frequently they are seeking nothing more than a relaxing atmosphere away from their stressful lives. They want the guide basically to take care of them for the day.

A sticky issue often arises with regard to whether the guide himself should fish. There is no simple answer to this dilemma. Western guides commonly fish alongside their customers. They usually have to. The bass are typically scattered and it helps to have another rod on the water. You might try to have your customers fish a time-tested traditional pattern, working the prime water. Use different baits, looking for emergent patterns and probing secondary water. It is important not to steal your client's fish.

When the fishing is tough, it also helps to boost the customers' confidence level if they occasionally see the guide reel in a bass. You must constantly make them believe that the fish are really out there waiting to be caught. Whatever your decision, clear it with your clients beforehand as to whether or not they want you fishing with them.

When Fish Don't Bite

The most disheartening feature to being a professional bass guide is dealing with those trips when the fish shut off. You know they're there and you've given it your best shot. They simply won't bite. This is an inherent element of the "fish for pay" game and good guides learn to live with it. Perhaps the position to work with is that regardless of how good the fishing is you should want your clients to receive the maximum in instruction, patience and, above all, courtesy.

Believe it or not, most customers understand that you are not a magician. They realize that much of your success is contingent on the whims of nature. Try to be a good conversationalist when guiding. Leave your clients with the feeling that they have learned something from you, even if the bass don't cooperate. They may then be able to apply this information the next time they fish on their own. Good guides enjoy a solid repeat clientele—even when bass can't be guaranteed.

A Bass Guide's Inside Tips

Veteran guides often find that there are certain ways of attacking a given body of water that seem to help their clients catch fish. Let's examine these basic approaches and how guides utilize them to get their customers hooked up.

Light and Polite

By now you can see that bass fishing is clearly not an exact science, but too many recreational anglers seem to over-complicate the sport by amassing huge tackle arsenals. It is not uncommon to see the novice basser walk out of a tackle shop with sacks of lures in a variety of sizes, shapes, and colors.

Smart guides try to encourage their clients to develop a narrow repertoire of baits. They want them to repeatedly throw these lures, and to develop a high level of confidence in using them. Far too often, the neophyte bass fisherman purchases so much tackle that a kind of "sensory overload" results. Put simply—he can't decide which lure to use.

By working with a limited selection of "confidence baits," the rookie basser will learn to develop and how to perfect the basic skills used with each kind of offering. As proficiency of presentation improves, so does the catch ratio, and confidence is built up.

For example, stay with a basic array of black, brown, purple, and salt and pepper worms in 4, 6, and 8 inch lengths. Next add a tandem and single-bladed spinnerbait in white and chartreuse. A crankbait in shad color and another in crawdad round out the plug line up. Throw in a floating minnow, surface popper, chugger, and stickbait to complete the menu for reaction lures. Finally, add a couple of salt and pepper grubs, a smoke/sparkle tube bait, and a chrome 1/2 to 3/4 ounce spoon and you're ready to go.

Be Experimental

Ironically, after we have recommended a compact war chest of artificial lures, we are now going to tell you to be more experimental. At times, bass can be super sensitive feeders. With increased angling pressure, the fish can frequently "shut off" to the time-proven baits. In this situation, consider abandoning your confidence lures and try something new. Remember, throw out the book!

Sometimes the change can be subtle. For example, you can switch to a salt and pepper worm but use one with a chartreuse tail. Other times, the lure change can be more dramatic, like tossing a buzzbait over 40 foot depths in gin clear water. The point is that frequently it will require some imagination and a radical departure from tradition to wake the bass out of their doldrums.

Watch for Emergent Patterns

Most pros feel that the single most important factor in successfully nailing fish is to learn how to "pattern" the bass. Throughout the day the shrewd angler will try to decipher what type of pattern the bass are on. This could be shallow or deep, around brush or rocks, in the sun or shade, eating little plastic worms or larger "snakes," or preferring black-colored baits instead of purple ones.

Sometimes it seems that the novice basser expects to find a pattern that will hold true all through the day. This may be the case for waters in less populated parts of the country, but don't expect such simplicity in areas with a lot of boat traffic and heavy angling pressure.

Veteran guides are constantly on the lookout for new emergent patterns to form when they are with their clients. For instance you may start out fishing shallow shoreline in the morning, then move to the deeper points as the day progresses. Later in the day you may have to move back towards the shoreline structure. You have to be able to change baits and sometimes outfits to come up with new patterns.

Slow Down!

Some bassers will frequently try to emulate their favorite bass fishing television shows by rapidly "running-and-gunning" down the bank. There are times when this tactic may work such as when using a spinnerbait or crankbait over a large expanse of shoreline. Day in and day out, it will pay to dramatically slow down in retrieving artificial baits.

Keep in mind that many lakes have limited shoreline structure. Hence, there are not that many prime targets at which to throw. When you find such potential cover, it is important to carefully dissect it by casting from every angle. The popular finesse baits such as reapers, grubs, Gitzits, and Slinkees are designed to be slow-moving offerings. If soft plastic lures in this genre are retrieved too quickly, the subtle dying and fluttering action of the baits is lost.

It is also important to slow down the tempo due to the intense pressure on many of our lakes. The pressure on the fish from the human population is one reason to slow down. Also, the number of presentations the bass see in a single day means you have to present the bait very slow and deliberate.

Thus, many professional local guides will encourage their customers to throttle down when it comes to working both reaction lures like crankplugs and spinners, and finesse offerings such as tube baits and grubs.

Use Light Line

Weekend bass fishermen will find that they will get more strikes by scaling down in line diameter. Many guides rarely ever have their clients throw anything heavier than 8 pound test monofilament.

Many lakes across the country are deep and clear. The fine diameter line will obviously get bit better in the clear water. There is another reason for spider web-like mono. Many of the diminutive soft plastic lures mentioned such as grubs and darter worms "swim" better with 6 to 8 pound test monofilament.

Both the doodling technique and traditional split-shotting strategy are perfectly matched to the light string. Both of these methods have accounted for numerous limits when the bass are otherwise in a lockjaw state.

Buy Quality Line

Serious guides urge their clients to invest in premium grade monofilament. Far too often they encounter a customer with state-of-the-art equipment only to have their reels spooled with cheap, bulk mono. These large economy spools sell for only a few dollars. However, there are significant drawbacks to this low quality line. It can lack uniformity, suppleness, and knot strength, as well as abrasion and weather resistance.

Bass guides, like other serious anglers who fish for money, often claim that the line is the most important link between the angler and the fish—not the rod, the reel, or the hook. Conscientious guides should emphasize to their client that with all the money spent in preparing for a trip—the tackle, the boat, and all of that—the one place not to cut back is the cost of the line. All you have to do is pick up a cheap line and you can tell it's cheap by the way it feels, the way it casts, and the lack of abrasion resistance. If you fish around a lot of rock your line has to stand up to the abrasion of rubbing against rocks. You must use a quality line.

It is tough enough getting bit on some lakes only to lose a fish due to a bad investment in low grade monofilament. Spend the extra money and purchase top-quality line to insure the maximum in performance.

Don't Horse the Fish!

Half the battle is getting the bass to bite; the other is playing the fish out. Serious bass fishing is an exciting sport. The angler can never really tell what is on the end of the line until he or she starts to fight the fish. The adrenaline is flowing and, with strikes at a premium, recreational bassers have a tendency to try to "horse" the fish in. This can be a big mistake.

Some guides feel that clients have a tendency to rush the fish to the boat. The best way to make them take their time and not lose a good fish is to lighten up on the drag so they can't "horse the fish."

For deep-water action while split-shotting or doodling tiny worms, you have to keep steady pressure on the fish. Instruct them to minimize making any jerky movements with the rod and let the bass fight the drag. It is imperative to be alert for a "hot" fish that decides to skyrocket to the surface. You may be amazed to see bass stuck at 45 foot depths bolt to the top. In this case you have to reel fast to gather up the slack line; otherwise the fish will often throw the small hook.

Sharpen Those Hooks

Serious guides continually remind their clients of the necessity of sharpening all their hooks. The bass have hard mouths and it is sometimes difficult to get a good hook set into the fish. This is particularly true in using scaled-down lures with small hooks, combined with the stretch of light monofilament.

Recurrently check your hooks throughout the day. The points can become dull from the lure banging into rocks or similar structure. Carry one of the new automatic sharpeners or a hook hone with you to re-touch the point as needed. Don't try to salvage a bad hook. Throw it away and re-tie with a new one.

Move Off the Bank

Too many weekend fishermen relegate their activity to shoreline targets. This approach may work on Southern waters with lush vegetation and prolific structure, but it has limited application other areas in the country. For one thing, most deep granite reservoirs have minimal targets along the bank. Secondly, much of the boat, water-ski, swimming, wading, and sailing activities originate near the shore making the bass quite wary.

The trick is to move off the bank and concentrate on outside structure. There is an entirely new underwater world awaiting the angler beyond the 20 foot mark. The bass in this deep-water environment are less pressured and may be more prone to bite.

Professional bass guides encounter some hesitation on the part of neophyte anglers to willingly fish outside structure. The problem seems to be that to the novice all the water "looks the same." This is especially true when the angler is some distance from the bank. Here's where sophisticated electronics help to build the client's confidence in this type of deep-water approach. The guide will carefully show his customers the underwater terrain and fish-holding structure as it appears on his instruments. Once clients can actually see the bass on a ledge, a pinnacle, or a submerged rock pile, their confidence is buoyed in fishing deep structure.

Stay Alert

Don't always expect the bass to clobber the lure on our highly impacted lakes. Quite frequently the fish will barely "mouth" the bait, particularly with the latest parade of soft plastic offerings. The "strike"—if you can call it that—with a reaper, darter worm or tiny grub may be nothing more than a little "tick" in the line.

With the slightest amount of pressure or unusual resistance on the line, smart guides encourage their customers to set up on, hopefully the fish. Remember, the bottom topography of many lakes is basically long stretches of soft mud. Thus, there are limited obstructions for your deep-water baits to hang up on. More than likely the resistance you feel is a bass mouthing the lure.

Well, there you have it—ten key points to becoming a more successful serious bass fisherman from the perspective of professional guides. Anglers who get paid to find fish for other people employ these approaches on a routine basis. However, keep in mind that there is no substitute for practice, patience and perseverance when it comes to serious bassin'.

Becoming a Serious Bass Pro

We are often asked by recreational bass fishermen, "How can I become a pro?" This is a rather complicated question since high stakes tournament bassin' differs significantly from most other sports.

Many professional athletes develop a fairly clear cut view of what it takes to reach the pinnacle of success in their particular endeavor. For instance, basketball and football players realize that to make it to the NBA or NFL much will depend upon the training they receive in a top-name college. Likewise, young baseball players understand that strong performance in the minors is their direct ticket to the big leagues. The route to professional stardom in the bass fishing world isn't exactly this precise.

Unlike the NBA or PGA, there is no single governing body that delineates the credentials and rules of behavior necessary to becoming a bass pro. To date, there are at least a half dozen major tournament organizations that promote professional events. Each has its own following, geographical niche, rules for competition, and standards of behavior. Bass anglers in this country need some kind of universally acceptable set of guidelines for becoming a professional.

Similarly, the bassin' community really doesn't have a farm system like other major sports where the professional ethos is taught to upcoming stars. About the closest we come to this is the bass club concept. As diverse as these local clubs are, to some extent they serve as a sort of training ground for a would-be tournament pro. Here too, many of the critical issues involved in acquiring that professional image are rarely addressed in most club formats.

Even though bass anglers are a somewhat fragmented group, as far as professional unity is concerned, there are still certain ways the angler must perform to achieve pro status. I'm not talking about proficiency in presenting an artificial lure. Rather, there are ways that bassers must act before they are respected as bona fide professionals. This code of conduct involves the issues of sportsmanship, integrity, public image, and sponsorship. Let's examine how serious anglers can learn to deal with these situations while becoming professional bass fishermen.

Sportsmanship

Perhaps foremost, professional bass anglers must demonstrate sportsmanship among themselves. Football players are penalized for pass interference, baseball pitchers are ejected for scuffing a ball, and basketball stars are given technical fouls for swearing at courtside. These are all examples of improper sportsmanship. Bass anglers, because of the structure of a tournament, are not typically policed by a referee, a line judge, or an umpire. Much of the enforcement of proper sportsmanship has to occur among the tournament fishermen themselves.

For example, pro bassers have to learn to respect each others' "water." In a pre-fish situation, if one contestant sees that a fellow angler has discovered a spot and is trying to guard it for the first tournament day, professional courtesy suggests that he stay away until the first person has had a chance to fish it. Pros can find their own water. This is a major challenge of the sport. It is one feature that distinguishes professional bass fishermen from novice anglers.

The issue of encroachment also enters into the sportsmanship picture. True pros wouldn't think of crowding another boat either at anchor or with marker buoys set out. Some high level tournament anglers may even ask permission to quickly pass in front of another boat so as to not disturb the other person's water.

Professional bass anglers must also be willing to share the prime fishing water with their non-boat partners in a draw tournament. The non-boaters have paid an equal amount of money to fish the contest. The rules usually stipulate that they deserve an equal chance at directing the activity by fishing frontseat for one half of the day. Some non-boaters will insist on their turn up front. Others grudgingly relegate themselves to the stern in deference to the "pro" who owns the rig.

These are only a few examples of how the issue of sportsmanship among fellow anglers contributes to the professional posture. All of these situations require that bassers take responsibility to insure an atmosphere of "fair play."

Personal Integrity

The term "professional" in itself conjures up an image of personal integrity and honesty. Many tournament anglers lose sight of this element in their quest for victory. This short-sighted, win-at-all-cost attitude often backfires with tragic consequences.

Some so-called "pros" have let their personal greed dictate their tournament ethics with illegal fish planting scams, etc. which have been publicized in the media. These are the more extreme examples when the fisherman's sense of honor or integrity is thrown aside. There are other, less talked about practices that mar the professional image many anglers are trying to maintain.

For example, is it "professional" for bass fishermen to intentionally change their productive lures with "decoys" as they motor into the weigh-in area? Is it "professional" to fabricate an outright lie about where the fish were caught to purposely mislead other contestants? Finally, is it "professional" to violate basic rules of boating safety to reach a prime spot first, traveling with great risk at high speed under dangerous conditions? I have actually heard some veterans brag that they would power their rigs through the worst weather if it meant a shot at the dough. It didn't matter that their non-boat partners expressed serious reservations about personal safety when such a decision was made.

Too many times otherwise competent bassers justify such little ploys in exchange for a high finish. As tournaments become more popular and moneys increase, professionals from across the country will invariably meet at the more prestigious contests. The overall number of players is still small by comparison to other major sports. There is a lot of "networking" that occurs in the pro bassin' ranks. The anglers share information to try to help each other. One guy knows his lake real well; another is an expert on other water. The concept of "you help me today, I'll help you tomorrow" is in effect throughout professional bassin' circles.

Thus, because this fraternity is so limited and tightly knit, it doesn't pay to sacrifice one's integrity for a one-time tournament win. The adage "everything that goes around, comes around" couldn't be more true than it is among professional bass fishermen.

The Public Image

Sports superstars have a responsibility to perform both on and off the field. It shouldn't be different for professional bass fishermen. Tournament level bassin' has suffered from a negative image at times. This is often fostered by a misinformed press. Some recreational anglers still feel that the bass pros are raping the lakes with their hi-speed boats and sophisticated electronics. Forget the notion of catch-and-release. John Q. Public sometimes only sees the "catch" part of the equation. This makes some novices envious of the pro basser's prowess but does not acknowledge the fact that "release" is also an important part of the sport.

It is essential for the tournament professional to become an ambassador of sorts, representing his sport to the public. The weekend bait dunker has to be educated to the merits and long-term benefits of the catch and release philosophy. Respected tournament pros can do this through seminars, personal appearances, and through casual conversation near the water, as well as through their conduct while fishing.

The dedicated bass professional must be willing to share information with the public. I am not advocating giving away all the trade secrets. Obviously, the touring pro needs every legitimate edge possible to excel over the competition. There are many general facts and tips that can be given at seminars, tackle stores, informal gatherings, etc. which will make the pro appear to be more like a hero in the public eye.

In sum, part of the "professional package" entails that bassers become respected role models for the sport. If big time tournament bassin' is to expand and prosper in the future, much will depend upon public acceptance of this kind of fishing. Pro bassers, as roving diplomats, help to greatly enhance the overall public perception of bass fishermen and their tournaments.

Sponsorships

Tournament anglers know they have "made it" in the sport when manufacturers ask them to use their products in a promotional relationship. This is a very sensitive area in the professional bassin' arena. Many fishermen fail to contemplate the ethical aspects of sponsorship and thus make some critical mistakes when they reach this level.

Most sponsors are business people. They deal in bottom line return-on-investment. They understand that bass fishing fame, in terms of tournament victories, can be a fleeting thing. The basser that is hot on the tournament trail today can hit a bad streak of luck tomorrow. There is a fascinating, unpredictable quality about bass fishing that makes the sport so challenging. Therefore, once sponsorship is established, the manufacturer may be more interested in how the fisherman will represent his product and less in tournament performance.

Professional anglers must be willing to conduct themselves in a business-like manner in working with sponsors. The "good ole boy" stereotype of the bassin' man won't cut it anymore in the world of Madison Avenue advertising. Sponsors expect and deserve pro bassers to look and act the part of representatives of their product. They want neat appearances with their logos proudly displayed. They anticipate that their pros will be able to converse with the public. This is all part of the selling tactic that manufacturers hope to parlay in exchange for fishing sponsorships.

You will find that, like pro bassin' ranks, the fishing tackle and related boating industries are fairly closely knit. Manufacturers talk among themselves and compare notes. Thus, it is imperative to maintain an ethical and honest position in these relationships. Think twice about trying to play one sponsor off the other in attempting to stage your own, miniature bidding wars for your loyalties. These people are sharp and will usually see through such maneuvers.

Use their product with commitment. This is also an important feature of being professional. If the product doesn't meet your needs, then be honest and discuss it with your sponsor. Avoid hoarding, trading, or worst of all, selling merchandise in exchange for other goods or cash. A line manufacturer once noted that some of his field staff members were trading bulk spools of monofilament for shot gun shells at a local sporting goods store. Their dealings were reported and a valuable sponsorship went down the drain!

To Be a Pro—Act Like One

In sum, being a serious professional bass fisherman involves much more than being an accomplished caster, wearing caps with logos, participating in big time tournaments, and owning an expensive boat. To reach that milestone in this sport, much will depend upon personal deportment. Professionals are judged more in terms of how they act, than how well they fish.

Hopefully, we've given aspiring pros something to think about while veterans might reassess their current behaviors. If tournament bass fishing is to evolve into a dynamic sport in the next few years, it will take a serious effort by those dedicated pros to set an example for the next generation of serious bassers!

Backseat Blues

An overwhelming majority of bass fishing contests are staged as draw tournaments. This simply entails putting all the names of the anglers who wish to fish from their boats into one pool. This group is then paired through a random drawing with those contestants who don't have a rig. Invariably, there is an overabundance of bassers who want to fish from their own boats. In this situation, two boaters will be drawn together. A coin is flipped to determine whose boat will be used in the tournament. The loser of the toss assumes the role of non-boater.

Thus, for most club level or professional meets, there will be an equal split of boaters and "backseaters." There can be many heated exchanges, dubious ethical practices, and some overall bad feelings generated from this rather asymmetrical relationship.

Some boaters unfortunately maintain the posture that since they supply the rig, they should get to call all the shots. Most tournament rules clearly stipulate that each angler has the right to direct the boat and/or fish from the frontseat position regardless of ownership for one half of the day.

This becomes a rather sensitive topic, rarely ever discussed publicly in bassin' circles. On one hand, some anglers feel that owning a hi-tech bass boat is their major credential of having "made it" in the sport. Far too often this is an erroneous assessment, since some boaters are struggling tournament fishermen at best. On the other hand, novice bassers who don't own a rig are often intimidated by the boat owner's equipment and assumed status in the bassin' world.

The problem becomes even more compounded in the case of two boat owners that are matched together in the rig belonging to one or the other. Egos can really clash on the water with this combination during the tournament day.

The backseat issue has a number of dimensions worth exploring. Let's examine both the pluses and minuses of being relegated to the rear of the boat. Then, we'll pass along some tips for boaters and non-boaters that might make this relationship more palatable for both parties.

The Pluses

Riding "shotgun" in a bass boat under tournament conditions does not necessarily put the angler at a major disadvantage. Some neophyte bassers can definitely benefit by going into the draw as a non-boater. Many boat owners are indeed accomplished bass fishermen. They often have valuable first-hand knowledge of the tournament lake gleaned from years of experience. These boaters are typically proficient with a variety of techniques that may be unfamiliar to the backseater.

In some sense then, the non-boater might have much to gain with this type of draw. It can be almost like getting a free instructional "guide trip" while still competing in a tournament. It is thus in the beginner's best interest to go non-boat and learn from these pros.

Many recreational bassers also lack the boat handling skills necessary to pilot one of these powerful rigs through rough water over long distances on big lakes. Here again, from a sheer safety standpoint, it might be better going as a non-boater and leave the driving to the veterans.

There is also another reason why fishing from the rear platform may not be such a bad idea. Some highly skilled bass fishermen actually prefer the backseat because it removes them from the pressure of running the boat. We have heard anglers often comment that they were relieved not to have had to worry about working the trolling motor. These fishermen feel that they can concentrate better on their techniques when they aren't fighting the elements of the wind, waves, etc. that confront the frontseater.

Finally, with certain tactics, the seat position in the boat makes little difference in terms of effectiveness. Fishing over deep structure with spoons or jigs, for example, leaves a lot of open water that can be mutually shared. Similarly, fan casting in a circular fashion while sitting on top of a shallow flat minimizes any distinct advantage the frontseater may otherwise have.

The Minuses

Fishing from the rear end of a bass boat creates problems under certain situations. If the non-boater remains in the backseat position during a flippin' bite, he may be aced out of fishing some of the better "virgin" water. This is especially true as the frontseat man maneuvers the rig, bow first, into a narrow cut or channel. The backseater is left with "seconds" as the driver flips the most viable targets first. If the bass seem to be keying in on reaction lures such as crankplugs, spinners, or top-water baits, the non-boater can receive a royal "backseating" if he isn't careful. A selfish frontseater can keep the bow headed up the bank picking off those "first strike" aggressive fish, leaving leftovers for his partner.

Another drawback facing the backseat angler is that he may ultimately be at the mercy of the boater with regard to the style and pace of the day's bassin'. The frontseater can orchestrate the dominant style simply by his selection of baits. For example, if he decides to throw a crankplug, it might be tough for the backseater to slowly crawl a worm from the stern. The backseater will then have to quickly adapt to the crankin' program if he wants to stay competitive.

The frontseat man can also establish the pace for the day's bassin' by his choice of lures. Speed of movement is also determined in part by how fast the boat owner wants to cover the terrain with the trolling motor. Here too, the backseater is often resigned to fishing at the boater's pace or he may literally be left behind.

Peaceful Solutions

There are a number of things that non-boaters can do to insure an equal opportunity to catch bass during the tournament. First, backseaters shouldn't be intimidated by the boater. He has laid down an equal sum of money as an entry fee and has just as much of a desire to do well. If the non-boater has found some fish during the practice period, he should communicate to his partner that he too would like to try certain water. Interestingly, most boaters will agree to take their draw partners to a particular area without many reservations. And why shouldn't they? It is always better if two people are on fish rather than just one.

At this point, if the boater seems agreeable to sharing the water, discuss your feelings about being a backseater. Explain that if you're treated fairly while fishing in the rear, you'll be content to stay there. Tell the boater that you expect to have ample opportunity to make casts toward the front of the bow, emphasizing that you can alternately throw to the prime targets.

If there is resistance to this straight forward proposal, reiterate the tournament rules. If a "hard line" must be taken, simply request to fish from the frontseat for half of the day. Quite often the boater may reassess his reluctance to share the water after the formal tournament rules are cited. Don't be surprised if a more agreeable attitude results in the promise that no backseating will occur if you let him run the front. You see, some boaters simply treat having to "fish backseat" as tantamount to a sentence to Siberia! Most are willing to negotiate once they understand that their draw partner expects a fair shake. All of these discussions should occur *prior* to the morning launch so as to clear the air from the start.

Even in a friendly atmosphere, you may find yourself being backseated as a result of the boat unavoidably pointing into the bank, bow first. No problem. Walk up into the front section and inform the boater that you will be fishing up here, slightly behind him until the boat is repositioned more parallel to the bank.

Consider using longer rods from the backseat to make further casts. This little ploy often helps when you are tossing light baits from the stern and the boat is slightly angled away from the shore. Ask your partner to slow down somewhat if you are getting too much belly in your line from running and gunning too fast. You can also very subtly turn the steering wheel to cock the outboard skeg inward. This will also quickly pull the rear end of the boat more parallel to the bank giving you a better shot at the shoreline.

Above all, non-boaters should be assertive, yet diplomatic. Be sensitive to the fact that the boat owner has a lot of money tied up in his rig. He probably also bought it with the idea that only he would be running his boat. Explain your position and be negotiable. As I mentioned, you can also benefit from the experience of a long-time bassin' man.

Boaters, on the other hand, try to be less selfish and more sensitive to your backseat partner. Tell your partner that you will both catch fish if you work as a *team*. Never intentionally position your boat to hurt the backseater. Boat owners should learn to divide the water and avoid conflict. Understand that non-boaters have an unequivocal right to receive just treatment in the tournament. At a prestigious national contest, a high-level touring pro once thanked the non-boaters in front of a large audience for participating in the event. As he said, "Without you guys, there isn't any tournament."

Visualize Success—The Inner Game of Serious Tournament Bassin'

There is often debate as to whether or not the serious tournament fisherman is indeed an athlete. A compelling argument can be made that the physical, mental, and social dimensions involved in pursuing fish for money and/or fame is on parity with other professional sports.

As with pro football, baseball, or basketball, the serious bass fisherman on tour must contend with routine issues of travel and time away from home, sponsorship contracts, and financial support, periods of intensive practice and the overall pressure of competition. Like other pro athletes, the bass angler who fishes for money must also deal with winning and losing.

The question arises, what does it really take to become an accomplished winner in the professional bassin' ranks? What else is needed besides the latest hi-tech gear, the hottest boat and motor, financial backing, familial support, and time to compete? The secret ingredient may be one that is increasingly used by athletes in all major sports — the ability to visualize success.

Winners and Losers

In recent years, coaches and managers of professional athletes have discovered a training ingredient that goes beyond physical conditioning. It can make the difference in determining why one player might "get on a roll" while another becomes entrenched in a spiral of declining performance.

Sports psychologists along with lay professionals have begun to train athletes to develop a mental approach to improving their performance capabilities. For example, batting instructors may encourage the slumping hitter to first remember what it felt like to really hit the ball well. The player is encouraged to recollect the sight of the ball coming over the plate; the eyes fixed on contact with the bat; the sound of the ball flying off the bat; and, finally, the flight of the ball into fair territory as the batter tallies a "hit." The player creates a detailed picture in his mind as the entire scenario is reviewed mentally without actually contact with a bat or ball.

This mental imagery is practiced time after time until the slumping player has totally absorbed the scenario of the perfect hit and can both see it and feel it as if it were real.

The next step is to then transfer this scenario to the actual game situation. As the batter steps up to the plate and awaits a "real" ball from a "real" pitcher he is filled with confidence, because he knows how the scene will play having already "lived" it in his mind numerous times.

Can this visualization process have some application to serious bass fishing? The answer would appear to be an emphatic YES!

Take the case of a prominent pro who was competing on the prestigious B.A.S.S. national circuit. He confided that he seemed to have an unusual "problem." He related that lately he had become quite concerned over what he considered to be some weird coincidences with regard to his tournament results.

He claimed that although he seemed to be on a "roll" lately, having placed well in a series of events, he was bothered by having "imagined" such success days before the actual tournament. He mentioned how he would have "waking dreams" of finding the best water, stalling the fish with the right baits, "sticking" the bass, and even accepting his prize money on the victory stand! The most amazing thing was that these scenes tended to come true when he was actually fishing the tournament a few days later.

Certainly this veteran pro was not having some sort of breakdown or strange "mystical experience." Rather he was inadvertently constructing a positive scenario of the impending tournament. He was unconsciously using those techniques now being practiced throughout the sporting world to *visualize* his own success!

So, the question is how can the serious basser begin to practice and develop the art of positive visualization?

Well, to begin with, the pre-tournament period is the most critical time to construct a positive approach for the impending contest. In a quiet moment, sit down, close your eyes, and relax. Think about days past when everything seemed to be in perfect synchronicity as you caught bass with great proficiency.

Next, begin to transfer this imagery of the perfect fish-catching day to the upcoming tournament site. Imagine having all your tackle precisely organized the night before. Each individual rod, reel, and lure is perfectly matched for the next day's prevailing conditions. Imagine this in as much detail as you can.

Now, flash forward even further. Picture yourself leaving the starting line and cruising to your favorite spots on the lake. The locations are yours to own. You are motoring to *your water*.

Once there, see yourself selecting the appropriate outfit from your precise arsenal of rods and reels and baits. Visualize your boat position, pinpoint accurate casts, and the bass striking your lure. Savor the image of fighting the fish and finally landing your catch.

With your mind is in this dream-like state, continue, visualizing the entire tournament day. Imagine the exact locations to which you will travel as the hours pass by. Anticipate the different kinds of terrain you will cover as well as the specific rigs and baits you will use to fool your prey.

Eventually, with your limit in the live well, let your mind take you to the weigh-in and conjure up an image of victory. This is *your* dream—make the ending as spectacular as you like!

Some bass fishermen may wonder what happens next. Is this merely a lot of hokum or semi-hypnotic speculation going on? You may now find that once on the water under actual tournament conditions you are now carrying a highly positive image of yourself, your abilities, your equipment, your prime fishing spots, and your overall tournament prowess. Put simply, you may now begin to attack the water with a level of confidence quite possibly never experienced in previous tournaments.

More importantly, this positive vision of one's ability and future success serves to short-circuit the potential for falling into a slump or minor depression that might otherwise occur during the tournament day. If a strike is missed or a bass throws the hook—it's okay. There will be other chances to rectify this minor setback.

The serious bass angler who masters the visualization process learns to "go with the flow." The "positives" offset the "negatives" if an affirmative frame of mind is maintained throughout the contest.

More importantly, there seems to be a certain "domino" effect that goes hand-in-hand with positive visualization. Success generates more success. This is the phenomenon of the fisherman-athlete being "on-a-roll."

Although some serious level bassers would appear to be able to visualize naturally, as in the example above, most of us must practice the process to make it work. Tournament grade anglers are not necessarily born with the ability to visualize in a positive manner. For most, it will take a belief and a commitment to the process to make it effective.

Understand that the more precise and detailed mental image you can construct, the greater the likelihood of attaining the positive results portrayed in your picture. Practice focusing on the image you have created frequently and completely for maximum effectiveness.

Positive visualization is being employed in such diverse fields as medicine, education, and business as well as sports to help people to obtain positive outcomes. Competitive bass fishing is by nature a somewhat secretive sport. It has been noted that some pros have quietly experienced the results of positive visualization but may not be talking about it. Any edge the touring competitor can master—physical or mental—is guarded well in the pro bassin' fraternity.

The art of positive visualization, however, is accessible to any angler who is willing to give it a try. Anyone can become a player in the "inner game" of serious tournament bassin'.

Tournament Burnout

There are many reasons why men and women decide to become serious tournament bassers. For some, fishing at a highly competitive level is a simple extension of a lifelong love of the sport. For others, the thrill and glory of the competition is the attraction. Dreams of super-stardom with big cash paybacks and full sponsorship lures many anglers into the tournament game.

These are some of the features that draw anglers to the tournament ranks. There are also a few competitors that eventually "hang up their guns" leaving the tournament rat race, and perhaps bass fishing all together.

What causes tournament burnout? Why do some bass pros suddenly decide to quit after years of competition? The reasons are complex and varied.

Not surprisingly, there aren't too many former professionals that even want to talk about their exit from the bassin' world. As with any sport, part of one's heart and soul remains in the game. When you leave it, some of that competitive spirit is left behind. Sometimes this is followed by a painful readjustment to non-tournament life. The reasons why pro bassers burn out are worth examining.

Finances

Professional bass fishing is an expensive sport. The basic price of hi-tech equipment has increased dramatically in past years.

For example, it is hard to find decent baitcasting reels and graphite rods for under $40.00 any more.

It is also difficult to compete at this game with only one or two rigs. You can count on needing somewhere between four and six outfits to be prepared for the different conditions encountered in the field. The sport has become so specialized with reels made solely for crankin', rods designed primarily for flippin', and whole rod and reel systems engineered for tube bait tactics. The top anglers invariably have the latest in innovative equipment. To compete, the budding pro must keep up with advanced technology. This entails spending considerable funds.

Bass boat owners can certainly relate to how expensive it has become to operate this piece of equipment. The purchase price of a high speed rig has skyrocketed in past years, along with the cost of fuel and oil. Other hidden expenses can also make a dent in the pros' pocketbook. Engine repair is costly. Wear and tear on the towing vehicle also adds up along with the escalating fees for boat insurance.

On top of all this, the touring pro must contend with expenses for motels, meals away from home, and the other incidentals associated with travel. The problem is that the average bass pro has minimal sponsorship at best to help offset these expenses. Furthermore, most tournaments have limited paybacks with only a few anglers even sharing in the "pot of gold" awarded to the top finishers.

One long-time Western pro recently decided to quit the ranks of the professional, stating that he felt the tournament game had become a "rich man's sport." "It's a burden to fish the tournaments unless you have a real high income job or you have someone paying your way for you," he commented. "It's just not economically feasible—there is not enough money in it. The biggest thing for me right now is that I just can't justify spending the money on it anymore. I'm not burned out about the competitive part, it's just that I feel at this point in my life I'm better off channeling my energies elsewhere."

The question arises then as to whether the anglers at the top of the sport are there because they have lucrative jobs to begin with which allow them to finance their dreams or do they have the money to compete in the sport simply because they are able to bring home the tournament bacon?

Travel

Apart from the expenses accrued in travel, life on the road itself can be quite exhausting and lonely. Some anglers simply do not have the mental or physical fortitude to spend days traveling, pre-fishing, competing, and then traveling home again. Many of the "older statesmen" in the sport feel that tournament bassin' is becoming "a young man's game." There is no question that the repeated travel can take its toll on even the most dedicated younger anglers.

This is not much different, however, from life on the road for rodeo cowboys, traveling salesmen, or long haul truck drivers. After a while, the miles start to add up and some anglers may question whether they want to subject themselves to the stress of this less glamorous facet of tournament level bassin'.

Family

The married pro may face an additional difficulty in trying to juggle both a heavy tournament schedule and his or her role in a relationship or as part of a family. Most contests are held on weekends. This is usually the only time families are able to relax and do things together. It is difficult to incorporate this familial concern with the tournament style.

One relatively young fisherman who was once a highly regarded "up-and-comer" in the tournament ranks mentioned that his commitment to the tournament life probably cost him his marriage. "It's tough on the marriage. They (wives) put up with it for a while — but there aren't too many girls who like to sit around a motel (or at home) waiting for you to finish up a tournament." Now separated, this would-be star has resigned from professional bassin' and rarely ever fishes for this species anymore.

Being a parent compounds the problem, especially for the male competitor with children involved in competitive sports. It can be frustrating for one parent to have to spend many weekends assuming the roles of mother, father, cheerleader and chauffeur for Bobbysoxers, Little Leaguers, or soccer players while dad is off chasing bass. This too can generate tremendous pressure and guilt on the pro, leading him to leave the tournament circuit for a more stable family life.

Stress

Some anglers decide to walk away from the tournament scene because they are tired of the stress often inherent in the competition. When an athlete takes money out of his own pocket and practically gambles on his own performance against other competitors, tension and stress inevitably build up.

Worse yet, high stakes bass fishing is an unpredictable sport. Unlike other athletic endeavors, a portion of the angler's success can be attributed to blind luck. Some days luck is with you; other days it's not. This unpredictable quality of the bass tournament makes the outing both challenging and frustrating. Some bassers may come to feel that they have minimal control over their own performance. So they figure, why go through the hassle of trying to fool these little green fish?

Other pros basically lose their competitive edge. This is especially true if they are on a poor performance streak as often occurs with professionals in this sport. They simply get tired of spending the time, money, and effort, and having nothing to show for it.

Other former pros note that somewhere along the line they lost a desire to compete because *it just wasn't fun anymore*. As one past competitor said, "It was too much competition. I just like to fish for fun . . . . The pressure, it just wasn't for me anymore."

Social Conditions

Finally there are some former pros who left the sport because of certain social conditions they felt to be inherent in the tournament world. Some mentioned the "psyche games" between competitors as a reason for burnout, while others couldn't tolerate the cliques that often develop among the pros.

One fisherman related that he was tired of being an outsider, looking in. "I just got burned out on it," he said. "I got tired of the B.S., the stories, the cliques, and the talk behind the back. The fishing and the catching part is great, but the rest—you can have it."

Taking Stock

Tournament bass fishing can be exciting, challenging, and rewarding. It can also be hazardous to one's health. Built-in stress, anxiety, and frustration is inherent in the professional pursuit of these gamefish. Mental health therapists often recommend to their clients that they "back off" from a particular endeavor in which they are closely involved if the "emotional tachometer" approaches red line proportions.

On this note, it may help to take a break from the serious tournament scene if you find that you are enjoying the competition less and less. Rather than reaching total "burnout" and leaving the sport, step back, take a break from the tournaments, and re-evaluate your commitment to the game. By doing this, you may discover ways to integrate your serious bass fishing with your overall life style, creating better balance. Then, when you return to the tournament circle, you may find you approach the game with renewed intensity, combined with enjoyment and a passion for the sport.

Good Luck!

Glossary

Bangin' - Using a heavy jig head and vertically shaking it off the bottom, banging rocks and similar structure.

'Blades - Another commonly used name for spinnerbaits (also lead'n blades).

Break - A ledge with a drop-off leading into deeper water. A prime fish-holding structure.

Bullet Weight - A cone-shaped sliding sinker designed especially for plastic worm fishing.

Buzzin' - Retrieving either a spinnerbait or a buzzbait along or barely under the surface.

Carolina Rig - A rig characterized by a sliding sinker butted by either a swivel, snap or similar device. A lengthy 18 to 36 inch leader with a soft plastic lure attached. (See illustration page 46.)

Chugger - A specialized topwater lure, combining the cylindrical body of a stickbait and the cupped mouth of a surface popper. (See illustration page 60.)

Crankin' - The retrieve associated with winding in a crankplug or similar hard plastic lure.

Curl Tail - The tail design on many soft plastic lures which makes the bait appear to be fluttering in the water.

'Dads - Another name for crawdads or crayfish.

Darter - A 1/16 to 3/8 ounce jig head, arrowhead-like in design, used with a small plastic worm or grub trailer.

Dead Bait - When a soft plastic lure such as a worm or grub is allowed to rest motionless on the bottom.

Doodlin' - The art of rythmically shaking a small 3 to 4 inch long worm vertically over deep underwater structure.

Drop Bait - Lures typically casted following an explosive attack and miss with a surface plug. The angler then casts a soft plastic lure into the commotion, letting it "drop" into the sport where the commotion occurred.

Fall Bait - A lure allowed to momentary sink midway through the retrieve such as fishing a spinnerbait "on-the-fall."

Fan Casting - Making repeated casts in either a semi or full circular pattern to thoroughly explore a potential fish-holding area.

Flippin' - Making short, vertical presentations to shallow, shoreline targets.

Floater - A soft plastic bait that will float above the bottom even with a hook in it. Air bubbles are injected into the plastic during the manufacturing process to create this effect.

Flyline - Presenting natural live bait without any additional weight or sinkers added to the line.

Grub - A short compact 3 to 5 inch long soft plastic lure designed to resemble a crawdad or baitfish. Can often be used in place of a plastic worm. (See illustration page 103.)

Jerkin' - Making rhythmic sweeps of the rod to drive a floating minnow plug down under the surface.

Jig'n Pig - A pork rind trailer laced behind a lead head jig. (See illustration page 83.)

Kneel-and-Reel - Intentionally extending the rod tip underwater to make a crankplug dive deeper while retrieving.

Lift-and-Drop - Lifting the rod, then lowering it when presenting a metal spoon in a vertical fashion. The "lift" raises the lure through the water; the "drop" lets it flutter down.

Line Feelin' - (also known as "stitchin'") Retrieving the line by hand in order to slowly pull a soft plastic bait along the bottom. Commonly practiced on the San Diego Lakes.

Live Rubber - The strands of rubberband-like material used in jig and spinnerbait skirts.

Lizard - Soft plastic replica of the land-based reptile. Used primarily for flippin'.

Pegging - Breaking off the tip of a wooden toothpick into the head of a bullet weight. This makes the sinker immobile when using a Texas rig. (See illustration page 44.)

Paddle Tail - A flat paddle-shaped tail portion found on certain plastic worms used with doodlin' technique.

pH - The acid or alkaline quality of the water, which can affect the areas where bass will seek cover.

P-head - A small round pea-shaped lead head jig in 1/32 to 1/4 ounce used with subtle soft plastic lures. (See illustration page 100.)

Pitch - A gentle underhand or side-arm presentation involving a short cast to nearby shoreline targets.

Plastics - Another term for soft plastic lures such as worms, grubs, tube baits, and lizards.

Glossary (continued)

Plowing - A slow methodical retrieve of a jig being inched along the bottom.

Popper - A surface lure with a prominent cupped mouth to create a "popping" sound when retrieved. (See illustration page 60.)

Pork - Another term for any pork rind trailer used behind a jig, spinnerbait, or other lure.

Pressure - Any dull resistance on the end of the line when bass mouth a soft plastic lure.

Reaper - A small 2 to 3 inch soft plastic lure shaped like a feather or leach. Commonly used with the split-shot method.

Rippin' - Using short rhythmic rod twitches to keep a floating-diving plastic or wood minnow under the surface.

Riprap - Any broken rock that lines the bank in continuous fashion.

Run'n gun - A rapid fire series of casts made quickly to cover expanses of shoreline.

Safety-pin Spinner - Common spinnerbait design with wire frame bent to resemble an open safety-pin. (See illustration page 94.)

Shakin' - Short repeated rod twitches that make the plastic worm "shake" as it is retrieved along the bottom.

The Sink - When a bass hits a lure while it is vertically dropping through a strike zone.

Skin-hooking - Barely embedding the plastic worm hook into the outer layer (or "skin") or plastic. This facilitates quick easy hook sets.

Slab Bait - Any hard plastic crankbait with a flat slab-like surface and without a diving lip. (See illustration page 53.)

Slide Sinker - Another term for a bullet weight. Can also apply to larger oval egg-shaped sinkers made to slide up the line when used with a Carolina set-up.

Snake - Any long 8 to 18 inch plastic worm resembling either an aquatic or terrestrial snake.

Split-shottin' - A variation of the Carolina rig A lead shot is crimped 12 to 36 inches above a soft plastic lure to suspend the bait slightly off the bottom.

Stitchin' - See "line feelin."

Spoonin' - Vertically presenting metal spoons in a lift-and-drop fashion.

Stickbait - Topwater lures without a diving lip, cupped mouth, or propeller (See illustration page 60.)

Stick-ups - Decayed brush that is exposed somewhat out of water.

Straight-tail - A plastic worm with a simple straight tail structure, resembling a live nightcrawler.

Structure - Any fish-holding area from docks and boulders to underwater ledges and grass beds.

Stop'n Go - A specific retrieve where the angler intentionally stops, pausing to allow the lure to rest motionless.

Subtle Baits - A variety of smaller soft plastic lures typically fished on lighter 4 to 8 pound test, including grubs, reapers and tube lures.

Suspend - When bass move off the bottom or from structure and position themselves at a mid-water level.

Texas-rig - Most common way to use a plastic worm. Comprised of a bullet weight, worm hook, and the plastic worm. The hook is embedded into the worm to make the lure virtually weedless. (See illustration page 40.)

Tail-Spinner - A jig with a revolving spinner blade attached to the rear. Also known as a "mattie." (See illustration page 97.)

Trailer - Anything used behind a jig, spinnerbait, or other lure.

Tube Bait - Any hollow soft plastic tubular lure usually with multiple "tentacles' in the tail portion. (See illustration page 105.)

Turnover - When the surface layer of water quickly chills and sinks to the bottom. The warmer bottom layer in turn rises to the surface. Typically this is a tough time to catch bass.

Twin-spinner - A spinnerbait with two distinct wire arms, with either one or two blades attached to each arm. (See illustration page 98.)

Walk-the-Dog - A specialized retrieve designed to make a stickbait or chugger sashay across the surface.

Worm Hook - A hook especially designed for fishing with plastic worms and similar soft plastic baits.

Yo-yoing - The lift'n-drop motion associated with vertically presented spoons, slab baits, spinnerbaits, and other lures.